MAKING IMAGES
MOVE

MAKING IMAGES

Photographers and Avant-Garde Cinema

M O V E

JAN-CHRISTOPHER HORAK

SMITHSONIAN INSTITUTION PRESS

Washington and London

Editor: Tom Ireland
Production editor: Jack Kirshbaum
Designer: Kathleen Sims

Library of Congress Cataloging-in-Publication Data
Horak, Jan-Christopher.
  Making images move : photographers and avant-garde cinema / Jan-Christopher Horak.
      p.   cm.
  Includes bibliographical references and index.
  ISBN 1-56098-744-8 (alk. paper)
      1. Cinematography—Europe—History—20th century.   2. Cinematography—United
States—History—20th century.   3. Experimental films—Europe—History—20th century.
4. Experimental films—United States—History—20th century.   5. Cinematographers—
Europe—History—20th century.   6. Cinematographers—United States—History—20th
century.   7. Photographers—Europe—History—20th century.   8. Photographers—United
States—History—20th century.   I. Title.
TR848.H67   1997
778.5'3'09—dc21   97-17444

British Library Cataloging-in-Publication data available

Manufactured in the United States of America
02 01 00 99 98 97 5 4 3 2 1

⊗ The paper used in this publication meets the minimum requirements of the American
National Standard for Permanence of Paper for Printed Library Materials Z39.48-1984.

Contents

Foreword

Chris Horak's remarkable book looks at artists who are never entirely happy to be simply photographers or filmmakers, who throw themselves into film-making but can never stop thinking about and reflecting on photographic practices. Eager to explore the intersection between the two forms, these photographer-fillmakers often cross boundaries in ways that throw critics off-balance and leave audiences slightly puzzled. Horak focuses on these artists' film work: on one hand, situating it within the larger context of their photographic oeuvre, and on the other, exploring how their films appropriate and rework photographic conventions, make use of photographs within their films, or allude to photography within the mise-en-scène or narrative.

The eight individuals whose creative output Horak examines all started out as photographers and moved on to film—an almost inevitable progression given such factors as the greater availability of still cameras as well as the relative expense and technical complexity of film. The book's title—*Making Images Move*—suggests this progression. In some cases, as with Helen Levitt's film *In the Streets,* the book's title perfectly matches the artist's intent. As Horak demonstrates, the visual components of Levitt's earlier street photographs are reworked and extended in her film. But just as often these film-makers try to make moving images become still. This seemingly perverse, countervailing theme—this tension between making still images move and stilling the moving image—provides much of the book's texture and insight.

There have been many books about the translation of different art forms into film. The move from theater to film was explored as early as 1949 in

A. Nicholas Vardac's *Stage to Screen: Theatrical Methods from Garrick to Griffith* and more recently in John C. Tibbetts' *The American Theatrical Film* as well as a wide array of essays. Numerous biographies trace the move from theater to cinema of directors (from D. W. Griffith and Sergei Eisenstein to Mike Nichols and Arthur Penn) and actors (Bette Davis, Marlon Brando, and Katherine Hepburn). The path from narrative fiction to film, both in terms of adaptation and personnel has also been explored (including Richard Fine's *West of Eden*, on East Coast writers who moved to Hollywood and encountered a radically different system of authorship). So it is astounding that Horak is the first author of a book-length work to explore similar kinds of relationships between photography and film.

There are several factors that help explain this long neglect. The adaptations of plays and novels engage problems and practices integral to mainstream thinking—both in Hollywood and in the feature filmmaking of other national cinemas. The kind of aesthetic problematics posed by relations between photography and film most often have to do with documentary and avant-garde cinemas—genres for which narrative does not have the same status or force, genres which have been relatively neglected areas of intellectual inquiry. If their photography and film work are considered as a single corpus, all of these image makers vacillate between documentary and avant-garde. Horak's task here—following his groundbreaking anthology, *Lovers of Cinema: The First American Avant-Garde, 1919–1945*—is thus far more difficult than tracing the shifting of narratives or personnel from one cultural practice to another. The displacements are more oblique, the artists less fixed in a single medium.

In each case Horak is dealing with an outstanding photographer who was in some sense dissatisfied with the limitations of the medium. This dissatisfaction is reminiscent of a debate between two sculptors, Paul Gsell and Auguste Rodin, in which Rodin asserted

> "People in photographs suddenly seem frozen in mid-air, despite being caught in full swing: this is because every part of their body is reproduced at exactly the same twentieth or fortieth of a second, so there is no gradual unfolding of gesture, as there is in art."
>
> Gsell objected, "So when art interprets movement and finds itself completely at loggerheads with photography, which is an unimpeachable mechanical witness, art obviously distorts the truth."
>
> "No," Rodin replies, "it is art that tells the truth and photography that lies. For *in reality time does not stand still,* and if the artist manages to give the impression that a gesture is being executed over several seconds, their work

is certainly much less conventional than the scientific image in which time is abruptly suspended."[1]

It is, Chris Horak suggests, the desire to make images move through time and space that drove many of these photographers to work in a related but also very different medium. And yet, as he makes clear, cinematic truth remains every bit as elusive as photographic truth. Film gives subjectivity even freer reign, making these artists gesture toward their initial love—photography.

Charles Musser
Yale University

Acknowledgments

This book has been so many years in the making that I'm not sure who to thank first. I'll begin with Ute Eskildsen, curator of the Fotografische Sammlung of the Folkwang Museum, Essen, Germany, with whom I have been working on various film and photography projects over the last twenty years and who has been a close friend almost from the moment we met. Many fruitful discussions with her and Timm Rautert on Helmar Lerski, Paul Strand, Danny Lyon, politics, aesthetics, and life have found their way into the pages of this book. Furthermore, I would like to thank the following "participants" and witnesses, who gave me their time and interest: Robert Frank, Helen Levitt, Danny Lyon, Chris. Marker, Hattula Moholy-Nagy, Leonard Rappaport, Naomi Rosenblum, and Anneke van der Elsken.

Thanks also to my readers, Charles Hagen and Charles Musser, who supported this project in a number of ways. Charlie Musser's long and detailed critique was particularly useful in helping me clarify the structure of the book, as was Chuck Hagen's use of the manuscript in a course taught at Bard College. Others who have contributed thoughts are William Johnson, Brigitta Kämper, Laura Marks, Constance Penley, Ulrich Pohlmann, the late George Pratt, Allen Sekula, Abigail Solomon-Godeau, Sally Stein, David Trend, Hillel Tryster, and my former students at the University of Rochester. Thanks to my coworkers at the Munich Filmmuseum, in particular Gerhard Ullmann and Heiner Gassen, who generated some of the stills for the text.

The research on this book was supported by the George Eastman House, where I had the pleasure of being senior curator for ten years, and the

Munich Filmmuseum/Stadtmuseum, where I am presently director. Other institutions supporting my research were the Folkwang Museum (Essen, Germany), the Goethe Institute (Tel Aviv), the Steven Spielberg Archive (Jerusalem), the Museum of Modern Art (New York), the Fotomuseum/ Stadtmuseum (Munich), the George Eastman House International Museum of Film and Photography (Rochester, New York), the Galerie Alvensleben (Munich), and the Nederlands Filmmuseum (Amsterdam). A special thanks goes to the editors of *Afterimage* (Rochester), where a number of chapters appeared in earlier versions, as well as the *Yale Journal of Criticism* and *Aperture.*

For film stills and permissions to use stills, thanks to the Helmar Lerski estate at the Museum Folkwang; Ronny Loewy; Chris. Marker; Anthony Montoya at the Aperture Foundation; the Paul Strand Archive; Hattula Moholy-Nagy; Danny Lyon, represented by Simon Lowinsky Gallery (New York) and Kesner Gallery (Los Angeles); Robert Frank, represented by Pace Wildenstein MacGill Gallery (New York); Mary Corliss of the Museum of Modern Art Film Stills Library; the George Eastman House, specifically Paolo Cherchi Usai and Barbara Galasso; Anneke van der Elsken; Helen Levitt; Anne Tucker at the Museum of Fine Arts, Houston; and Gerhard Ullmann at the Munich Filmmuseum.

Finally, thanks to my wife, Martha F. Schirn; my daughter, Gianna Mei Li Horak; my twin brother, Michael J. Horak; my younger brother, Peter Barkley; and my father, Jerome V. Horak. Without their familial support and love, I certainly would not have finished this project.

1   Photographers and Film

AN INTRODUCTION

The earliest film pioneers and inventors of what at the turn of the century became known as moving pictures were often photographers. Unsatisfied with the technical limitations of still photographic images, they were willing to make sacrifices in order to explore a new and potentially exciting form of expression: cinematography. Both the American scientist Eadweard Muybridge and the French inventor Etienne Jules Marey were photographers, whose earliest experiments with sequentially ordered photographic images were an important step toward the development of moving images. The Lumière brothers, Louis and Auguste, inherited their father's photographic business and, excited by a demonstration of Edison's kinetoscope, were among the first to present publicly projected film images to a paying audience when they introduced their "Cinematographe" on 25 December 1895 in Paris. Many of the Lumières' first, globe-trotting newsreel cameramen had been photographers—for example, Edward Doublier and Auguste Moisson. Louis Lumière also continued his experiments with photographic color slides.

In the United States, the pioneering film producer Sigmund Lubin founded a photographic lantern-slide business in Philadelphia in 1882 before turning to film production at the turn of the century. W. K. L. Dickson, Edison's coinventor of the motion picture camera, was a photographer. In Great Britain, G. A. Smith and Eammes Collings were prominent portrait photographers as well as film pioneers.[1] The world traveler, adventurer, and educator E. Burton Holmes commenced his lectures with photographic slides as early as 1893 but soon integrated motion pictures into his travelogues.

Frame enlargement from an untitled Lumière film (1896), taken from Leopold Bridge in Munich, with the Bavarian Parliament in the background.

Indeed, the early history of motion picture projection (at least until 1905) is inseparable from the history of the projection of photographs (lantern slides), a fact noted by recent historians of early cinema.[2]

The German photographers Max and Emil Skladanowsky traveled throughout Germany with their father, an exhibitor of photographic magic-lantern slides, before inventing a motion picture camera and projector in 1892. Two other German film pioneers, Oskar Messter and Guido Seeber, also started in the photographic lantern-slide business. Messter was to become one of Germany's most prolific producers: he "invented" the Maltese Cross, an essential element for all motion picture projectors; built motion picture cameras and projectors; invented a high-speed 60mm camera for producing scientific slow-motion studies; produced and distributed a whole catalogue of films over more than a twenty-year period; produced the first successful and popular sound film series (Biophone) between 1903 and 1909; and contributed to the founding of the modern film industry by organizing his company vertically to include production, distribution, and exhibition. Guido Seeber's career as a cameraman spanned nearly fifty years of German film history.

Once the commercial film industry was institutionalized on the shores of the Pacific at Los Angeles, photographers flocked to Hollywood. Many enjoyed prosperous careers working as still photographers for the motion picture studios (including George Hurrell, Ted Allen, John Engstead, Clarence Sinclair Bull, Otto Dyer, Jack Freulich, Eugene Robert Ritchie, and Laszlo Willinger), producing glamour portraits of the stars for the studio's insatiable publicity machine as well as film stills. In Weimar Germany, Hans G. Casparius filled a similar role as stills photographer for G. W. Pabst and others before being forced to emigrate to England, where he became a documentary filmmaker. Such stills did not exactly duplicate shots from films but were specifically composed to create interest in a given film. Because of this practice, which came into vogue in Europe and the United States in the period shortly before World War I, photography has always functioned as advertising, too, for the cinema.

Other photographers worked in the film industry as art directors, for example, Cecil Beaton and Alexander Rodčenko (in Moscow), or as color consultants, like George Hoyning-Huene. Many, however, moved into motion picture production as cameramen and directors. Some of Hollywood's finest cameramen started as photographers, including Karl Struss, James Wong Howe, Stanley Cortez, Floyd Crosby, and Farciot Eduart. Others became directors, the best-known examples being Stanley Kubrick, Ken Russell, Freddie Francis, and David Hamilton. In almost all of these cases, photographers

Portrait of Luise Rainer, taken by George Hurrell, ca. 1938. Courtesy of George Eastman House.

gave up one medium to become successful in the younger medium, usually forsaking their previous involvement in photography.

Photographers and photography have often been the subject of fiction feature films. In some cases, the occupation of the hero helps develop the plot, as in Alfred Hitchcock's *Rear Window* (1954) and Michelangelo Antonioni's *Blow Up* (1966). In both cases, a photographer believes he has seen something through the lens of his camera that turns out to be very difficult to prove, leading both films to explore the nature of truth in photography (and, by extension, film). Other films, like Roberto Rossellini's *La macchina ammazzacattivi* (1948) and Roger Spottiswoode's *Under Fire* (1982), are concerned with the ethical and moral obligations of photographers and, more specifically, photo-journalists.[3]

Just as photography is a subject of fascination for the cinema, so too have photographers been intrigued by the medium of film. Some of the world's best-known photographers—for example, Eve Arnold, Brassai, Anton Bruehl, Margaret Bourke-White, Fritz Henle, or Harry Callahan—made only one or two films before returning exclusively to photography. Like many artists curious about media related to their own, they dabbled in film without changing their self-image as photographers. Not surprisingly, these photographers most often attempted documentaries, since this form most closely approximated their work as photographers.

However, as the filmography at the back of this volume indicates, numerous photographers have comfortably moved back and forth between media, becoming accomplished filmmakers as well as photographers. Common to most is the fact that, rather than working in Hollywood or the commercial film industry, the great majority of these photographer/filmmakers have chosen to work in avant-garde or documentary film and television. The establishment of a modernist, avant-garde movement in cinema, both in Europe and America, is unthinkable without the participation of photographers. Indeed, many photographers experimented with film, defining themselves essentially as cinema amateurs dabbling in another medium. Not only did they produce films; many of these artists wrote theoretical and practical essays on the possibilities of the new medium. Among the many photographers making substantial contributions to avant-garde and documentary cinema in Europe are Francis Bruguière, Jan Dibbets, Paul de Nooijer, Raymond Depardon, Paolo Gioli, William Klein, Helmar Lerski, Eli Lotar, Chris. Marker, László Moholy-Nagy, and Man Ray. In the United States, the film avant-garde has benefited from the participation of such photographers as Thomas Bouchard, Irving Browning, Bruce Davidson, Robert Flaherty, Hollis Frampton, Robert Frank, Roman Freulich, Hy

Film still from *Light Rhythms* (1930), directed by Francis Bruguière.

Hirsch, Helen Levitt, Jay Leyda, Danny Lyon, Gion Mili, Stella Simon, Ralph Steiner, Paul Strand, Edward Steichen, Charles Sheeler, and Weegee.[4]

This book looks at professional photographers who ventured into the field of cinema without relinquishing their interest in photography. Unlike many of those named above who only trained as photographers before moving more profitably into the field of moving pictures, these photographer/filmmakers have traveled across the borders of both media, learning from each mode of expression, wholly allegiant to neither. Some have attempted to incorporate photography into their film work, for example, Chris. Marker, Raymond Depardon, Robert Frank, Silke Grossmann, and Ed van der Elsken. Ferenc Berko's film *Time Capsule* (1965) utilizes his own photographs exclusively to create an impressionistic portrait of the Westinghouse Pavilion at the New York World's Fair. Depardon's film *Les années declic* (1983) reprises the photographer's twenty-year career as a photo-reporter, using still images exclusively, much as Chris. Marker narrates his career in photography in *Si j'avais quatre dromadaires* (1966). Ed van der Elsken describes both his career and his photographic aesthetics in *De verliefde Camera* (1971) but also appears in frame as a subject. These films are, however, the exception rather than the rule. Most photographer/filmmakers have maintained a clear division between their lives as photographers and as filmmakers.

If the truth be known, few highly successful photographers have established critically acclaimed careers as filmmakers, and, vice versa, few established filmmakers have earned exceptional reputations as photographers. Some of the exceptions to the rule are discussed below, including Paul Strand and Robert Frank. It's almost as if the two media—alike as they may seem—are too different, demanding wholly different ways of seeing. And yet, the number of artists working in both media belies this assumption.

I would like to suggest that this difference in vision is much more of a problem for critics than for the artists in question. Despite the wealth of activity, and the undeniable contribution photographers have made to the history of avant-garde and documentary cinema, few photo or film historians have dealt with this phenomenon. Many academics in the field of cinema studies are unfamiliar with the work of even well-known photographers, while photography specialists often flaunt their ignorance of film history, preferring to treat film as a subject for film-star fandom. Historians of photography have preferred to ignore the films of photographers, while film historians have discussed the films of photographers—if at all—outside the context of the artist's photographic career. Just why this has been so is unclear.

Photography, according to Charles Wolfe, "has comfortably fit into the critical assumptions and curatorial practices of art historians."[5] The reluctance of photo-historians may, therefore, be explained by the fact that they have often come from the field of art history and are hesitant to tackle a medium that is both technically complex and culturally suspect (because of the taint of commercialism and the difficulty of establishing exact author- ship). Photography historians have tended to focus on their own area of ex- pertise, the still image, thus avoiding the difficulties of reading moving im- ages, which require an analysis of film syntagmas. In discussing the films of Danny Lyon, Pamela Allara has suggested another reason for the split be- tween film and photo history:

> Curiously, contemporary criticism makes a firm distinction between still photography and film, and critical writing on the two is likely to appear in separate publications addressed to different audiences. This is due in part to the fact that film is frequently interpreted in terms of its narrative structure . . . whereas photography is considered to have an iconic structure and there- fore has been analyzed in the formal terms generally applied to painting.[6]

The predominance of narrative film analyses in film criticism is certainly a contributing factor in the lack of intelligent criticism found in the film press, on the one hand, and the neglect suffered by photographers' films in the aca- demic discipline of cinema studies, on the other. Thus, a *Variety* film re- viewer of Chris. Marker's *Si j'avais quatre dromadaires* (1966), which is made up entirely of still photographs, seemingly misses the point when he writes: "There are too many precious descriptions and observations on photos that do not always support the cleverness. And there is a final flatness to the un- moving stills that do not always make up in composition, surprise and visual elegance for the lack of movement."[7] Mainstream film critics were never sympathetic toward film experimentation, as evidenced by a review in *Monthly Film Bulletin*: "There is very little to be said about photographer David Bailey's cinema experiment [*G. G. Passion*, 1966] other than it is a bad case of would-be 'significance' run riot."[8]

However, the problem seems broader. Until recently, most film historians focused on the mainstream film industry, while much of the historical writ- ing on avant-garde and documentary film has not risen above the level of hagiography. Thus, one possible reason why photographers who are also filmmakers have been left out in the critical cold is that they have most often chosen to work in film genres that can be loosely termed experimental—for example, avant-garde, documentary, and ethnographic films—while rarely venturing into mainstream, commercial, narrative film production, where the demands of the marketplace are greatest.

This makes sense for several reasons. First, the work of the photographer is for the most part solitary, allowing for a great deal of aesthetic freedom.

Second, the division of labor in independent cinema is less well-defined than in the commercial arena. Third, modern cameras and film stocks in semi-professional formats have allowed filmmakers to experiment at relatively low cost. Such liberated working conditions are rarely available to a commercial cinematographer or filmmaker, who is bound by a whole catalogue of economic factors and production conditions, including "talent" contracts, union crews, studio bosses, the tyranny of the Hollywood system, extremely expensive 35mm equipment and film stock, high-priced actors, and narrative conventions. Photographers working in more independent forms of film production, on the other hand, have the freedom to experiment, because budgets are smaller and crews are minimal. The Swedish photographer and filmmaker Rune Hassner notes: "After about two decades as a documentary photographer and photojournalist, I was very much tempted by the new medium, television, and by the new technique, the Arriflex on the shoulder and the Nagra tape-recorder on the other shoulder. Being able to work as earlier with the Leica, alone when it was needed."[9]

A further reason for the neglect of photographer/filmmakers in film studies might be the emphasis in the past fifteen years on feminist and psychoanalytic criticism, which has shifted critical concern away from the work of individual artists toward broader issues of gender, sexual preference, and ethnic empowerment. In other words, while traditional photo-historians rarely ventured beyond the conservative realms of aesthetic-authorial analyses, such auteurist criticism fell into disfavor in film studies. Interestingly, a new generation of photo-historians have come to recognize the artificiality of these lines of demarcation and attempted to cross borders through such disciplines as cultural studies.[10] Film historians have, likewise, broadened their perspective to look at the many forms of cinematic discourse at the margins of mainstream cultural practice. There seems to be a growing awareness of the need to examine the way photographers have utilized film and other media.[11] In particular, it becomes a question of discovering how an artist's vision is transformed when a different medium is employed. To look at the work of photographers who make films, then, is also to think about the relationship of these two media to each other.

Within the art and exhibition world, too, the reception of films made by photographers has been scant, indeed. An early attempt in a New York University exhibition, *Photographers Who Make Films,* included photographs and films by Moholy-Nagy, Ralph Steiner, Robert Frank, Robert Mapplethorpe, Danny Lyon, and Mary Ellen Mark.[12] Reaching a much larger audience was an American Federation of the Arts traveling film program mounted in 1990, *Moving Pictures: Films by Photographers.* That film program presented films by no less than thirty-seven photographers, including

Man Ray, Gordon Parks, Eikoh Hosoe, William Wegman, Ruth Orkin, Margaret Bourke-White, Susan Meiselas, John Baldessari, Michael Snow, Robert Mapplethorpe, Bruce Weber, and Raymond Depardon. Divided into seven feature-film-length programs of film shorts, the series was organized along stylistic and thematic lines: "Surrealistic Tendencies," "Visions of America," "Street Scenes," "Photojournalism," "Definitions & Experiments," "Portraits," and "Three Meditations."[13] As the program headings indicate, however, the structure was more a matter of finding similar films to fit into a program than of creating a rigorous typology. The inclusion of László Moholy-Nagy's *Ein Lichtspiel schwarz-weiß-grau* in the "surrealism" program, for example, is questionable, since that film is clearly an example of constructivist art, not surrealism. Paul Strand and Charles Sheeler's *Manhatta,* on the other hand, could just as easily have fit into "Street Scenes" as it does into "Visions of America." Furthermore, a heavy concentration on the films of American photographers was undoubtedly the result of film availability, since few European films are in distribution in the United States.[14] To its credit, the program traveled throughout the United States to numerous museums and exhibition spaces, introducing films by photographers to audiences used to compartmentalizing their aesthetic experiences.

On the other hand, retrospective exhibitions of well-known photographers who have made films often still ignore or give short shrift to the artist's film oeuvre. Recent retrospective exhibitions on Paul Strand and Helen Levitt failed to incorporate adequately their film work. While the Strand exhibition at the National Gallery in 1990 was accompanied by a symposium, no attempt was made to show Strand's films in the exhibition.[15] And the curator's cursory nod to only one of Levitt's films in the Levitt retrospective at the Metropolitan Museum of Art in 1992 led directly to the writing of the essay included in this volume.[16]

Given the strong historical connections between film and photography, it is indeed surprising that a thorough theoretical discussion of the relationship between these two media has yet to occur. Just what draws a photographer to experiment with the film medium, when he or she has found success in still photography? In what way are these media formally similar? In what ways are they different? How is audience/viewer reception structured by the characteristics of each medium? In order to explore these questions, we need to delve into a bit of theory. Since the invention of cinema, theorists and aestheticians have continued to formulate ideas and concepts concerning the nature of film, at times touching on its exact relationship to still photography. With each passing generation, the parameters of debate have been redrawn, the postulates reformulated, thereby revising our understanding of the uses and pleasures of film and photography. Yet, there seems to have been little consensus on the subject, and no sustained critical debate.

Surveying film theoretical work over the past eighty years, it becomes apparent that few film theorists have overtly addressed the relationship between film and photography. For early theorists, such as Béla Balázs or Rudolf Arnheim in the 1920s, the question of photography in relation to film seemed immaterial, because their primary theoretical objective was to promote the cinema as an independent and culturally respectable art form, separate from theater, literature, and photography (which also suffered from cultural negligence). Rudolf Arnheim, while noting that the medium of photography was not merely a mechanical copy of nature, as postulated by most nineteenth-century theorists, did not concern himself with photography *expresis verbis* until the 1970s, when he argued that the photographer cannot escape the subjectivity of his position within the space of the action he is documenting.[17]

Likewise, Soviet theoreticians of the 1920s, for example, Sergei Eisenstein and Vshovolod Pudovkin, posited the editing of individual shots as the defining element of cinema as an art form. Their interest in the single image went no further than to postulate formal criteria for composition within the film frame as the most basic element of film form. It was not until the post–World War II period, when a generation of film critics, influenced by realist film and film theory, began publishing their work, that the relationship between film and photography became an overt theoretical agenda.

The classical film theories of André Bazin and Siegfried Kracauer posit an inherent structural connection between photography and film. Indeed, the ontological similarity between the two media is central to their argument that these media are realistic art forms with deep phenomenological connections to the real world, thus separating them from other art forms, such as painting, music, or literature, which have no such relationship to reality. Both critics theorized photography as a photochemical process that captures light and fixes it on a piece of paper, thereby rendering a visual impression of reality. The role of the photographer is not that of a trafficker in signs and symbols, but merely that of a facilitator to photographic vision, which parallels natural vision. The subjectivity of the maker is either denied or deemed inappropriate when too heavily foregrounded.

Not the medium itself, but the pro-photographic event, is seen as the focus of attention. Photography is perceived to have the capability of pulling a moment in time out of an unstructured reality, of creating the impression of three-dimensional space. The object depicted, the reality behind the image, the real world seen through vision, documented through chemistry, is what moves human emotions. Bazin writes euphorically: "Only the impassive lens, stripping its object of all those ways of seeing it, those piled-up preconceptions, that spiritual dust and grime with which my eyes have covered it, is able to present it in all its virginal purity to my attention and consequently to my love."[18]

By extension, film is seen as merely moving photography, where light is documented on a piece of celluloid in time, as well as in space. The frame of the film image functions similarly to the edges of the photographic image, except that the film image can look beyond the edge of the frame, like a human observer sticking his head out of the frame of a window. As Kracauer writes in his introduction to *The Theory of Film*, "Film is essentially an extension of photography and therefore shares with this medium a marked affinity for the visible world around us. Films come into their own when they record and reveal physical reality."[19]

Such a focus on the pro-photographic or pro-filmic scene indicates that aesthetically both Bazin and Kracauer valorized film realism. As realist theoreticians, both viewed the primary function of photographic media to be the reproduction of reality in all its complexity and ambiguity. Since both film theorists also interpret the history of painting teleologically, from its beginnings to the late nineteenth century—when it is relieved of its reproductive duties by photography and film—as a progressive movement toward the re-creation of reality, it is not surprising that they value film realism as the highest form of the art. Bazin writes:

> The guiding myth, then, inspiring the invention of cinema, is the accomplishment of that which dominated in a more or less vague fashion all the techniques of the mechanical reproduction of reality in the 19th century, from photography to the phonograph, namely the integral realism, a recreation of the world in its own image, an image unburdened by the freedom of interpretation of the artist or the irreversibility of time."[20]

Due to their investment in realism as an aesthetic, Bazin and Kracauer draw the theoretical equation between photography and film without a proper investigation of their technical, aesthetic, semantical, and syntactical differences. Indeed, such an investigation would have injected a degree of empiricism into a project that borders on the mystical. Bazin and Kracauer have, in fact, been classified as transcendental phenomenologists, since they identify the photographic object as synonymous with consciousness, with the essence of vision. The problem with transcendental phenomenology, according to Vivian Sobchack, is that it describes "only the irreducible ground, the essential structure, the static 'sameness' of consciousness—much as a still photograph describes the irreducible field of its vision, its invariant relations, the immutable 'sameness' of its gaze."[21] In other words, there is a false assumption that photographic media actually reproduce the world as it exists, that is, as it supposedly exists in its totality, as a unified whole without the intervention of human consciousness. The dynamism of reality and the constantly shifting perception of reality through human consciousness are somehow lost in the process. Furthermore, the technical characteristics of film and photography simultaneously tie them to and distance them from the reproduction of reality, since the technology must be guided by a human eye, brain, and hand.

Clearly, then, both theorists contribute to an understanding of just how film and photography are similar—they both create images that reproduce an approximation of human perception of the world—and offer a possible explanation of why photographers would be drawn to the related medium of film (it, too, is a realistic medium), but they fail to account for differences between the media. Generations of photographers, maybe even more than filmmakers, have thrived on their ability "to see" images in the real world, and to then capture them on a photographic negative. Film has the possibility of increasing this reality quotient and thus provides a challenge for those photographers interested in pursuing such an aesthetic. But Bazin and Kracauer do not clarify the exact attraction the cinema has had for photographers, if only because their discussion of photography is merely a starting point for their subsequent film theoretical deliberations.

While Bazin and Kracauer see film as an advance over photography, and both media as an aesthetic advance over painting, another phenomenological theorist, Stanley Cavell, has analyzed the photograph's specific accomplishment in relation to film. Cavell notes that a photograph shuts out the world, revealing within a frame only that which the camera (and its user) has chosen to expose, while forever denying access to the space beyond the frame.[22] In doing so, the photographer freezes a moment, not only in time, but also in space, transforming three dimensions into a two-dimensional picture. More importantly, a photograph can create a self-enclosed and self-sufficient world that needs no other referent, other than itself. Both time and space are fixed, allowing for the production of a unified point of view.[23]

A motion picture, on the other hand, continually peers beyond the horizontal and vertical borders of the photographic image; indeed, it revels in its own possibilities of movement, in continually discovering the terra incognita beyond the limited vision of the immediate frame. Discovering that other space can be accomplished a number of ways: through camera movement, through editing, through lighting. A movie camera can pan to the left or the right, move forward into an image or away from the object depicted. Through a shot-reverse shot construction, the filmmaker can simply turn the camera around, exposing what was previously behind the camera, what was invisible. By changing lighting patterns, the filmmaker can reveal things previously hidden by shadows. Thus, according to Cavell, the cinema is more than just a frame or window onto the world; it is indeed a multidimensional construction of spacial and temporal relationships that have the ability to create a seamless vision of the world or fragment that vision into a multitude of points of view.

An important ontological difference between the two media, which also influences the work of the photographer/filmmaker, is, therefore, the relative "openness" of the film image versus the insularity of the photograph. The photographer is always composing images as a closed system of meaning, where the edges of the frame also define the relationship of the objects depicted to each other and to the subject. While such meaning need not be one-dimensional, its parameters are limited to that which is visible within the frame. Once a photograph has been fixed on paper or celluloid, or as an electronic impulse (CD-Rom), these relationships remain static, the position of the subject frozen for all eternity at a particular distance. As Roland Barthes has noted: "Photography is impenetrable. My gaze can only roam over its quiet surface. Photography is flat in every sense of the term; this is what I must accept.[24]

Films, on the other hand, allow for an open-ended structure, both within the image and through time. The objects depicted within the film image may lose their specificity of meaning, because they are subject to change as the images moves. The position of the subject is also constantly shifting with the camera's changing point of view. The work of Robert Frank is perhaps most instructive here. While Frank's photographs, for example, in *The Americans,* are static in their construction of meaning and today appear to be particularly rich examples of a historically definable moment in American history—Eisenhower's 1950s America seen through the eyes of a European expatriate member of the beat generation—Frank's films defy easy semantic interpretation, even as the filmmaker attempts to control meaning. Indeed, Frank's films are studies of the way his subjects escape those meanings the filmmaker wishes to attach to them. In contrast, his photographic subjects are literally trapped in his gaze, within the structural frame the photographer has created.

This formal difference between film and photography is crucial, because it points toward another phenomenological characteristic of film in relation to photography, which has been explored by the phenomenologist Gilles Deleuze—namely, the element of time. While photography expands a split second into eternity, freezing the moment forever, film functions in time and can only be perceived through time. It may speed up time through stop-motion cinematography. It may slow it down through slow-motion, but it can only exist in time, because it is based on a temporally based illusion of perception that turns a series of physically static images into perceived motion. Moving images on a screen are more than an illusion of space and time, that is, they are more than an image to which movement has been added. Rather, in the words of Deleuze, they are "a movement-image."[25] In opposition to photography, where the single image retains its materiality, the sequencing of separate photographic images in the cinema renders them individually invisible through the process of projection. In other words, the film image is rendered in the act of perception as light and shadow, rather than in a concrete material form.

Phenomenologically, the ontology of the photograph is predicated on the photograph as an object. It is a physical representation of perception, rather than the act of perception itself. As an object it can be held, turned around: it has its own materiality. Film, on the other hand, lacks that materiality, at least in the moment of reception. Rather, according to Deleuze, it functions at three different levels: "(1) the sets or closed systems which are defined by discernable objects or distinct parts (frame); (2) the movement of translation which is established between these objects and modifies their respective positions; (3) the duration or the whole, a spiritual reality which constantly changes according to its own relations."[26] Deleuze discovers the essence of cinema not in the image, itself, but in the movement from one image to the next. Without that movement, the actual experience of seeing film is lost. As a phenomenologist, it is Deleuze's goal to rescue the experience of cinema, as a form of knowledge, from those theoreticians who wish to abstract it beyond real experience.

The aspect of time is crucial. Photography takes a moment out of time, $1/100$ or $1/60$ of a second, and transports it into infinity. The image, frozen as a sign within the frame, is untouched by time, although of course the context of reception through time may indeed change its signification. The photographic moment is fixed in timelessness, without a past, a present, or a future. Its formal design is, therefore, not subject to time, to change. This fact is central in the phenomenological theory of the relationship between film and photography presented by Vivian Sobchack. She argues that in photography, time and space are essentially abstractions, since the photographic object is both outside time—that is, timeless, without a present or a past—

and outside space, existing in two-dimensions that can never compensate for a lost third dimension. In contrast, film images exist only in the action of seeing, of becoming, in the act of perception itself. As Sobchack notes: "The images of a film exist in the world as a temporal flow, within finitude and situation. Indeed, the fascination of the film is that it does not transcend our lived experience of temporality, but rather that it seems to partake of it, to share it. Unlike the still photograph, the film exists for us in the act of becoming."[27] Sobchack calls her theoretical point of view "existential phenomenology," because the experience of film viewing is seen as a process of perception, of continual change and momentum, and, thus, as life experience.

However, one can argue that film is not reality, and therefore the filmic moment of perception cannot be equated with the act of natural perception. Indeed, the great problem with phenomenological critics is their willingness to ignore the cinema's essential discontinuity. Film is not a flow of moving images, but rather the illusion of movement, created through single static images. Twenty-four photographic images must pass before a lens in a single second to create the visual impression of movement on the screen, where in fact there is none. While most filmmakers are interested in covering up this discontinuity central to the cinematic apparatus, experimental filmmakers have emphasized the discontinuous nature of the cinematic experience. Such filmmakers as Peter Kubelka, or such photographer/filmmakers as Hollis Frampton, have indeed used the film medium to theorize just how the cinema's sleight of hand forms the particular aesthetic experience that is film.

Finally, one can argue that Deleuze and other phenomenological theorists are totally focused on human "experience" in a philosophical sense and must therefore ignore all those aspects of experience that are culturally and historically defined. The fact remains, however, that no human experience exists in a vacuum. Instead, it occurs in the real world, where both ideology and subjectivity color perception and reception. Yet in the work of Deleuze and most other phenomenologists, reception and the role of the subject disappear completely, since their "subject" is an ahistorical construct, a philosophical abstraction defined as a human being, capable of cognitive thinking.

In the last thirty years, the primary focus of film studies has been on the position of the spectator in cinema, and less on the ontology of the medium. Structuralist and post-structuralist shifts in theoretical emphasis have meant that individual "photographic" images are of little concern to the film theorist. If photography is mentioned at all, then it is only to note that film and photography are culturally determined, that vision itself is inscribed in ideological structures. Both photographic media are seen as languages with grammatical structures, as systems of signs.[28]

Such recent film theoretical discussions have generally evolved in two different directions, focusing either on semiotics or on the construction of subjectivity, as postulated by film theorists utilizing the methodological tools of psychoanalysis. Another fruitful area of inquiry for a historically grounded film theory, however—less so for photographic theory—has been reception studies. Reception studies look at a historically specific audience to make sense of film's narrative structures.[29]

Interestingly, most film theorists working in the area of structural linguistics have failed to make any meaningful distinctions between film and photography. In this regard, they have taken their cue from Ferdinand de Saussure, who in his *Course in General Linguistics* (1916) provided the basis for a general theory of signs.[30] By theorizing that all articulated languages *(parole)* are based on underlying structures—that is, on certain rules, conventions, grammars— Saussure defined the necessity for exploring these deep structures. According to Saussure, the basic element of every language is a sign composed of two elements: the signifier linguistically represents an object, phenomenon, or fact in the real world—the signified. While the relationship between the signifier and the signified is purely arbitrary in most spoken and written languages, that is, defined by ideology, there is a much closer relationship between the two in the photographic media of film and photography, given the visual similarity between the two, making the sign appear "natural." Saussure would have argued that Bazin, Kracauer, and other phenomenologists equate the signifier with the signified.

Charles Pierce, another linguist, followed up on the work of Saussure, attempting to more precisely identify the exact nature of signification in visual language. Pierce defined all visual languages in terms of three major classes of signs: icons, indexes, and symbols. With icons the relationship between signifier and signified is one of physical resemblance; indexes are signs based on existential bonds; while symbols are purely arbitrary signs. According to Pierce, photographs belong to the class of indexical signs, although other semiologists, for example, Roland Barthes, have argued for their iconic nature. Indeed, Barthes labels himself a realist, since the photograph is for him a message without a code.[31] In point of fact, photographs can be characterized as both iconic and indexical. The cinema, while relying most heavily on indexical signs, also employs iconic and symbolic signification. Indeed, the complex narrative structure of cinema makes it possible to incorporate all three classes of signs in the same film and at the same time, since images in film are subject to multiple levels of interpretation.

Investigations of film and photography through the methodologies of structural linguistics thus analyze film and photography as separate systems of signs that function within a whole range of textual and cultural practices. Most instructive here is the work of Jean-Louis Baudry, who postulates that photographic media are a priori ideological, given the specific historical structure of their apparatuses.[32] According to Baudry (who here is basing his work on Béla Balázs), photography's ideological base is grounded in the utilization of Renaissance perspective as a so-called normal point of view. The cinematic apparatus, on the other hand, produces an ideological effect by its very invisibility: "Couldn't we thus say that the cinema reconstructs and forms the mechanical model (with the simplifications that this can entail) of a system of writing *(ecriture)* constituted by a material base and a counter-system (ideology, idealism) which uses this system while also concealing it?"[33]

As a result of such studies, the realist theories of Bazin and others are now interpreted as treatises supporting what some theorists have called classical film narrative. David Bordwell and others have defined classical film narrative as a system of conventions in Hollywood cinema that create the illusion of a seemingly unified text, an apparently seamless representation of reality.[34] The issue of photography as a single-image system no longer arises, since the focus of theoretical inquiry has shifted to the larger issues of systems of meaning. Rather, classical Hollywood narrative is seen as an ideological strategy, since it employs a formal aesthetic that it passes off as "natural" vision. Much the same could be said for central perspective in painting and for realist photography. Stephan Heath notes, for example, that photography's predilection toward the creation of a unified point of view is essentially based on fourteenth-century codes of perspective, which are profoundly ideological: "In a real sense, the ideological force of the photograph has been to 'ignore' this in its presentation as a coherent image of vision, an image that then carries over into a suggestion of the world as a kind of sum total of possible photographs, a spectacle to be recorded in its essence in an instantaneous objectification for the eye."[35]

This concentration on larger textual systems and their ideological implications also became the focus of the work of Christian Metz, one of the most influential film theorists of the last two decades. Metz, too, completely ignored the relationship of photography to film in his initial development of a grand-syntagmatic, influenced as it was by transformational grammar studies in linguistics and the attempt to discover deep structures for film language. Indeed, in Metz's *Film Language: A Semiotics of the Cinema,* the author not only passes over the issue of photography, but, like Eisenstein fifty years earlier, neglects the single film shot, since his primary agenda is to identify an underlying structure governing the creation of film syntagmas.

Film still from *Battleship Potemkin (1925)*, directed by Sergei Eisenstein.

As a result, Metz postulates that it is only through the laws of editing that the cinema can construct meaning.

In contradistinction to Metz (in his early structuralist phase), Roland Barthes refused to make the leap of faith necessary to claim that not the individual shot but the process of editing is the essential ingredient of cinema. Barthes certainly sees movement as central to the cinema, just as the immobility of photography is its strength. As a post-structuralist theorist embracing a realist aesthetic, Barthes is unable to ignore the power of the single image, which has a power that cannot be fully understood. As Barthes has noted: "If the specificity of cinema is not to be found in movement, but rather in a third undefinable sense, . . . then 'movement,' which has been turned into the essence of cinema, is by no means animation, flow, portability, 'life,' copy, but rather only the outline for a series of permutations, and a theory of the photogram is necessary.[36] In other words, Barthes, without returning to a simplistic realist analysis of the image, is calling for a film theory based on the iconic value of the film image. As stated above, Barthes assumes that the photograph is essentially denotative in its meaning, "a message without a code"—that is, its message cannot be further reduced to a linguistic code. At the same time, he suspects that the objectivity of the photograph is mythological because of the structural paradox of photography being denotative as well as connotative.[37] Connotative meaning is the result of coding through choice of subject, technical treatment, framing, layout, and accompanying text. In order to understand the difference between film and photography, then, Barthes suggests a theory of the photogram that would explicate film and photography in terms of movement (life) and stasis (death). A photograph reduces life (the signified) to death (the signifier) through "a simple click" of the camera.[38] But film, too, while retaining the element of time and movement, transports the real into the realm of a timelessness that can be reproduced at will.

Christian Metz, meanwhile, has also retreated from his earlier position, approaching cinema from a seemingly completely different angle. In *The Imaginary Signifier,* Metz drew on the achievements of psychoanalysis to consider photography in relation to film. Metz begins by noting that photography's perception register is more limited than the cinema's, because the element of time and the element of sound are missing.[39] Reception in the cinema is therefore more complex than in photography, because it is sensually speaking more intense, involving optic and aural channels, and because it is subject to continuous change. However, Metz then goes on to equate film and photography in terms of the construction of the photographic/film apparatus. All vision, according to Metz, consists of a double "movement" involving the actual physical stimulus of the optic nerve (projection) and the perception of things through consciousness (introjection)—that is, through desire. In photography and film, the camera becomes a mere extension of the physical body:

> The technology of photography carefully conforms to this (banal) phantasy accompanying perception. The camera is "trained" on the object like a fire-arm (= projection) and the object arrives to make an imprint, a trace, on the receptive surface of the film-strip (= introjection). The spectator himself does not escape these pincers, for he is part of the apparatus, and also be-cause pincers, on the imaginary plane (Melanie Klein), mark our relation to the world as a whole and are rooted in the primary figures of orality.[40]

Given this argument, it is clear for Metz that neither the photograph, nor the cinema, can ever be a simple reproduction of reality or even a representation of reality. Rather, photography and film exist within the realm of the sym-bolic, of desire: "In order to understand the film (at all), I must perceive the photographed object as absent, its photograph as present, and the presence of this absence as signifying. The imaginary of the cinema presupposes the symbolic."[41]

Metz is of course constructing an analogy between the filmic viewing ex-perience and Freud's theory of disavowal: a male child notices the absence of the phallus in the mother and assumes that she has been castrated. However, unable to believe what he has seen, he denies the supposed castration, con-structing instead a fetish as a substitute for the missing penis. Like the child caught in a circle of believing and disbelieving what he has seen, construct-ing a presence where there is only an absence, the film viewer chooses to be-lieve in the illusion, even when he "knows" that it is an illusion. The sym-bolic is predicated on the spectator's belief in an illusion of a physical presence. It is generally thought that the illusion of a physical presence is much less sustainable in photography than in film.

While the similarities in the apparatuses of film and photography are ac-knowledged, the varying contexts for reception of the two media offer a key to their difference: in general, the positioning of the subject is completely different. Film addresses an audience in a darkened space whose awareness of itself is colored by its collective response, while photographic reception speaks to individuals. It is exactly this difference that Christian Metz takes up in his essay, "Photography and Fetish." Metz hypothesizes that pho-tography functions much better as a fetish object than the cinema because of its size (it can be held), and because it can be looked at again and again for as long as the viewer wishes, thus increasing its suitability for obsessive behavior. Gazing at a film image, on the other hand, does not allow for that kind of staring, because it moves within a space-time continuum over which the viewer has no control.[42]

As Ben Singer has noted in a perceptive critique of Metz, however, the question remains whether a photograph can be defined at all as a fetish object in the classic Freudian sense, since it is not located near the site of disavowal.[43] Singer ultimately accepts Metz's thesis with qualifications, identifying three areas of similarity between photographs and fetish objects: photographs cut off space beyond the frame, just as the fetish pushes the memory of castration and female lack out of view; photographs are instantaneous impressions, just as the sight of female lack burns instantaneously into the memory of a child; a photograph is both a reminder of a lost moment of time and a protection against that loss, just as a fetish is both a reminder of castration and a protection against it.[44] Does cinema work equally well as a fetish? No, according to Metz, because cinema does not have the power of concentration that photography has, allowing for psychic energy to be spent all at once on the same object.

This hypothesis has also influenced Raymond Bellour, who has written about the appearance of photographs in films and what perceptual mechanisms such an appearance sets in motion.[45] Bellour, like Barthes and Metz, understands that the photograph has a particular power of fascination all its own, even when it is seen in a film. He writes: "Yet the presence of a photo on the screen gives rise to a very particular trouble. Without ceasing to advance its own rhythm, the film seems to freeze, to suspend itself, inspiring in the spectator a recoil from the image that goes hand in hand with a growing fascination. This curious effect attests to the immense power of photography to hold its own in a situation in which it is not truly itself."[46] Bellour goes on to theorize that while the cinema functions only within time, the photograph suspends time, tearing the viewer out of the diagetic present, allowing him to linger in another time in the past, where time itself no longer has any meaning. In doing so, the photograph simultaneously distances the viewer from the illusion of the cinema, allowing him/her to reflect on the act of viewing. According to Bellour, the "stillness tempers the 'hysteria' of the film."[47]

In conclusion, it seems valid to point out that neither film theorists nor photography theorists have yet fully articulated a general theory that can account for the differences and similarities in both photographic media. Clearly, the structural characteristics of the two media define them as distinct textual systems, since the signification of space and time is not only completely different, but also affects the reception of the media in different ways. Yet, as this brief survey proves, such theoretic discussions appear, if at all, only in piecemeal fashion, usually in the context of wider discussions. Finally, it is not the goal of this book or this introduction to provide a complete theoretical discussion. Rather, it has been my goal to address the issues and point out some of the gaps and desiderata in the hopes that such musings will provide a fragile context for the essays that follow.

Central to the arguments presented in the pages below is the belief that photographers who make films have, thanks in part to their training as photographers, a singular and individual point of view. As noted above, photographers have most often tended toward avant-garde and independent documentary films, because only these film forms allow for the greatest degree of freedom from the constraints of an industrialized mode of production. In contrast to fiction feature-film production, in which the director can only exercise a controlling vision if he is able to resist the influences of producers and other persons with economic interests in the production, the avant-garde and independent film director can oversee all creative aspects. Given their position as cameramen or as directors, photographer/filmmakers are particularly sensitive to questions of composition, lighting, and camera distance— that is, they cannot help developing an individual style or point of view. Such a point of view is structural, the result of conscious and subconscious mechanisms. The more focused a filmmaker is on his inner eye, the less willing he/she will be to take on projects that are of no personal interest to them. The photographers discussed below are notable for both their willingness to explore and experiment at the formal level in the medium of cinema, identifying them as film avant-gardists, and for their consistent thematic concerns.

Even when photographer/filmmakers are careful to maintain their distance from the objects or persons depicted, coolly and objectively viewing their environment, they cannot escape their point of view, their own subjectivity. This is all the more true because the position of the spectator in relation to the producer of images has changed. No longer are producer and consumer abiding by the rules of the game that in traditional societies assumed a unified worldview, uniting subject and object, photographer/filmmaker and audience. Despite all the protestations of realist theorists, film and photography have in the twentieth century precipitated the breakdown in the belief that the world, that is, reality, can be objectively depicted. Too many competing media, too many competing messages, the deluge of visual images in photography, film, and video have injected a healthy proportion of skepticism in any reception of visual images. Rudolf Arnheim characterizes this change most cogently:

> Photography reaches into the world as an intruder, and therefore it also cre-
> ates a disturbance, just as in physics of light the single photon at the atomic
> level upsets the facts on which it reports. . . . Inevitably the photographer is a
> part of the situation he depicts. . . . Characteristically enough, however, our
> own century has discovered a new attraction in the very artificiality of pic-
> ture taking and endeavored to use it deliberately for the symbolic representa-
> tion of an age that has fallen from innocence.[48]

As a result of these factors, it is possible to hypothesize that the subjectivity
of the photographer is of crucial importance to the production of photographic imagery in the twentieth century as well as a given fact of life in the
reception of such images. Indeed, we can see a chronological development in
our history of films by photographers away from realistic narratives (even in
documentary) and discourses defined by objectivity toward an ever-increasing
awareness of the futility of objectivity, effectively embracing discourses of
subjectivity and voyeurism. Were such early practitioners as Lerski, Strand,
and Moholy-Nagy more interested in objectively visualizing the real world
or utilizing the creative means at their disposal to create a emotional bridge
between the artist and the viewer, then we can see ever more overt forms of
subjectivity influencing the work of post–World War II photographers.
While Helen Levitt still denies the subjectivity in her own work,[49] Robert
Frank, Danny Lyon, and Chris. Marker readily accept that their work is characterized by subjectivity, even when their subject matter is political. Indeed,
by coming to terms with their subjectivity, rather than repressing it in a discourse of supposed objectivity, they reflect a more "real" consciousness of
the relationship between subject and object. With the career of Ed van der
Elsken, we see a photographer whose work is unashamedly subjective and
voyeuristic to the point of narcissism. This trend toward subjectivity has also
brought with it an increasing unwillingness to communicate with an audience, since the terms of such a discourse are thought to be undefinable,
given the heterogeneous nature of the audience. Individual readings remain
necessarily incomplete due to private references in the work, on the one
hand, and the subjectivity of the reader, on the other.

   In the pages below, I have chosen to focus on a wide variety of photographers who have made substantial contributions as filmmakers, even when
these contributions have not been generally acknowledged. Each chapter introduces the work of a photographer/filmmaker. Clearly, the choice of photographers is a matter of personal circumstance and film availability, but it
can only be justified with some difficulty on theoretical grounds. Some readers, for example, may miss chapters on Raymond Depardon, William Klein,
or Johann van der Keuken, all of whom would have fit magnificently. On the

other hand, an attempt has been made to vary the methodological tools of my inquiry with each chapter, since the work being introduced is too heterogeneous to subsume under a single theoretical point of view, and I want to demonstrate that such a multiplicity of perspectives is productive when analyzing a wide variety of film work. It is my hope that the theoretical perspective employed in each chapter has been clearly stated and will focus the reader's attention on the points I wish to make.

Chapter 2 begins with an analysis of the films and photography of an artist who is better known in America as a filmmaker than as a photographer: Chris. Marker. Indeed, Marker's photography books are virtually unknown in the United States (and are hard to find in Europe also), as are most of his films, with the exception of such films as *La jetée* and *Sans soleil.* I have decided to begin with a discussion of photography in his books and documentary films, since this will allow me to continue the theoretical discussion begun here. Marker's work, in fact, affords a unique opportunity to look at the way these two media function and communicate differently.

After the theoretical discussions centered on Chris. Marker's work, chapter 3 moves back in time to the beginning of the century to look at the films of a photographer who moved freely from the commercial cinema to the modernist avant-garde. The Swiss-German photographer/filmmaker Helmar Lerski worked as a film cameraman in the German commercial film industry, as a technical specialist, and, in prestatehood Israel, as a filmmaker of what can loosely be termed propaganda films. Surprisingly, the evidence of Lerski's forty-year career as a photographer suggests that in virtually all cases he focused almost obsessively on his own aesthetic interests, regardless of what kind of films were being made.

Chapter 4 follows the film career of Paul Strand, who, like Lerski, was able to move from being a cameraman for hire in the commercial film industry to an independent producer of documentaries. The chapter begins with an analysis of Strand and Charles Sheeler's *Manhatta* (1921) and attempts to contextualize this film in the larger framework of the history of American avant-garde film. It is my contention—in contrast to the unqualified modernism of the European film avant-garde—that the American avant-garde has always been characterized by undercurrents of romanticism. Paul Strand's later political documentaries and photography books, which are the focus of the last third of the chapter, are similarly marked by Strand's romanticism, coupled with his undoubtably sincere Marxist politics.

In order to evaluate just what were the differences in the 1920s and 1930s between European and American modernism, as it pertains to film and photography, chapter 5 discusses the career of one of the most important photographer/filmmakers to emerge from Weimar Germany, László Moholy-Nagy. As a teacher at the famous Bauhaus School, Moholy-Nagy moved exclusively within the sphere of the modernist art avant-garde, seeing his efforts in film as part and parcel of his aesthetic experiments in a host of other media, including photography, painting, and architecture. At the same time, Moholy-Nagy, like Strand, attempted to bring together his leftist political sympathies with his modernist aesthetics.

Chapter 6 looks at the career of another American photographer whose career as a filmmaker has been previously totally ignored: Helen Levitt. Levitt's *In the Street* (1946) has long been a favorite selection in the Museum of Modern Art's film circulating library, like *Manhatta*. Yet despite their popularity, little serious analysis has been published on either film. As a woman working in a mostly man's world, Levitt has followed a more underground career than most. At the same time, she forms a bridge between the documentarist concerns of filmmakers and photographers in the pre–World War II era, and the subjective visions of the post–World War II film and photographic avant-garde.

Chapters 7 and 8 focus on two seemingly related photographers who have continued productive careers as photographers and filmmakers: Robert Frank and Danny Lyon. Yet, as these essays attempt to illustrate, their point of view and filmmaking aesthetics are quite different, despite attempts by some critics to lump them together. While Frank's films are analyzed as a continuing family drama in which the symbolic father (the filmmaker) attempts to create order, Lyon's films are much more overtly political, focusing on social groups at the margins of society.

Chapter 9 presents a photographer and filmmaker who is virtually unknown in the United States, although his first photography exhibition at the Museum of Modern Art was seen as early as 1955: Ed van der Elsken. This chapter is also somewhat of a work in process, since a number of van der Elsken's films have yet to be preserved, and others have still to be definitively identified. Like that of Robert Frank, Chris. Marker, and others, van der Elsken's work is radically subjective. In fact, both his films and his photography may represent the most extreme expression of an aesthetic that is almost solely focused on the artist's own consciousness.

The volume closes with a bio-filmography of over 130 photographers who have made films, and a selected bibliography on photographers who have become filmmakers. It is hoped that both the lexicon and the bibliography will provide the impetus for further research in this field.

2 Chris. Marker

PHOTOGRAPHIC JOURNEYS

Formerly a journalist, novelist, essayist, and assistant director to Alain Resnais, Chris. Marker has had a brilliant career as a politically committed, left-wing documentary filmmaker but is less well known for his work as a photographer. He has published at least six photography books, although none of them have been published in English, and his early books have been long out of print even in Europe. His first two photographic books, *La Chine: Porte ouvert (China: Open Door)*[1] and *Coréennes (The Koreans)* documented his impressions of visits to the People's Republic of China and North Korea, respectively, while a later book, *Le dépays*,[2] concerns Japan.[3] The latter two are photo-essays that juxtapose images and words to present both a real and an imaginary journey. Many of his documentary films, for example, *Dimanche à Pekin (Sunday in Peking,* 1956), *Lettre de Sibérie (Letter from Siberia,* 1958), *Description d'un combat* (1960), *Cuba Si!* (1961), *Le mystère Koumiko* (1965), and *Sans soleil* (1982), are similarly meditations about travel to China, Russia, Israel, Cuba, Japan, and Africa, respectively.[4] Like his photo-books, Marker's films are a mixture of documentary, diary, essay, memoir, and fiction. Whether photography or film, his works are constructed as multiple, even contradictory texts, consisting of juxtapositions of word and image, music and language, pictures and music, the whole coming together as a "stream of consciousness," which no longer differentiates between objectivity and subjectivity, reality and dreams, fact and desire, the past, the present, and the future. Similar to his erstwhile mentor, Alain Resnais—the director of *Last Year at Marienbad;* or Alain Robbe-Grillet, the writer of *nouvelle romans* such as *The Voyeur*—Marker leads the viewer into an imaginary world, which nevertheless reflects experiences in the real one.

One of Chris. Marker's earliest films, *Sunday in Peking,* begins with the statement: "For thirty years I have dreamt of Peking without knowing it. In my memory I had an image out of a children's book, without knowing exactly where it had come from, an image of the city gate of Peking: the path to the Ming Dynasty memorial. Suddenly one day I was there. It was a special feeling to wander through an image from my childhood."[5] The film's point of view, that of a subjective observer from France, is emphasized through the visuals: in the shot Marker pans over childhood toys, then up to the Eiffel Tower, then down again to an open book with a large photograph of the above mentioned Bejing street scene, before fading out and in to Marker's own reconstruction of the scene on film in 1955.

An image from childhood also defines Chris. Marker's science fiction short, *La jetée* (1963), which consists exclusively of photographs. As in *Sunday in Peking,* the whole story originates from the film's first image, an image remembered from childhood. The human ability to remember, to recall a visual, nonverbal imprint in the brain as experience and knowledge, is for Marker a never-ending theme. The narrator in *La jetée* says from off screen: "Moments in one's memory are like other moments. They remain conscious only because of the scars they leave behind." In *Sans soleil,* he writes: "He liked the fragility of those moments suspended in time. His memories, their only function to leave behind nothing but memories."[6] His four-hour, monumental documentary history of the New Left, *Le fond de l'air est rouge* (1977), released in Great Britain in the early 1980s in a three-hour version as *A Grin without a Cat,* also begins with a childhood memory, but one that is already mediated: it is the memory of an image of maggot-infested meat, followed by the aborted execution of Russian sailors from Sergei Eisenstein's *Potemkin* (1925). Likewise, Marker's latest project, the video installation *Silent Movie* (1995), has its genesis in memories from his childhood movie experience, film scenes with Clara Bow and Simone Genevoix reworked as still photographs on video—actresses whom Marker calls his "amours enfantines."[7]

According to Marker, all these images exist in his head in a precognitive state, at the level of pure perception; they are images between the subconscious and consciousness, between actual experience and the imaginary. Marker transforms these rediscovered images into a discourse on photographic images, a discourse about human imagination and the images in people's heads. In Marker's meditation on Akira Kurasawa, *A. K.* (1985), the filmmaker connects the very act of aesthetic creation with memory. Holding a close-up on a hand-held tape recorder, while a Japanese TV screen is seen flickering in the background, Marker notes at the beginning of his film: "To create is to remember. Memory is the basis of everything." In *Letter from Siberia,* he writes: "I write to you from a far country," a statement meant literally, as well as figuratively, since the past itself is a distant country.

Born in July 1921[8] in Neuilly-sur-Seine, a suburb of Paris, Chris. Marker's birth name is Christian-Françoise Bouche-Villeneuve. His early years are shrouded in mystery; indeed, Marker has made a career of fiercely guarding his anonymity. He has frustrated all efforts of individuals and organizations to compile a usable biography or to organize retrospectives.[9] It is known that during World War II Marker gave up his studies of philosophy to join the French resistance, eventually becoming a paratrooper attached to the American Army Air Corps. After the war he became a regular contributor to *Esprit,* a left-wing Catholic magazine, writing poetry, short stories, political commentaries, and film reviews (the latter alongside his colleague, André Bazin). He was also a founding member of the staff of *Cahiers du Cinema* and editor in the publishing house of Editions du Seuil, for which he began editing a series of travel books. His first novel, *Le coeur net,* published in 1949, reworked his experiences flying in the war. It was followed by a collection of essays, *Giraudoux par lui-meme* (1952). After codirecting and writing the commentary for Alain Resnais' short documentary about African art, *Les statues meurent aussi,* shot in 1950 but banned in France until 1963,[10] Marker participated in a documentary about the Summer Olympics in Helsinki, *Olympia 52* (1952). In the mid-1950s, Marker went to Beijing, where he shot a film, as well as photographic images for his first photography book, *China: Open Door.* At this time Marker apparently also met the photographer Robert Frank and—according to a letter Marker wrote to Bill Horrigan in 1994—realized he would never be as good a photographer as Frank.[11] Instead, he decided to dedicate himself to the cinema, but not exclusively, as we shall see.

Chris. Marker's cinematic oeuvre can be roughly divided into two broad categories: those films that are more personal and subjective, and the more overtly political films—the latter often made in collaboration or for hire. Such a division between personal and political films should not, however, be overemphasized, for it is equally true that all of Marker's "personal" films are also marked by his commitment to Marxism. Three of his early travel films, *Letter from Siberia, Description d'un combat,* and *Cuba Si!* (1961), are politically committed documentaries with highly personal, even idiosyncratic commentaries. *Cuba Si!* was edited immediately after the Bay of Pigs and banned in France and Germany for its overtly anti-American stance. *Le tonbeau d'Alexandre* (1993; the U.S. release title was *The Last Bolshevik*) is likewise a documentary of the Soviet filmmaker Alexander Medvedkin, yet it is clear that Marker is also writing his own cinematic autobiography through a description of Medvedkin's checkered career.

According to Richard Roud, *La joli mai* (1962) marks a turn toward less personal filmmaking, but this is only partially true. *La joli mai* begins with a lovely precredits sequence in which Simone Signoret recites a personal declaration of love to the city. Marker lovingly portrays Paris, the city of his birth, in long, panning shots and static, virtually abstract images. While Marker keeps these nonsynchronous sequences in long-shot, he moves in to close-up for his interviews. Shot in a cinema verité style, the film documents through street interviews with ordinary Parisians the mood of the country in May 1962, the first spring of peace after the loss of the Algerian War. The topics discussed are banal, everyday events that form people's lives, Marker constantly asking questions from off camera, animating the interviewees to express their feelings. Initially, the film's political message seems to be that most ordinary Parisians are not interested in politics, only in making as much money as possible. Only in the second half, when the topic turns to the Algerian War, do politics take on an increasingly important role.

In 1967 Marker formed a film collective, SLON (Société pour le Lancement des Oeuvres Nouvelles), which was initially set up to produce *Loin du Viêtnam* (1967), a collective work by Jean-Luc Godard, Joris Ivens, Yves Klein, Claude Lelouch, Alain Resnais, and Agnes Varda. Based on Dziga Vertov's concepts of radical leftist documentary, the SLON continued under Marker's direction as an effort to empower workers to produce their own films. Thus, Marker's personal artistic identity disappeared completely for several years while he supervised the production of shorts, for example, *Le deuxième procès d'Arthur London* (1969) and *Carlos Marighela* (1970); and longer documentaries, such as *La bataille des dix millions* (1970) and *Le train en marche* (1971).

After this intense political period, which culminated in Marker's personal analysis in *A Grin without a Cat,* Marker returned to his roots with *San soleil.* In the 1980s he turned his interest to the new medium of video, directing a cycle of short videos, *Zapping Zone* (1985–94), which has been exhibited as part of a multimedia project, *L'heritage de la chouette (The Owl's Legacy),* a thirteen-part series on Greek civilization; and *The Last Bolshevik.* Most recently he has produced a series of so-called video haikus, videos of one- and two-minute length, including *Petite ceinture* (1994) and *Owl Gets in Your Eye* (1994).

While the overtly political films, as well as Chris. Marker's move to video and television, are important facets of his overall career as a visual artist, this chapter does not and cannot discuss his cinematic oeuvre in its totality. Marker has to date produced nearly sixty films and videos. Instead, it will focus on Marker's utilization of his photographs in his films. This will allow not only for an analysis of a particular aspect of Marker's artistic persona, which has heretofore been underexamined—namely, his obsession with memory and subjectivity—but also for a more theoretical discussion of the similarities and differences between the two media of film and photography.

In Marker's films and photography, real geographical places are captured in images and transformed through the act of reception into subjective visions. The camera is utilized as a tool for the objective documentation of reality, but the result is a consciously constructed aesthetic subjectivity. This subjectivity is the result of the juxtaposition of word and image, the editing process, and the production of a sound track.

Like *La jetée, Si j'avais quatre dromadaires* (1966) consists exclusively of photographs.[12] Richard Roud has characterized these two films as among the most personal in Marker's oeuvre.[13] On the sound track of *Si j'avais quatre dromadaires,* three different fictional narrators, representing Marker's multiple personalities, comment on the images, interspersed with jazz, classical music, and animal noises. The photos are from the first ten years of Marker's career as a photographer (1955–65): his journeys to China, Korea, Russia, Israel, and Cuba. The use of photography in this film; in *La jetée;* in his political film-tract, *On vous parle du Brésil: Tortures* (1969); and in his video *Photo. Browse* (1990), as well as his intermittent production of photo-books, emphasizes Marker's continuous fascination with the medium of photography. In these films and books, Marker employs a highly personal essay form, which takes its cue from a specific geographical place in the real world to create space and time coordinates for the construction of a subjective perception of the world.

Time and space—better said, the human perception of time and space and its transformation through memory—are, likewise, themes that run through virtually all of Chris. Marker's work. In *Sans soleil,* Marker's fictitious narrator says: "He said, in the nineteenth century the conquest of space was paramount. In the twentieth century the challenge was the coexistence of different concepts of time."[14] Thus, Marker's work also considers just how such a perception can be translated into a photographic medium, that is, his work self-reflectively meditates on the relationship between film and photography. And finally, Marker questions again and again the medium itself, whether film or photography, in order to discover their similarities and differences. His documentary films thus never refer to a single, unified reality; rather they are representations of various realities, which contradict each

Film still from *Letter from Siberia* (1958), directed by Chris. Marker.

other, which are relativized through the act of aesthetic production, and which theorize photographic images as representation.

For example, in *Letter from Siberia,* Marker reworks a famous experiment, first devised by the Soviet film theorist Lev Kuleshov in 1923. An automobile and a bus pass each other on the street, Siberian construction workers level out sand for paving the street, an Asian man in a winter coat crosses a street. A montage of three separate images is shown three times in a row with three different commentaries: first a heroic-pathetic commentary about the Soviet Union's classless society; then an anti-Communist analysis regarding the lack of materials under the Soviet party dictatorship; finally an "objective" description of the actual conditions, a little bit positive, a bit critical.[15] However, since Marker is visually proving the semantic ambiguity of photographic images, he doesn't quite believe in the third possibility: objectivity. He says: "But this objectivity is not always the same thing. It does not deform the reality of Siberia, but it arrests the time for judgement, and that is the same thing as deformation."[16] Marker believes that every statement, every description deforms reality, if only unintentionally, because the world changes from moment to moment through time. An observation is at the moment of perception already an anachronism. The only objectivity, therefore, is a radical acknowledgment of subjectivity, a subjectivity that documents the relationship between the viewer and that which is seen, that acknowledges the culpability of the producer of images as representations. The central paradox in the work of Chris. Marker, therefore, is the instrumentalization of a belief in a photographic objectivity (documentary conventions) to communicate a radical subjectivity, thus placing the act of reception at the center of his aesthetic concept.

Marker had begun his filmmaking career with a documentary on African art, *Les statues meurent aussi,* that ruthlessly attacked Western colonialism and its racist and utterly subjective perceptions of black-African aesthetics. Shooting African statues in a high-key light, but completely motionless, as if taking photographs, Marker and codirector Resnais state that Western civilization burned the real history of Africa. What remains are works of art that are mute, because our eyes and ears cannot understand what they communicate. Torn from their cultural, historical and ritualistic context, these statues are degraded to the level of knickknacks in the white art marketplace; black culture becomes a site for "primitive" white desire. The true meanings of these creations are no longer accessible to the viewer, because the cultural context has been obliterated. Marker/Resnais can therefore only document the objects visually, while denying any interpretation.

The central thesis of *A Grin without a Cat,* on the other hand, is that the "revolution" of the 1960s was as a revolution merely a subjective experience, while at the level of objective history it was not so much an uprising as a revolutionary feeling that gripped the masses. In the film, Marker uses only found footage, that is, supposedly objective newsreel and documentary images, but through editing and the juxtaposition of word and image on his sound track, he creates a subjective history of the student and worker movements in France before and after 1968, the anti-Vietnam demonstrations worldwide, the leftist revolutionary movements in Latin America from Castro to Chile, the radical Baader-Meinhof cells in Germany, the Watergate hearings, etc. Marker's narrative strategy is to keep circling around his topic, to present a theory and then deconstruct it, to articulate a dream and then demonstrate its demise. Rather than despair at the "failure" of the revolution, Marker finds solace in the little victories, in the realization that what appeared to be a failure was merely only a subjective misinterpretation of the historical process, a misreading of the signs of history. What emerges is a sense that the meanings of objective images are in a continual state of flux, dependent on the historical moment of reception. Newsreel images that once seemed to be pregnant with meaning for the future suddenly only document a specific moment in time that failed to influence the future in any significant way.

The cinema becomes a site for reception, for the confrontation between an objective world of images and the subjective world of consciousness. The cinema is seeing. The cinema is a projection (objectively speaking) and a projection of consciousness (subjectivity).

La jetée opens with a view from the observation deck at Orly airport. The structure's clean, cool, even sterile modernist lines, so typical of 1950s architecture, blends into the horizon, giving nothing of itself or the personality of its creator, a tabula rasa for the projection of one's subjectivity. The film's title is ambiguous, referring simultaneously to the observation deck and to the film's hero, whose subjectivity is at stake here, who is catapulted through time like a projectile. Time/space travel thus also becomes a metaphor for cinema.[17] While the camera zooms back slowly, the narrator of *La jetée* begins his story: "This is the story of a man who had been marked since childhood by an image. The brutal scene that he would only comprehend years later occurred on the observation deck at Orly years before the Third World War."

Single photographic images follow: a family on a Sunday excursion, a close-up of a woman's face, an airplane, a man falling to the ground. For the viewer these images remain isolated, fragmentary, sequentially constructed, but seemingly without rhyme or reason. Their syntactical logic is no longer apparent, their meaning within a syntagma lost. They are mere memories without form, moments without continuity, signs of a space, of a scene. Thus, even in this first scene, Marker's decision to use photographs instead of moving images already seems to have a logic of its own: in our memories we seldom remember "moving images"; rather, our mental images often are frozen, isolated and fragmented in time. Only with difficulty can we reconstruct them into a film in our heads. The reference to images from childhood connects *La jetée* to *Sunday in Peking,* Marker's photography, and *Sans soleil,* all of which can be read as documents of memory. One of Marker's favorite films is Alfred Hitchcock's *Vertigo* (1959), an obsessive investigation of images and memory that Marker has paid tribute to in *Sans soleil.* In a fictitious interview with a computer, Marker states that he thinks of himself less as a documentary filmmaker than as a maker of documents, which contribute to the world's memory: "The word 'documentary' leaves a trail of sanctimonious boredom behind it. But the idea of making files like I do with you—to present data so that people figure out more or less how it was to be an earthling in the 80's suits me well."[18] In *Sans soleil,* the narrator states: "I will spend my life trying to understand the function of remembering. Which is not the same as forgetting, but rather its mining. We do not remember. We rewrite memory much as history is rewritten."[19]

Sans soleil also begins with an image evoking childhood, a black and white photo of three children in Iceland in 1965. Ironically, the narrator comments that this photo is an image that cannot be connected to other images, that is, it generates neither a series of images nor a film. Yet, a film commences with just this image. According to Marker's narrator, it would be best to surround this particular film image with black leader, "because if one can't see the happiness emanating from the image, one can at least see the blackness."[20] This image of innocence and happiness, which can only be read as such in the subjective moment of narration, and which is less pregnant with meaning if viewed by a sober observer, appears again and again in the course of the film. It becomes a sign for memory itself, an idée fixe, a secret, which will never quite be revealed. "At that point my three Icelandic children intruded and I picked up the shot once again. . . . It explains things better than anything else I saw at that moment, which is why I kept their outstretched arms in a long zoom to the last twenty-fifth of a second." Repeatedly, one finds in the films and photo-books of Chris. Marker images that do not reveal their secret, which can be objectively described, but whose semantics can only be partially deciphered, because Marker's images are inscribed by their subjectivity and the viewer's subjective ability to decode them.

Si j'avais quatre dromadaires also consists of single, photographic images whose semantic logic is not immediately apparent. Instead, they seem to be syntactically connected simply according to formal criteria. In quick succession one sees a close-up of a camera lens, a Korean man sitting in a sewage pipe, a bicycle, a man reflected in a fish-eye lens, a model of an atom, a bust from Greek antiquity. The circular composition of the images ties these photographs at a formal level together, but what do they mean? The act of photography itself is being theorized, according to the first narrator of the film: "Photography is a hunt, a hunt without the desire to kill. A hunt of the angels. . . . One tracks, aims, shoots, and click! Instead of a corpse, one has made something eternal."[21] Thus, one can read this sequence as Marker's visualization of the apparatus of the camera (photography and film), those human beings who utilize this technology, and its capabilities as a medium of representation. The result is art; its purpose is human communication—the single most important manifestation of being human.

A photograph takes a moment of time and transports it into timelessness. As a sign, the photographic image remains independent of time. Even a syntactical ordering of individual photographs, for example, in photo-reportage or photo-roman, does not change this fact. While photographs may be chronologically or thematically organized as single images, explanatory captions and the reader's cognitive capabilities are still necessary to create the temporal connections between these photographic moments frozen in time.

This principle is clearly demonstrated in *Commentaires 1 et 2*, the two volumes of Chris. Marker's collected screenplays (1953–66). Since Marker's films are not just dependent on his narratives, but rather consist of juxtapositions between words and images, he has attempted to visualize his film scripts through film stills. The photographs are integrated into the text in various sizes, sometimes taking up a whole page, sometimes only half a page, sometimes only as a small image at the edge of the text. The reader assumes that Marker has included all the most important shots in each film, yet the photographs remain strangely abstract, because they are single photographic stills and not moving images. In two-dimensional form they can only function as indexes of films scenes, giving the reader a visual clue, while he or she reads the verbal narration to the film. Any attempt to read the "illustrations" in *Commentaires* as a syntactical construction, however, is bound to fail, because the spaces between images are too great, precluding any semantic sense. The selection of films stills (why these and not other images?) remains mysterious. It is a mixture of long shots and close-ups, panoramas of cityscapes and landscapes, as well as portraits of human beings, interspersed with the products of visual culture: comics, advertising, propaganda bill-

Film still from *Sans soleil* (1981), directed by Chris. Marker.

Illustration from *Coréennes* (1959), a book by Chris. Marker. Also seen as a film still in *Si j'avais quatres dromadaires* (1966), *directed by Marker.*

boards, television, paintings, statues. These film stills hardly outline, even in general terms, the contours of the actual film; rather they are Marker's representation of the film as text.

The difficulty in making semantic sense of the illustrations is heightened when the reader realizes that individual photographs, that is, the film stills appearing in *Commentaires,* don't actually appear in the film. They are indeed film stills, rather than frame enlargements. For example, Marker published no less than thirty-five photographs in his film script for *Si j'avais quatre dromadaires,* which are not be found in the actual film, while others are framed completely differently, even though the film consists solely of photographs. In the script for *Sunday in Peking,* Marker likewise reframes many of the stills. One can therefore assume that he sees the film scripts in *Commentaires* as completely independent works, which have the privilege of being "incomplete." Not surprisingly, the book includes at least two film scripts for films that were never made and which Marker designates as *films imaginaires:* "L'amerique rêve" and "Soy México."

In contrast to other photographers who publish photo-books, it is noteworthy that Marker uses photographs relatively sparingly in his *Commentaires.* The published narration of *Sans soleil* (in German translation) eschews photographs and stills altogether. Even Marker's photography books, *Coréennes* and *Le dépays,* consist of very long texts in which photographs are inserted. They are neither independent image sequences with full-page photographs, as can be found in most other photo-books, nor merely illustrations to the text. Each level of communication, visual and verbal, remains to a certain extent independent. Marker writes at the beginning of *Le dépays:* "The text provides very little commentary to the images, just as the images hardly illustrate the text. In fact, they are two series of ideas, and at times they cross or point to each other, but to confront them [image and text] would be useless and tiresome."[22] One need not take Marker's statement at face value. Clearly, though, language and a literary aesthetic dominate the text, possibly because Marker's language creates its own images, and because the photographs need words to escape from their ambiguity. Word and image are related, just as they are related in Marker's films, which show a predilection toward a continuous flow of narration from off screen. His films use language and words, the way other films use sound as a continuous stimulus.

Significantly, Marker's most conventional photography book, *La renfermée: La Corse,* has a text by Marie Susini and merely photographs by Marker.[23] Photography and text are therefore rigorously segregated, Marker's forty-one images appearing without captions (one photo per page) in two sections at the beginning and in the middle of Susini's narrative. The sequencing of images from Corsica is structured as a slow zoom. The first section of photographs begins with vistas of the island, then moves to streetscapes, and ends with monuments and statues. The second section focuses on portraits of the island's inhabitants, both in close-up and in their environments, and ends with three images of animals in the Corsican landscape. The two sections are linked conceptually with a close-up image of Christ's head and a photograph of a Corsican man, framed by devotional candles. The overall layout of this book is thus, in contrast to Marker's other photography books, less conducive to a juxtaposition of image and text. The lack of captions allows the images to retain their ambiguity.

The ambiguity of the image is less apparent in the cinema, possibly due to the additional information heard on the sound track. Films consist of twenty-four frames per second, which form a continuum in the human brain and create the illusion of time, as well as space. The signification of time also allows for the signification of space, since only movement within the frame can create the illusion of space beyond the conventions of central perspective.

The question of space and time and their interrelationship is central to *La jetée*. In Marker's science fiction film, humanity searches for a refuge from its ruined environment (space) through time. The narrator relates the outbreak of the Third World War, the ensuing nuclear holocaust, and the plight of the survivors, who are driven underground by the radioactive contamination of the earth's surface. Cut off from the natural spaces of the planet, surviving scientists search for an escape hatch in time, but their experiments fail. It seems that the idea of waking up in another time is more than the imagination can bear, leading to the insanity of their subjects. Only when they discover a former soldier, obsessed with an image from childhood, are they able to knock a hole in time. The nameless hero travels into the past and falls in love with the mysterious woman on the observation deck at Orly whom he had seen as a child, and whose memory has haunted him. After successfully traveling into the past, he is sent into the future to bring back energy sources, medical supplies, and foodstuffs. His mission successfully completed, he is slated for liquidation, since he lives in a totalitarian society in which the individual serves the needs of an all-powerful technocracy. But he rebels and is able to escape into the past, to the woman he loves, one last time. Only at the airport, at the very moment he faces his lover and a killer, sent from his own time in the future, does he realize his fate: "When he saw the man from the underground, he recognized that one cannot flee from time, and he understood that that haunted moment from his own childhood was the moment of his own death."

Film still from *La jetée* (1962), directed by Chris. Marker.

La jetée thus deals with the human prison of time and space. The film's narrative dilemma is underscored through the use of photographs (as noted above). Yet these photographic images are composed as film shots, allowing the viewer a degree of identification—as in a *photo-roman*—while at the same time distancing the viewer through the "unnatural" lack of movement within the frame. Marker pulls his audience into the narrative through classical devices for the construction of cinematic space: the establishment of filmic spaces via long shots and close-ups, shot-reverse shot constructions, cutting on form, and invisible editing. The composition of individual photographs, which are indeed simultaneously film shots, occurs according to cinematic principles, rather than their photographic quality, thus allowing for the placement of the images in a syntagmatic relationship. The sequencing of images must not only conform to narrative logic, but also to the logic of filmic editing, so that the illusion of a third dimension can be maintained. Furthermore, the length of shots, the time each shot is visible on the screen, is calculated according to cinematic time. Finally, Marker utilizes numerous cinematic techniques, for example, zoom shots, double exposures, dissolves, fade-ins and fade-outs, pans over the photographic image, and special effects shots, to create a smooth transition from shot to shot. (According to one rumor, Marker originally shot the film as a film, but didn't like the results, so he froze each image into a still.)

In contrast to the approximation of a classical narrative style in *La jetée*, Marker utilizes a wholly different set of cinematic conventions in *Si j'avais quatre dromadaires*. The film does not present a fictional narrative, in which the audience must be inscribed, but rather a documentary commentary, which is constructed according to more or less formal and thematic criteria. This documentary essay is represented at one level by the three narrators— an amateur photographer and two friends: all three "voices" of Chris. Marker—and at another level by Marker's editing of the photographs into filmic sequences. In accordance with photography's timelessness, time remains an abstraction, even in those sequences where camera movement over an image implies a temporal framework. The length of time the shots are held on screen, likewise, does not signify time itself, as in a normal "moving" film image, but rather functions as the measure of time necessary for the viewer to explore the space of the frame. It is thus a measure of subjectivity, at times very short, at times extremely long, depending on its thematic importance within the documentary flow of image and text.

In those shots in which Marker utilizes a zoom, he does so again not to indicate the passage of time through movement, but rather to use movement to focus the audience's attention on particular details within the frame.

Paradoxically, Marker quotes one of the earliest well-known films of film history, Louis Lumière's *L'arrive d'un train* (1895), when he shows a photograph of a locomotive pulling into a suburban train station, then zooms to the left corner of the image, where the station's name, Le Ciot, is clearly visible. Time and again Marker uses a zoom shot to visually enter into a photographic space and thereby transform its meaning. However, just as a zoom shot has a tendency to unnaturally distort space—movement is not real movement, but only the changing of the lens's focal length—so too do the photographs in *Si j'avais quatre dromadaires* remain abstract in their signification of space, never really communicating the illusion of real space.

The editing is likewise based on abstractions, on formal and thematic connections between images, rather than on a representation of cinematic space. Examples of the kind of editing on form cited above are repeated over and over in the film, since Marker must use formal and thematic similarities from shot to shot, in order to create smooth transitions and to loosen up the stasis of his imagery. Unlike fiction filmmakers, who can direct the viewer's gaze from one image to the next through narrative, Marker must homogenize a potpourri of images taken at a wide variety of locations over an extended period of time. Interestingly, Marker only rarely utilizes the dissolve, a narrative device heavily used by nineteenth-century lantern-slide projectionists to create transitions between spatially separate scenes. One can hypothesize that Marker eschews the device, because a dissolve in film would overdetermine the semantic connection between two disparate images, whereas Marker is only interested in smooth spatial transitions.

Photography signifies not only time, but also space, differently from the cinema. Chris. Marker's utilization of photographic images in *La jetée* and *Si j'avais quatre dromadaires* allows him to reflect on the relationship between the two media, film and photography, in terms of their space and time coordinates. The conventions of central perspective allow for the projection of a real three-dimensional space on a two-dimensional surface that provides the illusion of a third dimension. In other words, it is through the cognitive capabilities of the viewer that a third dimension is abstracted. In *Si j'avais quatre dromadaires* Marker presents a whole catalogue of possibilities for the signification of space through photography, concentrated into a single sequence. Some photos demonstrate depth of focus (Great Wall of China) or depth of field through a wide-angle lens (Göte Canal in Sweden). Others lack any depth at all, thereby emphasizing an abstract pattern (the square in front of the Cathedral of Notre Dame, taken from above, the same shot used as a moving image behind the credits of *La joli mai*), or visually flatten space (the Negev Desert).

Film still from *Le joli mai* (1963), directed by Chris. Marker.

Marker's portraits of countless persons of all nationalities is also a demonstration of his sense of space. The preponderance of portraits indicates that Marker sees this genre as particularly suited to photography. But Marker's portraits, both in his films and his photo-books, almost never exclude their subjects' environment. The close-up portraits of other photographers, like Helmar Lerski, where the focus is on the landscape of the face, would be an anathema to Marker. Marker needs to include the physical space of the subject in his composition, since it is through the cultural definition of that space that he can engage his subjectivity. The same impulse feeds Marker's portraits of woman's faces in his video installation *Silent Movie,* only in this case, it is the fetishistic quality of Hollywood dreams that provides the context for his subjectivity. In the video installation, Marker imbeds these close-ups in a larger structure, including—significantly— video monitors titled "the face," "the gesture," "the journey," "the waltz." Portraits, body movement, dance, travel are also central themes in *Si j'avais quatre dromadaires.*

In contrast to Marker's film images, which are seemingly representations of real places, his photographs, especially those in his films, never actually signify a real space; rather they are visual documents of photographic representations of real spaces. Photographs in Marker's films are themselves merely objects signifying perception, the signs of cognition, never an actual experience of the world.

In *La jetée,* Marker calls his narrative into question and heightens the film's self-reflexive tone through the use of photography itself. Despite dynamic compositions and camera pans, the still images in *La jetée* remain "lifeless," like the many statues in the film, and like the stuffed animals in the museum of natural history, relics of another, lost time. These photographs can be read as moments from memory, but never as moments that have the power to call back life. For only one second in the film, significantly a moment filled with eroticism and love, does the film itself come to life. When the hero's girlfriend wakes up and bats her eyelids, the film suddenly moves, still photographs are transformed into film. In this single moment the hero bridges not only time, but also, for the first time, space.

The lack of movement, that is, the use of photographic rather than moving images in the film, further distances the viewer from the narrative. A film that utilizes the conventions of invisible, narrative editing, but then remains without movement, cannot help distancing the viewer. Apart from the static quality of the images, the film fails to conform to expectations due to the lack of synchronous dialogue. Without the ability to move, the actors are also unable to speak; they can only be quoted by the film's narrator. As a re-

Film still from *Si j'avais quatres dromadaires* (1966), directed by
Chris. Marker.

Film still from a video installation, *Silent Movie* (1995), conceived by Chris. Marker.

sult, another level of realism crumbles. The narrator functions, as in all of Marker's travel films, as an essayist who quotes, describes events and feelings, defining the meanings of the images through language. Thus Marker's films always function on two separate levels: through the montage of images, and through the verbal, nonsynchronous text of the narrator.

In the cinema, the signification of a third dimension is made visually much more plausible through the added element of time. By presenting movement within the frame in real time and through a seemingly real space, film is able to create the illusion of a third dimension much more completely than photography. Not only persons and objects are able to move about in this fictitious space, but also the camera itself can be mobilized in real space to create a representation of a physical space. While a photograph can never be more than a reflection of light and shadow within a fixed frame, demarcating a limited point of view that cannot ever be expanded beyond that frame, the film camera can pan and track to the left or the right, into the frame or away from the original scene. In summary, one can say that photography codifies reality through the conventions of central perspective and by freezing time, while the cinema is defined in terms of space and time coordinates that allow for a more complex signification of reality.

This reality consists for Marker not only of images of reality, but also of the reality of images. Not surprisingly, then, Marker mixes his photographic images with other forms of perception, that is, with other representations that make up visual culture. Indeed, he treats all these representations as existing on the same semantic level. Thus, in *Coréennes* Marker presents engravings, old maps, comics, propaganda posters, woodcuts, and Korean paintings. In *Sunday in Peking,* he includes an excerpt from a Chinese shadow play (shown as an animated film), historical genre paintings, and a sword-fighting demonstration that resembles a ballet. *Le mystère Koumiko* begins with Japanese comics, which visualize the prejudices and stereotypes foreigners have concerning the Japanese people. Later in the same film, Marker intercuts shots of newspaper advertising, a youth magazine (with a Japanese female astronaut), and other objects of popular culture. In *Le dépays,* he presents the chalk drawings of Japanese children, neon advertising in the Ginza, film posters, and the political banners of a Japanese street orator.

This mixture of high and low art, folk and popular culture, demonstrates Marker's attitude that such visual evidence documents a specific perception in much the same way as his films and photographs do. Many of the images in *Le dépays* appear again in *Sans soleil* and were probably taken on the same trip: the statues of cats, the Ginza advertising, the video games, television imagery. Finally, the illustrations for his two *films imaginaires* consist exclusively of found images. In "L'amerique rêve," Marker juxtaposes "dead or alive" posters, Mickey Mouse, Captain America, pornographic postcards, Li'l Abner, Marlon Brando in *The Wild One;* while in "Soy México," it is Air France advertising, drawings of Mexican costumes, an etching of Cortez, photographs of Juárez and Zapata.

For the viewer, such photographic "objets trouvés" are easily recognizable as such, yet at the same time they allow Marker to create his own personal grammar of signs: in *La jetée,* he concludes a scene with a pan up to the Arch of Triumph in Paris, which has been destroyed in the Third World War. It is of course a photo-montage, but the illusion works. This utilization of historical photographs with iconic character allows for a shorthand significa-tion of historical processes. At another point in *La jetée,* when the hero is shot on the observation deck at Orly at the end of the film, Marker pays homage—by recreating the scene—to a world-famous photograph of a Re-publican soldier falling, taken by Robert Capa during the Spanish Civil War. Two soldiers, two human beings from different epochs of history, are thus symbolically unified in the moment of their death, both of them trans-formed into representations of martyrdom, democracy, and freedom.

In *Si j'avais quatre dromadaires,* the viewer is not only exposed to art and popular culture in museums and on the street, but also simultaneously to the audience looking at the objects in question. Thus, Marker never per-ceives art in the broadest sense in a vacuum, or for its own sake, but rather as a mode of communication, as the physical manifestation of human com-munication. By visually connecting art and audience, viewer and represen-tation, he likewise distances his film audience, making them aware of their own subject positioning and allowing them to meditate on the relationship of high and low art.

The structural properties of film and photography are such that the ele-ment of narrative, of fictional storytelling, is more conducive to film than to photography. Even though much early projected photography, for example, the lantern slides of Alexander Black, was designed as a series, thus forming a syntagmatic unit capable of narrative continuity, most photography com-municates primarily and initially only as single images.[24] Photo-reportages in illustrated magazines communicate first as single images, which through an accompanying text can be brought into some kind of narrative order. Some modern photography books are organized in terms of narratives, for example, the books of Danny Lyon. The *photo-roman,* which is extremely popular in Europe, also develops its narrativity through sequencing of im-ages, but its formal conventions are more closely related to films and comics than to photography, which has discarded its early narrative conventions associated with lantern-slide lectures. Like the cinema or comics, the *photo-roman* consists of shots bundled into sequences, yet these single images are read first as individual images, and only the reader's cognitive abilities allow for the construction of a chronology. This process of reading images in the *photo-roman* benefits, of course, from language, the captions and/or speaking balloons that make up the text.

It is not an exaggeration to state that Chris. Marker's photo-books and films are heavily dependent on language, on words: the commentaries of the author and the dialogues of invisible speakers, which consist of written or spoken language. In contrast to modern documentary forms, which communicate primarily through synchronous sound (dialogue or direct address) while rejecting the ever-present but invisible commentators of traditional documentary forms, Marker's films are inscribed by the presence of their invisible narrators. However, it is not the "voice of God" of classical newsreels and documentaries that is heard, but rather the personal and highly recognizable voice of the author, Chris. Marker, who speaks to his audience directly from offscreen. At other times, Marker has chosen a female voice as his own, as in *La joli mai.* This is also true in the more obviously political documentaries, for example, *Cuba Si!* or *Le fond de l'air est rouge,* where Marker's political analysis is less personal, but definitely understood to be his own. The subjectivity of the imagery is also the subjectivity of the text, of the author's physical voice. The film draws its perceptual realism through his point of view, as expressed in language, and through those images documenting what he has seen. It is his radical acknowledgment of subjectivity that allows him to deconstruct the classical modes of address and thereby establish another kind of reality.

Time, however, changes not only the meaning of the images seen, but also the subjectivity of the narrator. In *Le dépays,* Marker admits to the reader:

> If from the beginning of this text I have used the romance personal mode of address, it is not because I have read too much Jorge Semprum, but rather in the instinctive need to draw a line of demarcation between that person who took these photographs in Japan between September 1979 and January 1981, and that person who is writing this particular text in Paris in February 1982. The two are not identical.[25]

That the author of the written text is different from the maker of the photographs can also be said of the relationship of the three speakers in *Si j'avais quatre dromadaires* or the epistlers in *Letter from Siberia* or *Sans soleil* to the images in those films, since the narrators are all more or less fictions.

Illustration from *Le dépays* (1982), a book by Chris. Marker.

Terrence Rafferty describes this complex relationship between narrators and images in *Sans soleil* as follows:

> The far-flung documentary images of *Sans Soleil* are assembled as an autobiography— the film has no subject, except the consciousness, the memory of the man who shot it—yet Marker attributes this consciousness to the invented "Sandor Krasna," removes it from himself to a yet more spectral entity. And then he adds further layers of mediation: "Krasna" himself is often made to attribute his thoughts to others. . . . And the entire narration is read by another invention, the nameless woman receiving Krasna's letters.[26]

The author is a fiction, even when Chris. Marker's voice is repeatedly heard on the sound track. It is indeed no accident that even the name Chris. Marker is fictitious. Marker is emphatically stating that his subjectivity is dependent on his position within space and time. The writer and filmmaker exist only for a moment in the act of writing in Paris, while the cameraman lives briefly in Japan or China or Siberia in 1955 or 1965 or 1979.

Having said that, it is also abundantly clear that the fictional author Chris. Marker can be easily identified in film after film, indeed in everything he has done throughout his career. His obsessions, attitudes, themes, and stylistic characteristics mark his film and photographic work as surely as a signature on a painting. James Quandt has called him "the last auteur."[27] This manifest subjectivity, however, can have its negative aspects, for example, in *Si j'avais quatre dromadaires* and *Sans soleil*, when space and time become meaningless, when the specifics of geography and culture disappear in the mix of Marker's montage. All the sites of Marker's films, whether China or Israel, Japan or Russia, China or Africa, belong to a fictional geography. Place and time function as mirror images of the author's subjectivity, not as iconic representations of a specific reality. Marker is not so much exploring foreign cultures as he is reacting to them. They are merely the raw material for the author's essays and philosophical flights of fantasy.

Not surprisingly, music functions similarly to the images, mirroring less the specific cultures Marker is reacting to than his own subjectivity. For example, in *Sunday in Peking*, Western classical music is heard almost exclusively, except for a very brief synchronous sound sequence and the opening and closing credit sequences, which utilize Chinese music. Clearly, Marker is not adding music as an emotional support for the film's credibility as a document of reality, but rather to emphasize his own subjectivity. This may in fact be Marker's method of avoiding the colonization of consciousness, as he first theorized it in *Les statues meurent aussi*. By clearly identifying the parameters of his own subjectivity through indicators like music, rather than creating a seamless narrative through image and sound, Marker once again reminds the viewer of his own subject positioning that reception, too, is wholly bound up in cultural context.

Like the hero of *La jetée,* whose transgalactic travels through space and time are only possible due to the strength of his inner subjectivity, Marker's focus in many of his films is inward rather than outward into the real world. Not surprisingly, then, it seems that Marker ultimately utilizes film and photography interchangeably, since in the subconscious, in memory, both media function similarly. As a result, he has no qualms about inserting photographs into a film or freezing silent film images as stills on a video monitor. The photographic journeys of Chris. Marker lead us not into the great wide world; rather they present us with the inner world of illusion.

Having looked at a filmmaker whose utilization of photography is indivisibly linked to his aesthetics of cinema, who again and again incorporates photographic images into his film texts, we might now fruitfully turn to a photographer who applied his photographic aesthetics to his work in the cinema. Helmar Lerski worked for hire in the commercial film industry—in this respect he represents an anomaly among the artists discussed in this book—as well as a semi-independent documentary filmmaker. Yet, in both cases, Lerski endeavored to pursue very personal aesthetic agendas, which can be characterized as experimental in the broadest sense. Whether working in fiction features or on documentaries, Lerski successfully applied his photographic techniques, especially his lighting and compositional techniques, to cinematography.

3 Helmar Lerski

THE PENETRATING POWER OF LIGHT

Helmar Lerski's first book of photographs caught the imagination and the spirit of the intelligentsia of the late Weimar Republic with its mixture of reality and artifice, working-class solidarity and high-art aspirations, black-and-white earthiness and ethereal lighting. The book, *Köpfe des Alltags* (1931), roughly translated as "everyday heads,"[1] brought together intense, close-up portraits of supposedly normal working people—not the dregs, nor the celebrities of society, but rather those nameless masses who go about their daily chores: the butcher, the baker, the charwoman, the tailor, the stoker. Marked by strong lines, rough, weather-beaten skin textures, deep shadows under pensive eyes, these faces of the commonplace were true to life and, at the same time, larger than life, made heroic through Lerski's extreme camera perspectives and chiaroscuro lighting, which turned physiognomies into breathtaking landscapes of human desire and despair.

Lerski, whose portrait studio was frequented by the intelligentsia and celebrities of Weimar Germany, had increasingly begun photographing the unemployed and other "common" people.[2] After presenting the *Everyday Heads* series in a one-man show at the Kunstbibliothek in Berlin in 1930, the book received rave reviews from Germany's arts press. One well-known critic, Curt Glaser, perceived "images that enrich our knowledge of visible existence, images that seem to uncover spirituality by effectively revealing the opinion of their creator."[3] While the republican literary journal, *Das Tagebuch*, discovered "a new German type, the proletariat from the street, the factory and office," the left-wing *Arbeiter-Fotograf* perceived in Lerski's

photographs "the fighting, defying, enduring, suffering soul of the proletariat."[4] The critics, whether conservative or left-wing, each saw what they
wanted to see in the images, indicating a certain ideological ambiguity inherent in the project. In point of fact, Lerski was less interested in the social
and ideological context of his images or improving through political action
the living conditions of his subjects than in the undefinable "inner structure" of their physiognomies.

Lerski's ambition went beyond the documentation of individual human
faces to the depiction of the universal in humanity: his subjects are given occupations, but no names. In his photographic *opus magnum, Metamorphosis
through Light,* Lerski took this tendency to its logical extreme, photographing
the same face of a Jewish worker he named "Uschatz" 175 different ways.
Working in a rooftop studio, he bent and sliced the rays of sun over Tel Aviv
through mirrors in such a way as to create radically different personalities.
Not the specific historical moment, but rather the eternal verities were to be
discovered in the landscape of the face. Light functions like an X-ray machine on the soul. *Uschatz,* a bowdlerization of *Ur-Schatz,* means "original
treasure" in German, indicating Lerski's search for the universal in the particular and vice versa. *Metamorphosis* was too radical for its time: it was exhibited in it entirety only once, in Jerusalem in 1936, and shown in excerpts
in London as a slide show at the Academy Cinema in 1938. *Metamorphosis
through Light* was not published as a photography book until long after Lerski's death.[5] This same dichotomy between the desire to create an image
from reality and the artist's need to transform that image into a metaphorical sign, displaying eternal values, characterizes much of Lerski's work, both
as a photographer and as an independent filmmaker.

Prior to working as an independent filmmaker, Lerski spent nearly fifteen
years as a cinematographer in the commercial film industry of Germany,
working with a limited number of film directors whose aesthetic conceptions were complementary to his own. In this respect his career parallels
those of such American photographer/cinematographers as Karl Struss and
Floyd Crosby. Working as a cinematographer for feature fiction films, Lerski
had to place his aesthetic ideas in the service of a film director who was responsible for the ideological and narrative content of the films. Lerski was
able to maintain a large degree of control of the images, that is, of the style
and look of a film. Indeed, as shall be seen below, Lerski's distinct photographic style was appreciated by most of the directors he worked with. The
final aesthetic results could be mixed, however, depending on the talent of
the director and/or his aesthetic and ideological concerns.

After returning to photography full time in the late 1920s and emigrating to Palestine in 1932, Lerski produced films only occasionally. Lerski photographed, directed, and edited these independently produced documentaries, thus allowing him a much greater degree of freedom than had been possible earlier in his career. At the same time, since filmmaking in prestatehood Israel was only in its infancy, Lerski's film work was subject to a whole other set of constraints, namely conforming to an ideological agenda established by the Zionist film propaganda agencies funding his work. As will be seen, Lerski was only partially able to fulfill the requirements established by his funders, leading to conflicts that kept a number of his films from receiving wide distribution in the form originally envisioned by the filmmaker. Thus, while Lerski's film work can be seen as avant-gardistic in terms of its formal experimentation, it is equally clear that his films were subject to many of the constraints of commercial and state-funded propaganda film producers. This chapter will therefore focus on the way a photographer has been able to realize his artistic concerns, in spite of such constraints. What will emerge is a view of a filmmaker whose deep humanism is visible through the formal design of his images, whether photographs or films.

Born on 18 February 1871 in Strasbourg—his real name was Israël Schmuklerski—the son of Polish-Jewish parents, Helmar Lerski spent his childhood in Switzerland before going to the United States in 1893, where he was soon apprenticed as an actor on the German-language stage.[6] After more than fifteen years on the stage, much of it in Milwaukee's Pabst Theater, Lerski was going nowhere fast as an actor. Still in Milwaukee, he gave up his thespian ambitions and began a career as a photographer in 1910 by opening a studio with his wife, who came from a family of photographers. There he found his first clients by shooting portraits of his former colleagues from the German Pabst Theater. Even his earliest surviving portraits display formal elements that would later be associated with the Lerski style. Almost immediately, Lerski's portraits appeared in the local German-language press and photography trade journals. The photography critic Sadakichi Hartmann wrote about Lerski as early as 1912 in an article, "A New Departure in Light and Shade Arrangement," noting that the concentration on the face in connection with contrasting lighting was unfamiliar.[7] Using mirrors to focus and shape light on the face, Lerski was already molding his subjects. As he later noted about a portrait of a friend made around 1911: "Thus, I managed to create John the Baptist from the head of a scientist friend of mine. . . . The lively, blooming countenance was transformed into a face marked by death, using only light to give him the characteristics of life passed away."[8]

In 1915 Lerski decided to move to Germany, where he had his first one-man exhibition in the Grafik-Verlag in Berlin in the autumn of that year. However, it was not photography, but cinematography that was to preoccupy his creative energies in the next period of his life.

Helmar Lerski's film career can be divided into two periods. In Germany from 1916 to 1929, Lerski, who found employment as a cameraman in Berlin's film industry, subordinated his artistic persona to the commercial demands of his directors. He was a technician who, in the best of situations, could develop elements of a visual style with directors who were sympathetic to his concerns. In Palestine after 1932, Lerski, the independent documentary filmmaker, ideally had control over his films, but that freedom was often subject to the propagandistic demands of his Zionist financiers. Common to Lerski's film practice both in Germany and Palestine were his consistent formal strategies: extreme close-ups in the style of his portraiture, and chiaroscuro long shots, which rejected the prevalent industry practice of evenly lighting a scene.

In March 1916, Lerski was hired by William Wauer, a well-known painter and film director who hoped Lerski's radical ideas would add artistic flair to his films. Responsible for "managing all photographic and technical aspects of the operation," Lerski apparently also produced a portrait of Wauer (the only surviving photograph from this period) for a company press release.[9] Although Lerski was a novice cameraman, his interest in the aesthetic manipulation of light seems to have matched Wauer's. But Lerski also seems to have shaped the company's goals, as noted in a press release: "As its specialty, the W.W. Film Co., Berlin, presents an original photographic treatment of the human face, with all the richness of its expressive features and forms. The photographic artist . . . achieves this perfection in living portraiture . . . through his artistically and technically new usage and placement of light sources, which allow him to capture the human soul, as reflected in the living reality of the face."[10] The human soul's reflection in a face—a lofty goal—was thus central to Lerski's aesthetic, even at this early date. Reviews of Wauer's films with Lerski (of which there are apparently no surviving copies) continually mention the masterly use of light and shadow effects, although in other respects Wauer's detective stories seem to have been less than ambitious.

In 1917 Lerski joined producer Hanns Lippmann's Deutsche Bioscop Film Co., Berlin, as technical director, producing both publicity stills and films for director Robert Reinert's film team.[11] Lerski's stills of the Bioscop film star Carl de Vogt were supposed to increase sales.[12] Between 1917 and 1921, Lerski and Reinert completed twenty-two films, including such popu-

lar successes as *Opium* (1919) and *Nerven* (*Nerves,* 1919). Based on their titles and surviving contemporary reviews, most of Lerski and Reinert's films
were somewhat pretentious and overladen with symbolism, although their
metaphorical style seems to have been popular at the time. *Ahasver* (1917),
for example, presents an epic and metaphorical narrative of the biblical figure. Lighting and design in Lerski's portrait of Carl de Vogt as "Ahasver, the
eternally wandering Jew," recalled Lerski's American portrait, "An Arab
Head" (1912), and looked ahead to his first project in Tel Aviv, *Jewish Heads*
(1931–35). In Reinert's film, which consisted of historical and modern portions, much like Griffith's *Intolerance,* Ahasver treks through the centuries,
while the melodramatic stories receive a semblance of unity through the visual symbolism of the wandering Jew. The film was praised by the press,
which proclaimed that the film proved that the cinema "would solve difficult, intellectual problems."[13]

In January 1919, *Opium* was released and, benefiting from a fad for exploitation films brought about by the end of police censorship, became a hit.
The film relates the story of an English scientist who falls prey to the very
drug he is studying. Lerski's style here is unmistakable: his long shots achieve
a depth of focus through chiaroscuro lighting, wide angles, and stop-down
lenses that was thought unachievable at the time. For example, when the
film's hero gives a public lecture, Lerski places a water glass on the lectern
and simultaneously keeps the audience in focus. At times he layers space to
define character motivations; at other times he metaphorically contrasts in-
door scenes (civilization) and outdoor views (nature) within a single frame
by keeping his windows open.[14] Thus, Reinert's penchant for highly emblematic images was supported by Lerski's deep-focus cinematography. For
example, Reinert repeatedly cuts away to an image of the villain (in the foreground), a Chinese opium dealer played by Werner Krauss, at the moment
he discovers his wife's infidelity (seen in the background with her European
lover). The scene motivates the villain's revenge against all Europeans, thus
driving the narrative forward. As the film's story moves from China to England to India, each location is identified with its own typography in the intertitles. While the melodramatic acting of the principals and Reinert's
nearly mystical belief in the healing powers of nature conflict at times with
the naturalism of Lerksi's images, Lerski seemed equally adept at creating
opium dream sequences that are reminiscent of late nineteenth-century
symbolist painting.

This tendency toward metaphorical rather than realistic narratives is even
more apparent in *Nerves.* Due to material scarcity after the German revolution of 1918–19, Reinert and Lerski worked for a whole year on *Nerves.* They

shot the film at real locations in Munich, Reinert having moved his base of operations to the Bavarian capital.[15] Two politicians—one a conservative, one a radical—use all legal and illegal means to combat each other, leading them to suffer mental breakdowns. The film is Reinert's conservative interpretation of the civil war that raged in Germany after the fall of the Imperial German government. His solution is for man to communicate more with nature, a conclusion he underscores by having the surviving politician and the widow of his adversary march off into a pastoral setting at film's end. The critics were again ecstatic, not only in their commendation of Lerski's cinematography, but also in their admiration for the film's content, which attempted to solve "metaphysical ideas, philosophical thoughts, and sociopolitical questions" through such simple phrases as "back to nature."[16]

Nerves was a blockbuster, and its success encouraged Reinert to plan a "monumental production," Sterbende Völker (Dying Peoples, 1921). However, in April 1921, a few months after shooting began on the film, Lerski left the production, supposedly due to scheduling conflicts. He turned to freelance work, following Hanns Lippmann to the Gloria Film Co. and working for such directors as E. A. Dupont and Hanns Steinhoff. Trade reviews noted repeatedly that Lerski achieved "beautiful, technically difficult" images, but the films failed "to rise above the well-trod paths of German costume pictures."[17] For example, Lerski's images in Neuland (Virgin Land) are easily identified: flatly lighted long shots precede close-ups in which the faces are sculpted by various light sources. Unfortunately, the technical and financial expenses of Lerski's light and mirror experiments were substantial, so that the cost-conscious film industry soon labeled him a "commercially feared employee," whose "Rembrandt atmosphere" embodied aesthetic pretensions that film producers could ill afford.[18] Lerski found it more and more difficult to find employment.

Not until 1924 did Lerski receive an assignment worthy of his talents when he collaborated with Paul Leni on Das Wachsfigurenkabinett (Waxworks), one of the most famous expressionist films of the era. The film relates the stories of three historical figures depicted in a fairground wax museum: Haroun al Rashied, the caliph of Bagdad; Ivan the Terrible; and Jack the Ripper. Lerski's cinematography has been unjustifiably ignored in favor of Paul Leni's highly stylized and abstracted sets, but Lerski's high-key lighting, especially of the close-ups, contributes much to establishing the dark atmosphere of the film. While the "1001 Nights" sequence at the film's beginning is relatively evenly lighted (except for later scenes in the catacombs), the Ivan the Terrible story gets much of its dramatic power from Lerski's expressionistic lighting patterns. And the final Jack the Ripper sequence would

Film still from *Opium* (1919), directed by Robert Reinert. Courtesy Gerhard Ullmann, Munich Filmmuseum.

Film still from *Nerves* (1920), directed by Robert Reinert. Courtesy Gerhard Ullmann, Munich Filmmuseum.

not have been possible without Lerski's lighting. Only roughly five minutes in length, the sequence is a densely constructed series of superimpositions, in which the hero and heroine are haunted by the phantom image of Jack the Ripper. Lerski creates filmic space here solely with light by shooting the murderer from different angles and camera distances against black backdrops, then superimposing the images onto a scene with the film's lovers. This manipulation of cinematic space created through light matched Lerski's practice in making close-up portraits, for which he often used black velvet, wide-angle lenses, and a battery of Jupiter lamps and mirrors to eliminate all superfluous visual information and thus better explore the landscape of the face.

Lerski continued to utilize such techniques in "art" films such as *Die Perücke* (*The Wig,* 1924) and *Die Abenteuer eines Zehnmarkscheins* (*Adventures of a Ten-Mark Note,* 1926), both shot for the poet/director, Bertolt Viertel; and *Der heilige Berg* (*The Holy Mountain,* 1925), directed by Dr. Arnold Fanck. *Adventures of a Ten-Mark Note* is lost, but the earlier film is a masterpiece of lighting.

Contemporary critics lauded *The Wig,* especially Viertel's script and direction, but also Lerski's cinematography, which had been produced on location in the Palace of Berlin-Charlottenburg: "Viertel has found in the photographer Helmar Lerski a fellow poet, a poet and a visionary of the camera.[19] The film tells the story of a poor clerk who is embarrassed and chided because of his baldness. When he buys a used wig, formerly worn by a duke, he returns, as if guided by some force, to the palace of the duke, who supposedly committed suicide. Once there the clerk is mistaken for the duke. The first scene, with Otto Gebühr, already demonstrates Lerski's technique: his high-key lighting on the actor's forehead and shiny skull accentuates the baldness that is the character's shame. Much of the rest of the film takes place in the duke's palace in a single night, again affording Lerski the opportunity to show off his skills with strong light and mirrors. On the other hand, unlike *Waxworks,* the film uses close-ups only sparingly—a shot of the hero lying in the hallway in front of his wife's locked bedroom door is an exception—since Lerski and Viertel justifiably wanted to also highlight the real interiors of Charlottenburg Palace. Through pools of light, Lerski manages to create chiaroscuro lighting in the spacious palace interiors, giving the image a strong sense of three-dimensional space and a sculpted, unreal quality. This was fitting, since the story turns out to be nothing but the clerk's dream.

Next, Dr. Fanck hired Lerski for his "mountain film," *The Holy Mountain.* In the film, two mountain climbers fall in love with a woman dancer (Leni

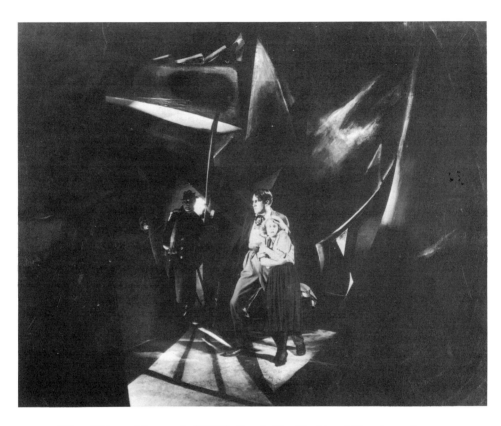

Film still from *Waxworks* (1924), directed by Paul Leni. Courtesy of George Eastman House.

Riefenstahl) without knowing that they are rivals. The moment of truth comes when they attempt a dangerous night climb up the North Wall, leading the younger man to fall off a precipice. After holding on for a whole night to his dead friend hanging from a rope, the older man, now delirious, plunges to his death in the frozen wilderness. In death the two men remain true to each other. Fanck sets up a dichotomy between nature and artifice, male and female, in the first two scenes, where Riefenstahl is seen dancing above ocean cliffs, and then on stage. The two men in the audience succumb to her erotic charm as Riefenstahl dances with transparent veils, highlighted by Lerski's sculpted light. The film's fiction reflected the actual rivalry between Fanck and Luis Trenker, the film's star, for Riefenstahl's sexual favors. Yet despite such autobiographical elements, Fanck's mountain fantasy clearly sets up a mythological view of nature in which the female is alien. Shots of the glistening walls of ice parallel Lerski's extreme close-ups of Trenker's weather-beaten face, the powerful lighting creating canyons in the wrinkles of a brow. Thus, Lerski's chiaroscuro lighting design for the studio scenes, which make up less than 25 percent of the film, supported a "heroic" ambience that found its correlative in the imposing exteriors, shot in the Alps by Hans Schneeberger and Sepp Allgeier. As in the case of Reinert's films, Lerski's lighting and camera work here served an intensely romantic, ideologically conservative project.

Siegfried Kracauer's view that the plot of *The Holy Mountain* borders on fascistic is overstated,[20] given the fact that not only *völkisch* and nationalist groups, but also liberals and leftists applauded Fanck's work. Unfortunately for Fanck's post–World War II reputation, though, the image of "men with faces of noblest bronze, who see visions before finding death in eternal ice"[21] became a central trope in the iconography of the death cult, which would be a defining facet of German National Socialism.

In 1926, Lerski filmed *Adventures of a Ten-Mark Note*. Influenced by "the new realism" and scripted by the film critic and theoretician Bèla Balàsz, the film was to objectively observe everyday life in the streets of Berlin. Published descriptions of the film imply that it was constructed out of numerous sequences, edited together from countless detail shots, based on Balasz's theory of the close-up.[22] True to his own style, though, Lerski shot close-ups of actors using black velvet.[23] The film also made compromises for the sake of commercial considerations (it was financed by the German subsidiary of Fox); for example, a love story framed the film's loose plot. Nevertheless, some critics thought the film too intellectual for a mass audience.

A year earlier, in October 1925, Lerski had begun working as head technician of the newly founded Deutsche-Spiegeltechnik Co., a subsidiary of Ufa

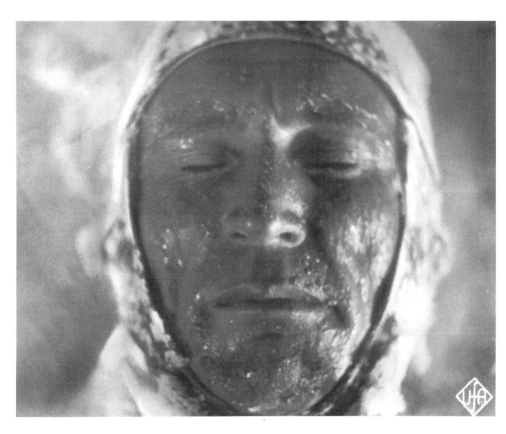

Film still from *The Holy Mountain* (1924), directed by Dr. Arnold Fanck.
Courtesy of Munich Filmmuseum.

intended to commercially exploit the "Schüfftan Process." Invented by the well-known cameraman Eugen Schüfftan,[24] the special effects system utilized a complicated set of mirrors to superimpose models, actors, sets, stills, and even other films onto one image. Given Lerski's predilection for mirrors, it seems natural that he should join the Schüfftan operation. Companies wishing to use the "Schüfftan photography" were required to hire the equipment and two technicians from the licenser. Although the process was featured in big-budget productions such as Fritz Lang's *Metropolis* (1926) and Joe May's *Dagfin* (1926), it was said that the Ufa staff had sabotaged the undertaking by failing to utilize the process when the opportunity arose. Whether this was true or not can no longer be ascertained. However, *Metropolis* would certainly have had a different look, had not the Schüfftan process been utilized in the numerous panoramas of the city of the future. After introducing the process in England in the production of *Madame Pompadour* in January 1927, Lerski left the company.[25] Since Lerski remained with the Spiegeltechnik for only a little more than fifteen months, it can be assumed that the work was ultimately not really challenging. For a cameraman interested in developing his own style, the purely technical work involved in the Schüfftan process must have been unsatisfying, once Lerski's initial curiosity wore off.

In the summer of 1929, Lerski completed his last "excursion" into German film before returning "regretfully" to photography. He was hired by novice film director and producer Carl Ludwig Achaz-Duisberg, son to the chairman of the board of the giant chemical combine, I.G. Farben.[26] Utilizing a Soviet style of editing, Achaz-Duisberg's vanity production *Sprengbagger 1010* (1929) presents a paean to a giant steam shovel that is capable of fantastic engineering feats. The narrative thus underscores the film's belief in economic progress and the redemption of the proletariat through a socially enlightened capitalism. Indeed, the film can be seen as a conservative, right-wing response to the revolutionary politics of Eisenstein, using the formal devices of Soviet film. While the film was generally undistinguished, it did give Lerski the opportunity to experiment with his lighting techniques out-of-doors, in real locations. The close-ups of faces—those of the workers and the engineer who is the film's hero—betray the typical signs of manipulation by Lerski's light and mirrors. The experience of making the film certainly influenced Lerski's work on his masterpiece, *Avodah* (1933–35), which would be a similar tour de force visualization of physical labor.

Sprengbagger 1010 proved to be Lerski's last German film, but his interest in film continued even after he took up his photography career. Again and again he argued for an artistically demanding cinema. In his seventies, after

World War II, Lerski lectured in Palestine on American films, disqualifying them as photographed theater. Cinematography, according to him, had to proceed from the phenomenon of light.

That dictum, in fact, is what makes his German film work problematical. Lerski's films are characterized by his personal signature, but the question remains, how to assess his dramaturgic lighting in relation to the aesthetic quality of a given film. In the surviving Reinert films, Lerski's dramatic lighting seems to push the naively symbolic images even further into triviality. Working with directors like Aschaz-Duisberg, Steinhoff, and Fanck, who all had a predilection toward highly metaphoric, nonnaturalistic images, Lerski's camera creates a heroic ambience, supporting conservative, at times nationalistic tendencies. In *Waxworks* and *The Wig,* on the other hand, Lerski's expressive lighting is in harmony with the consciously dreamlike visions created by Leni and Viertel. Given this tendency in Lerski's work, one can assume that his dramatic, expressionistic style undermined to a certain extent the conventions of New Realism in a film like *Adventures of a Ten-Mark Note.* The evidence of his German films, then, seems to suggest that Lerski's lighting was not ideologically neutral, but preferred by politically conservative directors with a predilection toward symbolism. Despite the questionable ambiguity of Lerski's denotation through light and form, his place in the forefront of film technical innovation is unquestionable. His technical lighting experiments, carried out with Wauer, Reinert, Leni, Viertel, and the Spiegeltechnik, also eventually led him back to photography.

Lerski first traveled to Palestine in mid-1931, planning a new photography book that was to "document the Jewish race." In point of fact, as in his earlier efforts, Lerski sought to discover "the eternal" in the physical landscape of the face. In this case, he was searching for the "prototypical Jewish character," as he noted: "I want to show only the prototype in all its offshoots, and what is more, I want to show him so intensely that the prototype is recognizable in all later branches."[27] While Lerski's motivations were certainly pure, the project seems to have been uncomfortably close to the anti-Semitic Jewish character studies found in *Der Stürmer,* which may have been one reason Lerski had trouble finding backers. In the spring of 1932, Lerski traveled to Zürich, where he established contacts with the World Zionist Organization (WZO), attempting unsuccessfully to organize a photo exhibition of *Jewish Heads* at the WZO Congress in Geneva. In late 1932, Lerski and his second wife, Anneliese, settled permanently in Tel Aviv, where they remained until 1948. Since efforts to publish *Jewish Heads*[28] had come to a standstill, Lerski began production in 1933 of a Zionist documentary film, *Avodah (Work),* possibly at the suggestion of Ernst Aaron Mechner, the head of the Berlin office of the Keren Kayemeth L'Israel (Palestine Land Fund).[29]

The film was to be a paean to the work of Zionist pioneers in the new "Erez Israel."

While in the Weimar Republic, Helmar Lerski the cameraman had subordinated himself to the rationale of a capitalist film industry and the aesthetic demands of his director. In Palestine, he directed films himself. The new production context resembled a state-owned film industry whose goal was to propagandize Zionist ideas. Between the world wars, Palestine was under British mandate, but at the same time, a state within a state was emerging: the Jewish Agency, allied with the WZO. The aim of Zionist film work was to advance immigration to Palestine and propagate the creation of a Jewish national homeland.

Practically all filmmaking, distribution, and exhibition activities in Palestine were financed under the aegis of the WZO. The Jewish National Funds, Keren Hayesod and Keren Kayemeth, had begun producing Zionist films in the early 1920s, yet these were for the most part the work of autodidacts with little experience in the commercial film industry. In the 1930s, German-exile filmmakers who had emigrated from Nazi Germany to Palestine professionalized Zionist film efforts. Surprisingly, Zionist film organizations were even able to continue their work in nazified Berlin, at least until 1938.[30] The WZO set itself the twofold task of convincing world Jewry of Zionist ideals and influencing Britain's foreign policy in Palestine. The suggestion of the *Jüdische Rundschau,* the official organ of German Zionism, in 1936 that a central, Zionist propaganda division be founded within the organizational structure of the WZO never materialized. Nevertheless, films financed by the Jewish National Fund and private investors in Palestine led to the growth of a real film industry in Israel.

Avodah was financed by Paul Boroschek, a Berlin banker who had set up Palestine Pictures Ltd. as an investment in the infant film industry of Jewish Palestine. Boroschek, who may have originally planned the project with another director and cameraman, also sought financial support for the production, which was to cost approximately £3,000, from Leo Herrmann, general secretary of the Keren Hayesod in Jerusalem.[31] Using a small, hand-held 35mm camera, which could only hold very short film rolls (50 feet), Lerski took on double duties as director and his own cameraman. He shot the film without synchronous sound. Although the camera allowed only for relatively short shots, its lightness gave Lerski the capability of moving unobtrusively among the workers in the fields to capture details and impromptu moments of the work process. Such images would have been inaccessible to a director working with a larger camera and crew.[32] Postproduction, including a very complicated sound mix, was done at the Hunnia Studios in Budapest, where the well-known German exile composer Paul Dessau wrote and recorded all the music in six weeks. The Hungarian Laszlo Vajda handled the sound direction, while Gerhard Goldbaum, formerly the head of Ufa's sound-recording department (before the Nazis kicked him out), supervised the exactly timed postsynchronization.

The press acclaimed the film, although its artistic and propagandistic goals were thought at times to be in conflict. A critic at the press screening in Jerusalem noted: "It is not a paradox, if one says that at times the artistry of Lerski is too great: viewing this supreme achievement one forgets the object of his depiction."[33] Berlin's *Jüdische Rundschau* wrote: "Work . . . That is the whole film's content, its images often intensifying to highest dynamism. Man and machine are its theme. The machine's stroke, the wheel's drive, the piston's hammering, the drill's clanking. Not since Potemkin have we seen such a rhythm."[34] The *Palestine Post* was equally ecstatic in its praise: "In this picture Lerski's artistic skill shows itself at its best. . . . Here the camera shows not only the light of the faces, but the very light of the souls."[35] Comparing the film to *Potemkin* (1925) and *Storm over Asia* (1928), the German film critic Hans Feld, formerly of Berlin, wrote: "I have never felt in pictures more forcibly the compelling suggestiveness of an epos."[36] The comparison with other propaganda films was not out of line. Indeed, the *Neue Züricher Zeitung* reviewed the film in the same breath with Leni Riefenstahl's *Triumph of the Will,* and both were screened at the Venice Film Festival in 1935.[37] The Zionist newspaper *Selbstwehr* (Prague), on the other hand, complained about its lack of propaganda value: "This Palestine film has the peculiar feature of not showing any Jewish cities, not a single settlement, and almost no human beings. Palestine is seemingly devoid of human life. One sees shoes, legs, hands, arms, faces,—not whole human beings but only parts—not whole settlements, but only rooms, windows, doors, not complete landscapes, but only fields, beds, weeds."[38]

This last opinion seems also to have been held by other members of the Zionist community. Arthur Hantke, in a letter to Leo Herrmann of Keren Hayesod, called the film "Bolshevist" and "a glorification of the working class," an opinion apparently shared by two other high-ranking Zionist officials, Ernst Mechner and Gal-Esser.[39] Efforts to distribute the film through the Keren Hayesod failed, although Paul Boroschek's belief that the National Fund was blocking exhibition in favor of its own feature-length documentary, *The Land of Promise* (1935), was apparently unfounded.[40] While Keren Hayesod correspondence demonstrated both positive and negative views of the film, Leo Herrmann agreed to distribute the film, but Boroschek lacked the financial means to supply prints or acquire the negative, which was held as collateral by the Hungarian lab.[41] After a private screening (attended by an enthusiastic John Grierson, the head of the British documentary movement) in the house of British Zionist leader, Harry Sacher, the film was shown at the Academy Cinema in London's West End[42] but otherwise failed to receive distribution in Germany, the United States, or South America. The film did receive limited distribution in Europe through Otto Sonnenfeld's Slavia Films, Prague.[43]

In point of fact, *Avodah* was not really suitable as Zionist propaganda, unlike *The Land of Promise,* which was a straightforward documentary with narration, emphasizing Jewish Palestine's economic boom and opportunities for capitalist investment, while downplaying the more socialist aspects of the kibbutz movement.[44] *Avodah,* on the other hand, was essentially a work of art with leftist tendencies and few references to Jewish reconstruction: a quote from Jessiah, a Star of David, a Hebrew prayer (the only spoken words in the film), and *chaluzim* singing the anthem of the Hashomer Hazair, the leftist, socialist wing of Zionism. Small wonder that one Zionist official at Keren Hayesod characterized the film's image of Palestine as "a glorification of the dictatorship of the working class, rather than a Jewish land of the future."[45] Scenes of Jewish communal life, customs, religious rituals, and social gatherings were almost totally absent. But three reels of outtakes reveal that Lerski originally shot much more traditional material, found in virtually every Zionist travelogue: a Purim festival, the Hebrew University, scenes of Tel Aviv, Allenby Street, the Jewish Agency Building, an Arab market, children playing, and the Wailing Wall, all of which were eliminated in the film's final edit in favor of a very narrow selection of formal themes.[46]

The film opens with a pioneer walking to Palestine—a stereotypical image of early Zionist documentaries—and a long, less typical sequence, portraying Arab life in the British Mandate. The film's main theme, reinforced through a recurring image of a water wagon and Dessau's musical leitmotif, is the need for water for survival. Following sequences on the building of roads and houses in Tel Aviv, the film's final two reels focus on the often frustrating search for water, culminating in a visual symphony of gushing water as a drill strikes a subterranean reservoir. Typical of Lerski's style, the film utilizes extreme close-ups of machines and men, their facial features, the sweat on their bodies, the dirt and oil of various apparatuses, highlighted by intensely reflected light. Lerski later circumscribed the photographer's aesthetic possibilities in the following manner: "The eye of the imagemaker is always looking at a portion of the whole, that area where his light falls. It is always merely a cut-out, a shot, a distant close-up."[47] The film is, indeed, nothing less than a visual symphony of hard physical labor in the desert, labor that is fragmented through editing into a formal play of movement,

Frame enlargement from *Avodah* (1936), directed by Helmar Lerski.

Frame enlargement from *Avodah* (1936), directed by Helmar Lerski.

physical shapes, diagonally composed camera angles, shadows and light, music and sound effects. Rather than constructing a unified view of the Zionist project, Lerski lifts the idea of work out of the historically concrete setting of Palestine in the 1930s into a timeless and idealized notion of human progress through labor, through which he was again striving to capture the human spirit in images of beauty. In its use of the film medium as raw material for concepts and formal patterns, instead of as a referent to the real world, *Avodah* has more in common with such avant-garde, new realist experiments as *Berlin, Symphony of a City* (1926) than it does with the propagandistic documentary common to the era.

Early in 1935 Lerski completed a short film, *Hebrew Melody,* which he coproduced with another German-Jewish refugee, Walter Kristeller. Cofinanced by the Jewish Kulturbund of Berlin, Lerski shot footage of the world-famous German-Jewish violinist, Andreas Weissgerber, walking through Jerusalem's old city. In front of Absalom's Pillar, he plays the popular tune by Joseph Achron that gave the film its title. Sound recording and postproduction were done by Shabtai Petruschka in Berlin's Tobis Klangfilm Studios when Weissgerber toured Berlin in March 1935 with Joseph Rosenstock and the Kulturbund Orchestra.[48] Consistent with the techniques used in *Avodah,* Lerski edited numerous close-ups of Weissgerber's hands, face, and body into sequences that emphasized fragmentation, rather than the unity of the musician's performance. While the film was distributed by the Keren Hayesod, it was apparently not widely seen.[49]

In spring 1939, after Lerski returned to Palestine from a long stay in England, the executive committee of the Histadrut (Jewish Labor Federation), under Golda Meir and David Remez, asked the sixty-eight-year-old filmmaker to help set up a film division. Lerski organized a modest 16mm film unit, where he trained young filmmakers including Robert Sziller, Rolf Kneller, and Naftali Rubenstein. In an interview Lerski noted: "At my age I cannot expect to make the Palestinian film of the future. I can only hope to train people who will stand on my shoulders. First small documentary films, then a real Palestinian picture. No Hollywood. Something springing from the soil. Born out of the strife and struggle of this hard land."[50]

In 1939–41, Lerski and his group produced at least four films: *Yaldei HaShemesh,* shot in the Kibbutz Givat Brenner; *Amal,* about a technical school of the Histadrut; *Kupat Cholim,* about Histadrut's health insurance; and *Labour Palestine,* a history of the Histadrut.[51] In November 1941, the film workshop was forced to close down because of the worsening war situation.

After World War II, Lerski directed another short film, *Balaam's Story* (1946), produced in conjunction with the puppeteer Paul Loewy. Financed by Keren Hayesod, the film was an adaptation of a puppet-theater play taken from the Old Testament's Numbers and probably based on Hugo Adler's play *Balak and Baalam* (1934). Kurt Weill was originally set to write the music, which was then composed by the German-exile composer Karol Rathaus based on Weill's motifs. Giving human expression to an inanimate puppet through light, Lerski constructed scenes exclusively through close-ups, thus hiding the puppets' strings and developing their dynamism through camera movement and action within the frame. The animation of the puppets was to create a new kind of cinema, as Lerski noted.[52] According to the film's narration, "This was a story of a curse, of a people who are cursed with no land and no right to govern their own wish to live together." While this overt Zionist message could be culled from the story, it is not known whether it matched Lerski's intentions, since the short was never released but rather incorporated into the feature film, *Out of Evil* (1951), directed by Joseph Krumgold. In that film, the puppet play is presented by a group of traveling puppeteers.

Lerski's final film, *Adamah* (1947), was produced by Otto Sonnenfeld for the Children's Village Ben Shemen and was to become the first feature-length film of the new state of Israel. Shot at the Ben Shemen Kibbutz, the film concerns the fate of a teenage boy who, having survived the hell of Auschwitz, must learn to overcome his psychic wounds and trust his fellow (wo)man again. The film's story, typical of the times, was to present Ben Shemen to the American Jewish community as a shining example of the work being done in Israel.[53] After completing the shooting assisted by pupils, Robert Sziller and Naftali Rubenstein, Lerski sent the rough cut to the United States for postproduction. As in the case of *Avodah*, Paul Dessau wrote the musical score, while Shabtai Petruschka handled the orchestration. In New York, the film was shortened and reedited by Hazel Greenwald and released by Hadassah, the Jewish-American women's organization, under the title *Tomorrow's a Wonderful Day*. According to Anneliese Lerski, her husband "was beside himself with anger at the film's premiere at the Locarno Film Festival" in July 1948, "since it had been completely chopped up, destroying Lerski's best and most beautiful intentions," with scenes missing and others (not shot by Lerski) added.[54]

Receiving a standing ovation at Locarno, the film was universally praised by the international press. The Swiss newspaper *Baseler Nachrichten* wrote: "The entire film makes the impression of a highly significant document through which a gifted film producer addresses to the world forum a life-affirming message in an emotional way."[55] After the Israeli premiere, the critic for *Davar* wrote: "This film teaches and elucidates in a sublime form

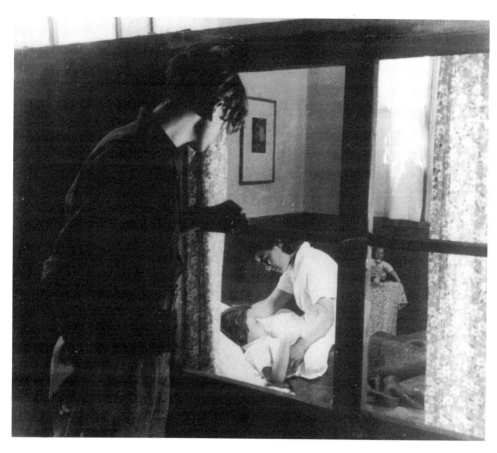

Film still from *Adamah, or Tomorrow's a Wonderful Day* (1948), directed by Helmar Lerski. Courtesy of Ronny Loewy.

the chapter of the absorption of the children from exile, and of love of the homeland."[56] The *New York Times,* on the other hand, claimed "the film's continuity and photography leave something to be desired" but otherwise praised the semidocumentary.[57] After opening in New York in April 1949, the film earned four times its original cost of 100,000 Swiss francs.

In terms of its lighting and photography, *Adamah* was a typical Lerski film. Utilizing numerous close-ups, reflecting the bright sun through mirrors into his youthful actors' faces, presenting the skewed vision of its young hero, Benjamin, through obtuse camera angles, Lerski gives the village of Ben Shemen a larger-than-life presence. At the same time, Lerski's fragmented editing and the multitude of spoken languages (reflecting the origins of the children) create a sense of emotional chaos that certainly reflected the atmosphere of the times. Only slowly does Benjamin learn to sort out at times confusing impressions and come to grips with his new reality. This subjectivity, which was reinforced by concentrating solely on Ben Shemen, seems to have been what Lerski was striving for, according to an early exposé—a subjectivity that was to a certain extent undermined by Hadassah's insertion of stereotypical and historical images of Israel's reconstruction. In other words, just as *Avodah* had been pared down to the essential theme of work, so was *Adamah* to be about the rebirth of hope, nourished in the soil of Ben Shemen. To include documentary shots that broadened and historically specified the film's view defeated Lerski's aesthetic intentions.

Of all the filmmakers to work in Israel before statehood, Helmar Lerski was certainly the most original. It was the single-mindedness of his artistic vision, his formal concerns as a "writer with light," his desire to shape his documentary visions into something timeless—a "metamorphosis into eternity," beyond the narrower propagandistic concerns of his Zionist funders—that have given his films their lasting values. It is clear that Lerski's Zionist films failed to accomplish their overtly propagandistic missions as advertisements for Erez Israel. Yet, for the Israeli cinema of the future, Helmar Lerski's aesthetic accomplishment as the nation's first gifted filmmaker was certainly an auspicious beginning.

Lerski's career as a filmmaker can be seen as very much in keeping with his work as an independent photographer, despite the fact that he worked as a cameraman and state propagandist, rather than an independent filmmaker. Possibly because Lerski had a distinctive photographic style, which was attractive to artistically ambitious film directors, he was also able to market his craft in the commercial atmosphere of the film industry. Beyond the formal play of light that characterized that style, whether in film or photography, one can recognize a tendency toward the creation of metaphorical rather than realistic images and a predilection for ideological conservatism. In his search for the prototypical, beyond the surface characteristics of the physical, Lerski sought to find the spiritual characteristics of humanity.

Somewhat younger than Helmar Lerski, the American photographer and filmmaker Paul Strand also moved freely from photography to film and back. Like Lerski, Strand worked as a commercial cinematographer (though with less personal investment) before directing his own independently produced documentaries. However, while Lerski gravitated to conservative aesthetics, Strand's were decidedly left-wing.

4 Paul Strand

ROMANTIC MODERNIST

While modernist art and photography explore fragmentation, multiplicity, juxtapositions, and the utilization of discontinuity as a principle of construction, classical narrative cinema strives toward unity and continuity as a formative principle. In the 1920s, though, the modernist avant-garde embraced cinema. The photographer and filmmaker Paul Strand was among the first to cross that frontier. *Manhatta* (1920), a seven-minute portrait of New York City, is acknowledged by many film and photo historians to be the first genuine avant-garde film produced in the United States. Initially, Paul Strand and his codirector, Charles Sheeler, were amateur filmmakers, working like their European compatriots outside the mainstream, commercial modes of film production, creating a work of cinema whose primary raison d'être was not the production of surplus value, but rather a modernist experiment in an unchartered medium. The avant-garde could be eclectic in its choice of media, whether painting, sculpture, photography, graphic design, or film, searching for new ways of seeing the ever-changing world, exploring discourses of a highly technological, highly urbanized environment. Like cubism, modernist photography and film deconstructed the omniscient point of view of central perspective, because—as was theoretically formulated—the vertical space of skyscrapers obliterated the horizon, leaving only extreme perspectives and angles, while the speed of modern transportation collapsed space into time.

Manhatta is central to film modernism's project of deconstructing renaissance perspective in favor of multiple, reflexive points of view. Yet, at the same time, Strand and Sheeler's work is mitigated by aesthetic concerns and philosophical premises that are archaic and antimodernist. In its conscious attempt to create an avant-garde, non-narrative, and formally abstract cinematic experience in opposition to classical modes of address, *Manhatta*, nevertheless, never quite relinquishes those structures that manifest themselves most visibly in the tension between the image and verbal text, between its modernist perspectives and a romantic longing for a universe in which man remains in harmony with nature.

Ironically, most published film histories give *Manhatta* short shrift, despite its acknowledged status, despite the fact that it is still the most popular film in the Museum of Modern Art's film distribution system. Indeed, film critics writing about the history of American avant-garde cinema either completely ignore the period prior to World War II or devalue its importance, claiming it to be essentially European in style and outlook, that is, derivative. The Anthology Film Archives, for example, lists only one early American avant-garde work in its pantheon of "essential works of the art of cinema," *The Fall of the House of Usher* (1928), implying that American avant-garde film begins with Maya Deren in the immediate post–World War II period.[1] As Janet Bergstrom notes, "This tacit critical and institutional consensus creates the impression that an official canon of important works and filmmakers has already been decided,"[2] a canon excluding Strand and other important early avant-gardists. This interpretation, which positions the genesis of the first American avant-garde to coincide with the rise of abstract expressionism in the United States, legitimizes by proxy its cinematic contemporaries in the "New American Cinema."

While the charge that early American avant-garde filmmakers emulated their European colleagues was not totally without merit, it is also true that only recently has an attempt been made to reappraise the early avant-garde on its own terms.[3] A similarity in both thematic concerns and formal applications does connect Europe and America quite naturally, given modernism's preoccupations on both sides of the Atlantic. But there seems to be in the American work a certain eclecticism, innovativeness, and naivete that heretofore have been misunderstood, although it is exactly these qualities that make it different from European work. Furthermore, as in *Manhatta*, many early American avant-garde works show evidence of an antimodernist current, a "romantic" subtext involving the desire to reconcile man with nature—a text totally absent in European modernism.[4] Finally, *Manhatta* actually predates much European avant-garde film and in a sense defines a prevalent style within both European and American avant-garde film practice, the so-called city film.

While focusing on *Manhatta,* this chapter will also analyze Paul Strand's later career as a filmmaker of the American avant-garde who, like many artists of the 1920s, gravitated toward documentary in the 1930s and 1940s, convinced that the worldwide depression was the first sign of the end of capitalism.[5] Strand's later films are also characterized by a dichotomy between modernism and a romanticism infused with revolutionary, left-wing politics. In his two most important works as film director, *The Wave* (1937) and *Native Land* (1942), Strand continues to explore man's struggle with nature and his alienation from nature through the forces of urbanization, industrialization, and laissez-faire capitalism. With the rise of McCarthyism in the United States, Strand exiled himself to Europe, where he continued to rework these themes in a series of photography books. This evolution should not, however, be seen as a relinquishing of avant-garde principles, but rather as a continuation of aesthetic strategies already present in *Manhatta.* That film ultimately constructs numerous, often conflicting texts, oscillating between modernism and a Whitmanesque romanticism, between fragmentation and narrative closure, that position the subject in the oblique perspectives of the modern skyscraper but simultaneously view technology as an event ideally in tune with the natural environment.

Those critics who discuss *Manhatta* usually write only the faintest praise, calling the film a "simple poetic documentary," "a relatively colorless documentary," or "a series of static photographs."[6] Other historians recycle information from Lewis Jacobs's ground-breaking, but now dated article, "Avant-Garde Production in America" (1947),[7] which does accord *Manhatta* some significant attention. Yet, the only attempt previous to my article to rescue the film from obscurity was Scott Hammen's *Afterimage* article, in which he provides a first descriptive analysis of the film.[8] Hammen, however, like a number of other critics, divorces the film's visuals from its intertitles, arguing that they are intrusive stumbling blocks to the flow of images, without recognizing—as I will argue—that their antimodernist meaning is in keeping with many of the images.

Less surprising is the cursory treatment *Manhatta* has received in books, catalogues, and monographs concerning the work of Strand and Sheeler. Both Nancy Newhall and Constance Rourke, two early biographers, devote no more than a paragraph (almost identical) to *Manhatta,* a pattern that has not been significantly altered by subsequent commentators.[9] Dickran Tashjian's discussion of the film in *Skyscraper Primitives,* for example, overestimates its modernist components.[10] An exception is Naomi Rosenblum's seminal but unpublished dissertation, *Paul Strand: The Early Years, 1910– 1932,* which presents a credible account of *Manhatta*'s genesis and Strand's relationship to Sheeler.[11] Rosenblum, however, shies away from both a close textual analysis and a contextual analysis, as it relates to the film avant-garde. Another exception is Theodore E. Stebbins Jr.'s discussion of *Manhatta* in the exhibition catalogue *Charles Sheeler: The Photographs,* which contributes valuable insights into Sheeler's participation in the project.[12]

Born on 16 October 1890 in New York City to Mathilde Arnstein and Jacob Strand, Paul Strand enjoyed a comfortable, middle-class childhood, attending the privately financed Ethical Culture School (ECS), which caters to nonparochial Jewish families.[13] At ECS Strand took his first photography course with Lewis Hine. After graduation in 1909, he embarked on a career as a photographer, having briefly worked in the family enamelware business. In 1913 he attended the Armory show and became acquainted with Alfred Stieglitz's gallery, 291. He had his first one-man show at 291 in March 1916.

Strand and Sheeler's mutual interest in abstraction and straight photography probably drew them together. Both had exhibited in March 1917 at Marius De Zayas's Modern Gallery, and both were considered protégés of Stieglitz. In 1917 Strand had won first prize in the Wanamaker competition, the *12th Annual Exhibition of Photography,* with his photograph "Wall Street" (1916), while a year later, Sheeler's "Buck's County House" (1915) and "Side of White Barn" (1915) won first and fourth prizes, respectively. After Strand returned from a stint in the army in July 1919 and Sheeler moved to New York in August 1919, the two artists became closer friends. Although Strand was seven years Sheeler's junior, the two struggling artists discovered their mutual fascination for cityscape architecture and its application to visual design. Then, according to Strand:

> One day I met him and he said, "You know I've just bought a motion picture camera. It's a beauty. It's a DeBrie camera, a French camera. It cost $1600." I said, "Well that's certainly very exciting, Sheeler. I'd like to see it." So we went to his place, as I recall, and saw this very handsome instrument. I don't remember any of the details, but the upshot of it was the idea of making a little film about New York. Who developed it, whether it was he or both of us together, I don't recall.[14]

Why and when Sheeler bought the DeBrie Interview type E camera remains a mystery. It is, however, more than likely that he had already intended to make a film about the city, since the DeBrie was an extremely lightweight, easily threaded and operated, wood-cased motion picture camera of the Parvo family, very popular with cameramen working on location or shooting newsreels outside of a controlled studio environment. It was thus ideally suited to the kind of project *Manhatta* eventually became, and if indeed it was Sheeler's intention to experiment with urban landscapes as seen through the motion picture camera, he could not have chosen a better camera.[15]

Sheeler and Strand worked on the film from early 1920 until at least September of that year. They shot the film from a series of rooftops and streets in lower Manhattan, specifically within a five-block radius around Battery Park, the Staten Island Ferry docks, Wall Street, Broadway, and Trinity Place. The film was probably edited in October, and apparently both artists took part in the process. Their lack of experience as editors is evident in the fact that at least one shot and possibly a few others were edited into the film with the emulsion the wrong way, causing the image to be reversed—unless, of course, this was intended for compositional purposes.

After completing the film, Sheeler and Strand gave a screening for various friends and colleagues, including Walter Arensberg and De Zayas, who owned an art gallery where Sheeler worked.[16] As Stieglitz notes somewhat caustically in a letter to Strand dated 27 October 1920: "So your film is in California. I'm glad Arensberg and De Zayas were so pleased. I'm sure the film is way above the 'usual' thing. But I do hope you and Sheeler will get more out of it than the applause of Arensberg and De Zayas."[17]

Manhatta opened commercially on 24 July 1921 at the Rialto on Broadway. The long delay between the film's completion and its public premiere surely indicates that Strand and Sheeler had difficulty finding an exhibitor willing to show the film. Though praising the film, critics seemed at best perplexed by this "scenic." Harriet Underhill's comments in the *New York Tribune* are typical:

> As a matter of fact it *[The Fall Guy]* wasn't nearly as interesting as the picture called *New York the Magnificent*. This showed scenes and related facts about what every New Yorker thinks is the greatest city in the world. Hugo Riesenfeld had the orchestra play all of the old favorites, like "Annie Rooney," "Sidewalks of New York," "She May Have Seen Better Days," "My Mother Was a Lady," etc. Two minutes more of it and there would have been community singing—a few intrepid souls were tuning up, as it was.[18]

Neither Underhill nor any of the other reviewers dealt with the film's construction, its particular view of New York, or the fact that popular tunes and a sing-along were hardly appropriate to the reception of an avant-garde work. Most of the critics in fact commented favorably on Riesenfeld's scoring, possibly because this was the most accessible element of the event. Not surprisingly, the reviewers could not conceive of the film in other than the commercial terms that inscribed its exhibition. Its avant-garde discourse was thus lost in the cadences of popular music. At the same time, its positive reception within the discourse of mainstream narrative cinema possibly indicates that its mode of audience address, its construction of the spectating subject, was possibly not as alien to commercial cinema as photo historians or the artists themselves would have us believe.

Only one critic recognized *Manhatta*'s importance as a modernist work. Robert Allerton Parker, whose perceptive review "The Art of the Camera: An Experimental Film" appeared in *Arts and Decoration* some weeks after the film's commercial run, wrote:

> In entering the field of the motion picture Sheeler and Strand sought to apply the technical knowledge gained from their experiments and achievements in still photography to the more complex problems of the motion picture. . . . The results have fully justified this daring adventure in a new art. . . . Here was no heroine, no villain, no plot. Yet it was all thrilling, exciting, dramatic—but honestly, gloriously photographic, devoid of trickery and imitation. They used no artifice of diffusion. They did not resort to the aid of the soft-focus lens. They did not attempt to make pictures that looked like paintings.[19]

Parker distinguishes *Manhatta* from the kind of narrative commercial enterprise then prevalent and the "soft-focus" pictorial photography that dominated contemporary photographic aesthetics, praising instead the values of the school of straight photography and its modernism: "The city, they discovered, reveals itself most eloquently in the terms of the line, mass, volume and movement. Its language is plastic. Thus it expresses its only true individuality."[20]

Like many American avant-garde works, *Manhatta* is both modernist and strangely romantic, even innocent in its view of the world. It is interesting to note that even before the film actually begins, *Manhatta*'s intertitles circumscribe the film's geographical space without inscribing its style. While the upper three-fourths of the image has been darkened to allow for the credits, the bottom of the frame presents an extreme long-shot of the lower Manhattan skyline and the Hudson River, including, from left to right, New York City Hall, the Woolworth Building, the Singer Building, the Equitable Building, and the Banker's Trust Building. Though abstracted to a degree, flattened through high-contrast printing, the long-shot of skyscrapers creates a unified space, positioning the viewer in relationship to the horizon in the manner of renaissance perspective and thus allowing him/her to establish spatial relationships among the individual skyscrapers jutting into the darkened sky. Nowhere in the film will this image be repeated, nor will spatial relationships be as clearly established. Nowhere in the film will a central perspective orient and position the viewer in the concrete and recognizable geographic space of the film's narrative. While the titles signify totality, inscribing the subject in a construction of a unified space and a centered point of view, the images of Sheeler and Strand's film signify (at first glance) discontinuity.

Manhatta does, on first viewing, appear to be a random selection of images taken in lower Manhattan, images that emphasize abstract elements of visual design in keeping with the modernist project. As Strand himself noted in his press release:

> Restricting themselves to the towering geometry of lower Manhattan and its environs, the distinctive note, the photographers have tried to register directly the living forms in front of them and to reduce through the most rigid selection, volumes, lines and masses, to their intensest terms of expressiveness. Through these does the spirit manifest itself. They have tried to do in a scenic with natural objects what in "The Cabinet of Dr. Caligari" was attempted with painted sets.[21]

Invoking the expressionist abstraction of *Caligari* may have been a way of establishing the film's aesthetic credentials, but it also points to the film's use of oblique camera angles, collapsed space, and static compositions. Curiously, Strand doesn't mention the film's many references to his own photographic work, as well as those of his mentor, Alfred Stieglitz. Other images anticipate Sheeler's paintings and drawings, indicating that he, unlike Strand, would continue to draw inspiration from the project for many years.

Two Stieglitz photographs, "City of Ambition" (1910) and "The Ferry Boat" (1910), can almost be mistaken for frame enlargements from *Manhatta*, foreshadowing the shot-reverse angle construction of the film's opening ferryboat sequence. In fact, both photographs were first published in an issue of *Camera Work* (no. 36, October 1911), which apparently offered Strand and Sheeler a blueprint for a number of other sequences. "Old and New York" (1910) and "Excavating New York" (1911), for example, presage the film's construction sequence, while the railroad yard sequence recalls "Hand of Man" (1902) and "In the New York Central Yards" (1911).[22] The *Acquitania* steamship sequence likewise recalls Stieglitz's photograph "Mauritania" (1910), published in the same issue of *Camera Work*.

Strand also borrowed from his own work. His photograph "Wall Street" (1910), taken from the steps of the Sub-Treasury Building, is literally remade in *Manhatta*, the blurred pedestrians of the original still dwarfed by the huge, dark windows of the Morgan Trust Company Building. "Fifth Avenue" (1916) resembles a similar film image taken on Broadway, both in terms of

Frame enlargement from title card of *Manhatta* (1921), directed by Paul Strand and Charles Sheeler. All stills from *Manhatta*, *The Wave*, and *Native Land* copyright Aperture Foundation, Inc., Paul Strand Archive.

Frame enlargement, "S.S. Acquitania," from *Manhatta* (1921), directed by Paul Strand and Charles Sheeler.

composition and its slightly low-angle perspective. "The Court" (1924), with its low-angle perspective, geometric construction of space, and rear view of buildings and rooftops, on the other hand, reprises an image in *Manhatta*.

Sheeler was more apt to reuse images from *Manhatta* in his photography and painting, as evident in an image taken from the Equitable Building and reproduced as a photograph in *Vanity Fair;*[23] as a pencil drawing, *New York* (1920); and as a painting, *Offices* (1922). Sheeler's painting *Church Street El* (1920) also was the product of a film image and a photograph, published in *Vanity Fair.*[24] *Manhatta*'s image of construction workers on geometrically arranged steel girders against a neutral sky appeared years later in his painting *Totems of Steel* (1935), while the shots of the railroad yard and factory indicate Sheeler's growing interest in industrial landscapes, manifested in his images of the Ford Motor Company Rouge River plant.[25]

These various cross-connections are interesting clues, establishing Sheeler and Strand's artistic preoccupations and their willingness to translate imagery into different media, thereby commenting on the specific limitations and successes of each medium's formal practice; but they cannot in every detail establish personal credit for *Manhatta*'s individual scenes or images. Both artists seemed at this point in their careers to be interested in an abstract construction of space, in which lines, planes, and solids dominated composition, and both used extreme perspectives extensively in their photographs and/or paintings. Breaking down images into their basic geometric construction, privileging abstract and formal compositional elements over the image's iconic signifying functions, while at the same time positioning the subject through straight photography conventions to read those images as "reality," Sheeler and Strand created visual interest through dynamic compositional force. More than half of the images are low-angle shots looking up at buildings or high-angle shots looking down at the city from elevated places. In either case, these extreme perspectives tend to visibly obscure spatial relationships and thus contribute to the fragmentation of the subject's perception. There is always in the first moment of reception a degree of disorientation before recognition and cognition of the image occurs, forcing the spectating subject to become aware of his/her own actions; caught, as it were, in the act of gazing. *Manhatta*'s extreme camera angles—and there are many more than in their paintings or photographs—thus contribute to the self-reflexivity of the audience's reception: a goal central to all modernist art. In this respect, *Manhatta* is a seminal film, predating even the extreme perspectives of European avant-garde films like *Berlin, Symphony of a City* (1926) or Dziga Vertov's *The Man with a Movie Camera* (1929), as well as László Moholy-Nagy's Berlin Radio Tower photographs. In photography

Frame enlargement, "Trinity Church Cemetery," from *Manhatta* (1921), directed by Paul Strand and Charles Sheeler.

such perspectives were more common, and Strand and Sheeler had probably seen Alvin Langdon Coburn's photograph of Central Park, "The Octopus" (1912), taken from an extreme high angle. Strand and Sheeler's extreme perspectives are still a function of their inscription of the visual conventions of documentary photography and film. They position the camera and, by extension, the spectator within the cityscape of lower Manhattan, as an observer would see it. In that particular environment, the architecture of skyscrapers defines not only the physical dimensions of space, obliterating the horizons through the construction of vertical structures, but also the actual perception of space. Normally, horizontal views become an impossibility: one must either strain to look up, or climb to look down through the concrete canyons of Wall Street and Broadway.

Given the intense verticals of skyscraper architecture, Sheeler and Strand are interested in capturing the play of light and shadow, forming geometric patterns of various shades of gray on the surfaces of buildings, highlighted by the dark squares of countless windows. At times the geometry of these patterns is broken up by rising columns of smoke that billow irregularly in the direction of the wind. Smoke from chimneys, smoke from railroad engines, and smoke from steamships and tugboats form a major visual motif: Strand and Sheeler are apparently fascinated by the motion picture camera's ability to capture its constant metamorphosis and dissipation into the atmosphere. This more natural play of light and shadow is also captured in *Manhatta*'s images of light reflected off the waters of the Hudson and in the film's final image of the sun's light bouncing off clouds and water. These highly romantic images of nature seem to contrast sharply with views of cityscapes elsewhere in the film, yet, as will be seen below, this dichotomy is not as radical as one might suppose. In any case, both the use of extreme perspectives and the emphasis on light and shadow tend to increase *Manhatta*'s level of visual abstraction.

These formal elements, though common to the modernist project as a whole, do little to clarify the syntagmatic structures ultimately governing the reading of motion pictures as a sequence of shots, rather than individual images. And because film images are embedded in a syntagmatic structure, *Manhatta*'s images have been criticized as too static, and lacking in dynamism and movement.[26]

Scott Hamen has correctly pointed out that a number of individual shots do incorporate subtle movement. The opening shot, taken from the Staten Island Ferry, for example, moves slowly to the right, while within the frame a barge steams through the image to the left. Sergei Eisenstein would later theoretically analyze the dynamic juxtaposition of movement within the frame in terms of a "montage of attractions."[27] A similar juxtaposition of movement, which, according to Eisenstein, increases the dynamic force of the contrasting movements, occurs later in the film, when the *Acquitania* and a tugboat steam past each other in opposite directions. More directly to the point of Eisenstein's theory of montage is another sequence of two shots in which horizontal movements of a steam shovel and a crane are juxtaposed from shot to shot. In another sequence the filmmakers juxtapose the movements of a crowd toward and away from the camera, while the camera pans down with the movement of the crowd in the first shot, then remains static.

Camera movement or movement within the frame, however, is only one aspect of cinematic dynamism. Another kind of dynamism, according to Eisenstein, can be achieved through formal contrasts from shot to shot. Strand and Sheeler juxtapose camera distances from shot to shot, increasing or decreasing the size of objects within the frame, establishing different sets of spatial relationships through varying focal lengths, as in the views of men on steel girders or the views of the Hudson River.

Finally, the film's rhythm, varying the length of the individual shots, indicates that the filmmakers were attempting to create another kind of dynamism through the temporal construction of images. Indeed, only two shots in the film last longer than twelve seconds, and both involve camera movement. Virtually every other shot in the film varies in length between four and twelve seconds, with shots usually alternating between shorter and longer images. These formal strategies of syntactical construction must, however, be contextualized within the film's overall narrative structure, if one is to make semantic sense of *Manhatta*'s rhythm.

Although on first viewing the film seems to be nothing more than an impressionistic sequencing of images, *Manhatta*'s overall narrative structure can actually be divided into four distinct movements of approximately equal length. Including intertitles, *Manhatta* consists of sixty-five shots, the individual movements breaking down into sequences of thirteen, fifteen, seventeen, and fifteen shots, respectively. Each movement focuses on a series of visual themes and motifs, while the four movements together resemble the structure of a symphony. The musical analogy, borrowed from Walter Pater, does not seem out of place here, given Stieglitz's exclamations that he wanted his later cloud photographs to recall "music! Man, why that is music."[28] The symphonic organization of visual images would indeed become overt in other European and American avant-garde films, most prominently *Berlin, Symphony of a City* and Herman Weinberg's *City Symphony* (1930).

The first movement begins with the camera approaching Manhattan from the deck of the Staten Island Ferry, followed by a sequence involving commuters leaving the ferry and dispersing into the streets of the city. The second movement centers on the construction of skyscrapers and their architecture. Images of modern modes of transportation, specifically railroads and steamships, compose the third movement. Finally, the fourth movement returns to lower Broadway and images of the Hudson River. The striking similarity between the first and fourth movement implies that some kind of narrative closure may have been intended.

Strand and Sheeler take advantage of another means of creating an overall narrative structure by using intertitles at eleven different points in the film. The intertitles have been lifted partially from Walt Whitman, although not only from his poem "From Noon to Starry Night: Mannahatta" (1860), as one might suppose, given the film's title, nor are they all direct quotes from Whitman. In almost every case the intertitles introduce individual sections, though they are not purely descriptive, but rather form a lyric counterpoint to the film's visual imagery. The first intertitle is taken from "A Broadway Pageant" (1860)[29] ("When million footed Manhattan unpent, descends to its pavements") and inaugurates a sequence of shots in which commuters are seen leaving the Staten Island Ferry. The skyscraper sequence is inaugurated with a stanza from the poem "Mannahatta": "High growths of iron, slender, strong, splendidly uprising toward clear skies." It continues with another stanza from "A Broadway Pageant." The third movement, focusing on transportation, is introduced by the second-to-last stanza of "Mannahatta": "City of hurried and sparkling waters!" Finally, the second intertitle and the last intertitle are taken from "Crossing Brooklyn Ferry" (1856): "On the river the shadowy group," and "Gorgeous clouds of sunset! Drench with your splendor me, or the men or women generations after me!"

The last intertitle is directly followed by two shots of the Hudson River bathed in light and clouds. As can be seen from these examples, as well as from other intertitles that may or may not be direct quotes from Whitman but certainly have a Whitmanesque flavor in terms of their themes and romantic exuberance, the intertitles do to a certain extent double this film's visual codings and thus give the narrative cognitive structure. This doubling of verbal and visual content has offended most later-day commentators,[30] leading them to hypothesize that the intertitles were added by commercial interests against the wishes of Sheeler and Strand. However, internal evidence and biographical information speak in favor of the theory that Sheeler and Strand chose the stanzas from Whitman and decided on their placement within the film's text. First, the fact that the intertitles have been plucked from a number of different Whitman poems indicates a degree of concern that would have been extremely uncommon for a Broadway movie palace simply needing a short subject. Second, the close correspondence between Whitman's verbal imagery and the respective visual imagery with which it forms a syntagmatic unit creates a narrative structure that hardly seems the work of a lackey at the Rialto Theater. Third, the poetic cadences of Whitman counterpoint the film's visual rhythm.

A transcendental view of the city as a natural phenomenon is very much in evidence in the intertitles taken from Whitman. *Manhatta*'s modernist vision of the city is thus "colored" through the Whitmanesque intertitles, reinforcing the anthropomorphic quality of many of the film's images. Technology is seemingly independent of human control, the film seems to say. Except for the early ferryboat sequence, with its teeming masses of commuters spilling out onto Broadway, and the later construction sequence, in which workers are actually seen in the act of production, *Manhatta* eschews images of human beings, images of the city as a physical manifestation of social relations.

The inhabitants of the city, their interactions and communications, their production of labor, are reduced to antlike movements, insects crawling between skyscrapers. The metaphor also applies to ocean liners and trains, which likewise move through the cityscape like living creatures, their technology apparently independent of human control. In this scheme of things, the skyscrapers become natural formations of concrete and steel, mountain peaks and deep canyons, surrounded by the glistening waters of the Hudson and East Rivers. Indeed, the film's final image is not of the cityscape, its manmade technological structure or urban squalor, but rather of natural elements: the river, clouds, the sun. This image of nature, like Whitman's "hurrying sea waves" in "Mannahatta," positions the subject in a transcendental reality, inscribed by the preceding intertitle: "Gorgeous clouds of sunset! Drench with your splendor me, or men or women generations after me!"

This yearning for a reunification with nature, inscribing technology, urbanization, and industrialization in mass society with naturalistic metaphors, is a not-uncommon feature of the "straight photography" advocates around Stieglitz, including Strand. While nineteenth-century pictorialism sought to exclude the economic and social discourses of American laissez-faire capitalism and manifest destiny with all their accompanying upheavals in class and social relations—retreating instead into subjectivity and individualism; privatized images of natural order; pastoral, idyllic landscapes; idealized historical and genre scenes; and harmonious family portraits of the haute bourgeoisie—*Manhatta* exemplified straight photography's desire to bridge the schism between city and country, nature and technology, man and mass society.

Steiglitz's description of how he came to make "The Steerage" (1907) expresses perfectly this perception of a possible synthesis, if only because his narrative articulates his desire, his own myth, rather than any historical reality: "And as I was deciding, should I try to put down this seemingly new vision that held me—people, the common people, the feeling of ship and ocean and sky and the feeling of release that I was away from the mob called the rich—Rembrandt came into my mind and I wondered would he have felt as I was feeling."[31] All the elements are here—mass society, technology, nature—but Stieglitz idealizes them in terms of a cosmic unity, so that the true condition of the urban proletariat dissolves into a vision of natural man, of genuine feelings, while the rich in Stieglitz's eyes appear false, out of time, ironically denoted as a mob: the very term usually reserved for the working classes. As Abigail Solomon-Godeau has pointed out, Stieglitz was far from the revolutionary modernist that traditional photographic history texts have made him out to be.[32] And so it is with Strand, as he points out in "Photography and the New God" (1922): "We are not, as Natalie Curtis recently pointed out in *The Freeman*, particularly sympathetic to the somewhat hysterical attitude of the Futurists toward the machine. . . . We have it with us and upon us with a vengeance, and we will have to do something about it eventually.[33] Is it any surprise, then, that Stieglitz should turn to the production of "Equivalents" and Strand forsake the city for pastoral landscapes once they realized that modernism would lead them to worship the machine? Strand, at least, sought another exit in his politically committed filmmaking.

In this context, the apparatus itself becomes for him a fact of nature, independent and anthropomorphic, rather than an instrument for the production of ideology. Strand's images of the Akeley movie camera (1921), the very camera with which he would earn his livelihood as a documentary and newsreel cameraman working for the mass media, concentrate on the sinuous curves and the feminine roundness of the camera's metallic body. Likewise, Strand's essay "Photography and the New God" is not so much a tirade against the machine god, its empiricist son, and scientific holy ghost as it is a call for a synthesis of nature and technology, with the camera acting as a catalytic force. According to Strand, pictorialism's crime was to deny photography's true nature, to obscure its technology, rather than embrace it: "At every turn the attempt is made to turn the camera into a brush, to make a photograph look like a painting, an etching, a charcoal drawing or what not, like anything but a photograph." The straight photograph, on the other hand, "has evolved through the conscious creative control of this particular phase of the machine a new method of perceiving the life of objectivity and of recording it."[34] Strand's idealist conception of the camera machine is thus that of the pencil of nature, able to capture human emotions through the science of optics and chemistry, able to overcome the schism between a dehumanizing technology and natural expression.

Paul Strand and Charles Sheeler's closing image in *Manhatta* is an image of nature, taken from high above the streets of Manhattan, that again raises the question of narrative closure. As stated above, *Manhatta,* far from being a non-narrative film, demonstrates a narrative structure that can be dissected into four distinct movements, in which the first and last movements demonstrate a strong degree of similarity. A closer look at this structure reveals that a number of images or locales appear both at the beginning and end of the film. For example, the image of Brooklyn Bridge, taken from the Brooklyn bank of the East River, finds its counterpart in an image from the Manhattan side of the Brooklyn Bridge. This doubling—positioning the subject first on one side then on the opposite side, inscribing the landscapes as the viewer/camera, both subject and object—is repeated a number of times at the beginning and end of the film: for example, the mirror-image pairs of crowds coming and going on Broadway or the high-angle views of Trinity Church Cemetery from opposite sides of the graveyard. Finally, and it is here that a sense of narrative closure comes most prominently into view, the first and last images of the film are mirror images of each other: in the first shot, the spectating subject is positioned on the Staten Island Ferry as it approaches Manhattan, while in the final image, the camera is placed on the Equitable Building, looking over and down the Hudson River toward Staten Island. The subject has thus come full circle; the object of the subject's gaze has become the subject, the subject has become the object. The filmmakers have inscribed the subject in an actual and a metaphoric journey: in time from morning to evening, in space from Staten Island to Manhattan, in the gaze from an urban cityscape to an image of a natural landscape. A symbiotic relationship is thus established. The schism between city and country, technology and nature, "whose coming together might integrate a new religious impulse,"[35] is thus healed in an idealized universe of the camera's gaze, Strand's machine god proven capable of achieving metaphysical unification.

Strand and Sheeler's visual equivalent of narrative closure violates the tenets of modernism's discontinuous and non-narrative aesthetic strategies. Yet *Manhatta*'s closure is only concretely realized in the gaze and seems hardly comparable to Hollywood's overdetermined narratives, in which the subject is necessarily returned to a fetishistic world of order, harmony, and

Frame enlargement from *Manhatta* (1921), directed by Paul Strand and Charles Sheeler.

unity, regardless of the chaos that might have preceded it. *Manhatta* merely approaches closure, implying a narrative that allows for the subject's inscription in the film's final transcendental image. This harmonious subtext is mitigated by and in conflict with the film's overall modernist design, its oblique and disorienting camera angles, its monolithic perspectives of urban architecture, and its dynamic juxtaposition of movement, light, and shadow. *Manhatta* is thus very much a heterogenous text, both modernist and antimodernist, its conflicting discourses never quite resolving themselves, as indeed they are never resolved within the discourse of twentieth-century American art.

Manhatta seems to be a highly ambiguous, even contradictory work. As the first consciously avant-garde film made in America, and as one of the first avant-garde city films created anywhere, its historical importance seems nevertheless assured. It is because of its avant-garde origins, produced as it was outside of the economic and ideological structure of mainstream, classical Hollywood cinema, and because of its urban subject matter that the film has for so long been misread as an unequivocal work of modernism. Such a reading must necessarily deny Walt Whitman's intertitles as a verbal and ideological intrusion into the film's visual text, compromising *Manhatta*'s modernism with lyric romanticism. Whitman's intertitles are in keeping with the film's overall narrative structure, its sense of closure, and some of its imagery. Retaining many other formal aspects of modernism, including its extreme angles of vision, its abstract play of light and shadow, its rhythmic montage, and its portraiture of the urban landscape, *Manhatta* nevertheless attempts to position the spectator in a discourse of symbiosis in which nature and technology harmonize.

When Strand took up personal filmmaking more than ten years after completing *Manhatta,* the romantic impulse would become more evident, exemplified in his turning increasingly to photographing and filming agrarian communities and the natural environment. As Sarah Greenough has perceptively noted of Strand's photography at the end of the 1920s: "Whereas in the 1910s he wanted to show that the nature of a city was monument, change, and impermanence, here he wanted to demonstrate that the nature of nature was permanence and endurance."[36] Virtually all of his political filmmaking and later photography concerns itself with preindustrial, nature-connected forms of civilization, rigorously excluding any signs of industrialization and modernity.[37] His peasants are shown to be in tune with nature, all empirical evidence to the contrary. The truth value of these images is signified through an aesthetic of realism.[38]

In the 1920s Strand was, of course, still preoccupied with earning a living with his Akeley camera, working as a New York stringer for Fox Films, Pathé, Metro-Goldwyn-Mayer, and Paramount, mainly as a newsreel cameraman. He photographed Princeton football games, boxing matches, the Kentucky Derby, and, occasionally, he shot "second unit" action scenes for Hollywood feature-length fiction films, for example, *The Live Wire* (1925) and *Where the Pavement Ends* (1928).[39] For *Manhattan* (1924), he climbed to the twenty-second floor to shoot Richard Dix's double holding on for dear life to a steel girder of the Telephone Building, which was then under construction. For *Janice Meredith* (1924), he went to Plattsburg, New York, to help shoot the sequence of the Battle of Lexington. According to Strand, "I accepted every job that came my way, and it didn't do me a bit of harm."[40] Strand earned thirty-five dollars a day and eventually worked his way up to fifty. It was a livelihood that allowed him to continue to photograph, but it never offered him any artistic satisfaction.

In late 1932 Strand moved to Mexico to photograph the people and culture, having become increasingly interested in that country and in producing images that would move beyond the narrow concerns of personal expression to make a meaningful political statement. Once there he was asked by Carlos Chávez, chief of the Department of Fine Arts in the Secretariat of Education, to produce a series of documentaries about the struggles of the Mexican people. While on a visit to Hollywood, Chávez had tried unsuccessfully to lure the German-émigré director G. W. Pabst to Mexico to make a motion picture.[41] Strand agreed to make the films, suggesting that they be made primarily for the country's sixteen million Native Americans and that they focus on the production of wealth.[42] Even though a new Mexican government eventually withdrew funding from the project in December 1934,[43] Strand was able to complete a short feature film, *Redes* (released in the U.S. as *The Wave*), which he photographed, cowrote, and supervised in 1934 with the Austro-German émigrés Fred Zinnemann, Henwar Rodakiewicz, and Günther von Fritsch functioning as director, scriptwriter, and editor, respectively.[44] Except for the two leads, who were a university student and an actor, the film was produced with working fishermen in the village of Alvarado, near Vera Cruz. Shot over a period of nine months with Strand's hand-cranked Akeley, the negative was processed by Roy Davidge in Hollywood (the same lab used by Eisenstein for *Qué viva México!*), and the Spanish dialogue was dubbed in Mexico City.[45] Due to problems in financing the postproduction, the film was not completed until sometime in 1936 and apparently created a huge sensation when it was shown in Mexico. Returning to New York in December 1934, Strand became heavily involved in the left-wing film production collective, Nykino, traveled to the Soviet Union in July 1935, and photographed *The Plow that Broke the Plains* for Pare Lorentz, beginning in September. *The Wave* did not open commercially in the United States until April 1937, when it premiered in New York. Sidney Meyers called the film "extraordinarily beautiful and moving as few films in our experience have been."[46]

The Wave is a drama about a group of Mexican fisherman who are ruthlessly exploited by a merchant who acts as middleman and by politicians indifferent to their plight. When a young fisherman's son dies because the local fish merchant refused to give him an advance on his next catch so he could buy medicine, the fisherman, Miro, begins to think about the conditions of his existence. He attempts to convince his fellow workers that they are being unfairly exploited and is shot by a sleazy politician for protesting the unacceptably low prices offered for the fish. As a result of his death, the fishermen are radicalized into united action.

As the compositions in the opening sequence with Miro demonstrate, Strand's fishermen are very much children of nature. Time and again we see Miro and the other fisherman photographed from slightly below against a seascape of water and blue sky, just as all the fisherman are shown in direct contact with the natural environment around them. This is particularly true of the final funeral sequence, where the fisherman are shown at the bottom of the film frame carrying Miro's body in a procession, while the major portion of the image is filled with a giant cactus in the foreground and a big, cloudy heaven above. The final image of the fishermen's armada repeats the big sky motif, giving the fishermen's struggle a heroic atmosphere. In contrast, Don Anselmo, the businessman who exploits the fishermen, is seen against man-made backgrounds or intercut with images of money, thus defining him as a product of civilization whose goal it is to make nature subservient to the demands of the system. Don Anselmo's pet parrot becomes a perfect metaphor for the condition of the fishermen.

According to many contemporary reviewers, the film had the look and feel of Paul Strand's photographs. Indeed, as William Alexander has noted, Strand actually quotes one of his own photographs, "Mother and Child," later included in *The Mexican Portfolio* (a reprint of *Photographs from Mexico*): "True or not, one is consciously aware throughout *The Wave* of Strand's earlier photography, for he composes with light, line, and frame very carefully, he lingers, and his actors move slowly."[47] However, given Strand's editing and narrative structure, it seems apparent that it was very important for him to make the viewer fully aware of the intense connection between his characters and their environment—something he learned from Robert

Film still from *The Wave* (1936), directed by Fred Zinnemann. Courtesy of George Eastman House.

Film still from *The Wave* (1936), directed by Fred Zinnemann. Courtesy of George Eastman House.

Flaherty—and something that was only possible by forsaking the fast-paced editing of American films.

The relationship between individuals and their environment (something missing from *Manhatta*) is also clearly visible in the portfolio *Photographs from Mexico*, which includes photographs Strand took in Mexico in 1932 and 1933.[48] Indeed, according to Katherine C. Ware, *The Wave* "was a major factor in the formulation of his mature style in addition to influencing directly the sequencing of images in the portfolio."[49] Ware argues that the ordering of images is cinematic, zooming in from establishing shots of landscapes to close-ups of individuals and religious wood carvings. As other critics, including John Rohrbach and Estelle Jussim, have pointed out, Strand's photography was increasingly influenced by film techniques, from his composition of images emphasizing frontality (Eisenstein) to the structure of his photography books, based on developing juxtapositions between people, places, and events (Flaherty, Hurwitz).[50] More importantly for the discussion here, though, Strand begins with an image of nature (a desert landscape "near Saltillo") and ends with a village gate in Hidalgo, composed in such a way as to emphasize the wide Mexican sky and the naturalness of the architecture. These images thus provide a context for the portraits of a people in tune with their harsh and rugged natural environment.

Working on *The Plow that Broke the Plains* was a less than satisfactory experience for Strand. Pare Lorentz, who had never before made a film, nevertheless had definite ideas about what he wanted to achieve with this documentary about land management in the high plains of the western United States. Strand and his colleague, Leo Hurwitz, found Lorentz's script unfilmable. After shooting the beautiful cattle and grassland sequences in Montana that open the completed film, they proceeded to write their own script, which emphasized to a much greater degree the role of capitalist exploiters in destroying the ecological balance of the West. Lorentz, however, read the pair the riot act and sent them off to film the dust bowl sequences, while Lorentz completed the production with photographer Ralph Steiner. Hurwitz and Strand initially wanted their names taken off the credits, but both changed their minds when they saw the finished film.[51] Even though Strand's compositional style was visible in several sequences, the film belonged to Lorentz, whose vision of America was more idealized than Strand's would ever be. In particular, shots of dust bowl farmers against a big sky suggest the intense struggle of man in a hostile environment and contradict the optimism of Lorentz's liberalism in later scenes.

In the summer of 1937, Strand and Hurwitz edited *Heart of Spain* (1937) using Spanish Civil War footage shot by Herbert Kline and extra film mate-

Film still from *The Plow that Broke the Plains* (1936), directed by Pare Lorentz. Courtesy of George Eastman House.

rial contributed by the Soviet cameraman Roman Karmen, outtakes from Joris Ivens's *The Spanish Earth* (1937), and commercial newsreels. The thirty-minute film is a celebration of the Spanish republican struggle against Franco and fascism and illustrates the use of new blood-transfusion technologies. The film was a commercial success but found even wider distribution through various organizations fund-raising for the Spanish Loyalist cause.[52] More important for Strand, *Heart of Spain* was a product of the editing room, where Strand learned much about constructing sequences out of highly heterogeneous material: "They built dramatic interplays by emphasizing oppositions between war and peace, virtue and evil, and town and countryside."[53] It was a lesson he applied to his later photography books.

Strand's next independently produced film, *Native Land* (1942), was politically more radical than *The Wave* yet, at the same time, continues his exploration of man and nature. Produced from 1937 to 1941 by Strand and Hurwitz in conjunction with Frontier Films—the collective founded in March 1937 by the two filmmakers with Ralph Steiner, Sidney Meyers, Jay Leyda, and Ben Maddow, among others—the film was more than four years in incubation because of a chronic lack of funds.[54] Initially based on the United States Senate's La Follette Committee, which conducted civil rights hearings on labor union busting and corporate labor spying, the film became a paean to the growth of the American labor movement. Constructed out of documentary and newsreel sequences as well as fictional sequences using professional actors to reenact events described in the La Follette hearings, the feature-length film opened commercially in May 1942 and quickly disappeared, its message of class struggle no longer in tune with the national unity politics of the home front during World War II.

Rather than discuss the film in its totality, I would like to briefly analyze the visual rhetoric in its opening sequence, which lasts close to eight minutes and sets the tone for the rest of the film. It is here that Strand's romanticism is most evident. The film opens with a series of images of waves crashing against the rocky cliffs of a primordial land. In the following shots, Strand cuts from the sea to the forest to majestic mountains, to rivers, to the arrival of the first pioneers, symbolized through images of bronze and stone statues memorializing the founding fathers. With Paul Robeson's strong voice booming on the sound track, the film develops a narrative of man struggling for freedom, struggling to tame a wild new country, attempting to stay in tune with nature. Cutting from shots of tall trees to the columns of New England neoclassical town halls, the narrator notes: "We built liberty into the foundations of our houses." The visual simile works: nature becomes art, the new American (wo)man lives in harmony with the environment, the product of his labor is visible to the eye. In particular, Strand again and again cuts away to shots of the open sky, tall trees, the land, and gravestones, creating a syntagmata that defines liberty (symbolized by the Statue of Liberty) as a continual struggle of the people in tune with nature. Liberty is given a Rousseauian definition as a natural right of man. Yet the development of cities and civilization, controlled by capitalist economics, alienates man ever further from nature and from those concepts of freedom. In the sequences in the middle of the film, nature disappears completely. Powerful political and economic interests exploit the land and its people; labor is cut off from the fruits of labor.

This intrusion into the natural order of things is already demonstrated in the film's second sequence, the murder of a Michigan farmer who had spoken up at a farmer's meeting. The sequence begins joyously: a farmer plowing his land, his wife and child working in the farmhouse. When some strangers from the city arrive, the boy, sent down to fetch his father, is hoisted onto the back of one of the white workhorses. The boy continues to play with the horses while his father walks off with the men, their evil intentions indicated by an anonymous diamond-studded hand in the window of a shiny automobile. A shot rings out, the car speeds off, the farmer's wife finds her husband as he falls dead in a stream. Thus, the idyll of man in tune with nature, working the fields, living off the land, is shattered by city folk, men who no longer have any connection to the soil, who remain invisible except for the visible signs of their wealth. Such dichotomies—country/city, nature/civilization, liberty/repression—are utilized consistently as tropes throughout the film, usually ending in defeat for the common people, that is, for nature. Except for the final sequences showing the founding of the La Follette Committee after massive protests, the film remains trapped in this negativism, a fact that was noticed by contemporary reviewers.[55] How was one to show a Marxist utopia, where (wo)man would again be in tune with nature, a fisherman and a poet?

Only at the very end of the film, after the union movement has been depicted through a series of small victories and major defeats, does the film return to its opening imagery of man and nature. As a union man is buried, the camera focuses on strong faces against a winter sky and bare trees. A union brother gives a eulogy, and once again Strand cuts away to ocean waves crashing against cliffs, images of misty mountains, a proud tree trunk, the soil, the Statue of Liberty, the American flag. Again the film makes the connection between nature, mortal struggle, and liberty.

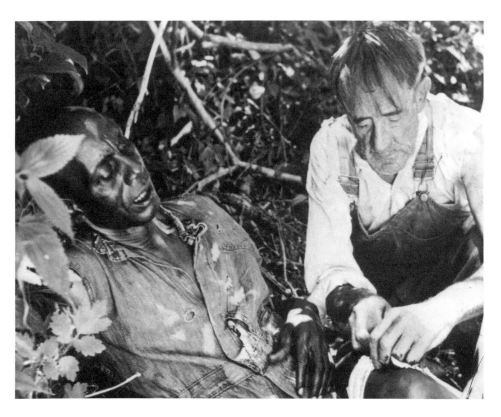

Film still from *Native Land* (1942), directed by Leo Hurwitz and Paul Strand. Courtesy of George Eastman House.

Strand thus moves away from his earlier optimism regarding an idealist synthesis of nature and technology. While *Manhatta* evidences a belief in man's ability to use technology in harmony with nature, rather than against it—a belief prevalent in his 1922 essay "Photography and the New God"— Strand later either excludes technology to uphold the myth of man's harmonious coexistence with nature (as in his photographs), or he illustrates the alienation of man from the natural environment through the forces controlling technology and industrialization. In essence, Strand throws off any pretenses to modernism and overtly embraces a romanticism that had, in fact, always existed as a more or less visible subtext in his work. While his romanticism is imbedded in a sincere belief in Marxism, Strand turned increasingly to documenting preindustrial societies.

In his photography books, many published in Europe after his exile from the United States during the McCarthy period, Strand looks at agrarian societies, as he had in *The Wave* and *Photographs from Mexico. Time in New England* (1950) can be directly linked to the opening sequences in *Native Land* in terms of its celebration of American individualism and a historical past in harmony with nature, but also to the portfolio, in terms of its crosscutting between images of the natural environment and portraits of stern-looking, weather-beaten New Englanders. In *La France de profil* (1952),[56] Strand searches for an ideal country village and ends up creating a composite portrait of a rural France untouched by modernity. With his photography book *Un paese* (1955),[57] he produces a portrait of the tiny village of Luzzara in southern Italy, the birthplace of the scriptwriter Cesare Zavattini, who supplied the text. Finally, in *Tìr a'Mhurain* (1962),[58] he traveled to the island of South Uist in the Outer Hebrides, creating a portrait of a rural society straight out of the archaic visions of Robert Flaherty's *Man of Aran* (1934). Certainly, Strand's last two published works, on Egypt and Ghana,[59] tried again to portray societies caught between rural life and industrialization, but even here the vast majority of images focus on the natural environment.

In retrospect, then, Strand's development from an ambivalent modernist to a politically committed artist with an undeniable nostalgia for a human society in tune with nature seems understandable, given the romantic currents in *Manhatta* and his politicalization in the 1930s, which drew him into a circle of dedicated and sincere left-wing artists and intellectuals. Apart from his increasing interest in agrarian societies, Strand's formal development as a photographer later in life was strongly influenced by his work as a filmmaker, just as his early filmmaking had been a product of his interest in modernist photography.

Like Paul Strand, László Moholy-Nagy was very much a product of his contact with various modernist art movements. Also like Strand, Moholy-Nagy hoped to create photographs and films that would be revolutionary, that is, lead to a changed political consciousness and the creation of social justice. However, Moholy-Nagy was a much more consistent modernist, even if that modernism, unlike Strand's, did not necessarily translate into leftist film-making.

5 László Moholy-Nagy

THE CONSTRUCTIVIST URGE

Of all the visual artists associated with the German Bauhaus in the 1920s, László Moholy-Nagy seems in retrospect to be most central to our understanding of modernist film and photographic theory and practice in that era. Moholy-Nagy's aesthetic theories, photography, painting and sculptures, and skill as an educator and organizer influenced a whole generation of young photographers in the Weimar Republic, as well as a post–World War II generation in the United States. Ironically, the prevailing view among art historians until a decade ago was that Moholy-Nagy's abstract paintings and montages were of much greater importance than his photography. Writing about Moholy-Nagy and Man Ray, for example, Barbara Rose notes in a 1971 article: "Yet such is our continuing prejudice against the reproductive arts that their claim to glory continues to rest with their decidedly inferior museum pieces."[1]

Due in no small part to a number of large retrospective exhibitions concentrating on avant-garde photographic media of the 1920s and early 1930s, Moholy-Nagy's photography and theory have now received their proper recognition. However, only recently have his film projects been analyzed, beyond a cursory mention of his film scripts. In fact, apart from his long-standing theoretical interest in cinema, Moholy-Nagy *did* work sporadically as a filmmaker in the years between 1929 and the end of his life. If we investigate the reasons for the prevailing knowledge gap, we are confronted with at least one obvious explanation: for years the films of Moholy-Nagy were virtually inaccessible; others have only recently been rediscovered.

But the problem of accessibility only partially accounts for the neglect. If we look over the standard histories of avant-garde and experimental film-making, Moholy-Nagy's work is strangely absent. If we further investigate primary source material concerning the German avant-garde in the late 1920s, it becomes apparent that Moholy-Nagy did not participate actively in the growing independent film culture but was, rather, an interested observer. Moholy-Nagy and, after 1930, his companion and second wife, Sibyl Moholy-Nagy, produced their films outside of both the commercial and in-dependent German filmmaking spheres, working essentially as amateurs. Not surprisingly, then, Moholy-Nagy elevated the role of the amateur film-maker—as contrasted to the crass commercialist—to that of a true savior of film art.[2] (Ironically, Sibyl Moholy-Nagy, née Sibylle Pietzsch, was a film pro-fessional, working as a writer for the Tobis Film Company in Berlin when she met Moholy-Nagy.)[3]

His films were undoubtedly screened in private gatherings, but only a handful of public screenings in 1932 of *Ein Lichtspiel schwarz-weiß-grau* and *Impressionen vom alten Marseiller Hafen* are documented for Germany,[4] while in England the Film Society of London screened only one of his post-Weimar films. Two other films from the late Weimar period were apparently never shown publicly before Moholy-Nagy's forced emigration from Nazi Germany in 1934, while his American films were apparently only screened privately. None of the various German avant-garde journals from the late Weimar Republic make note of any public presentations, although *Ein Licht-spiel* was widely reviewed in film industry publications and the Berlin daily press.[5] Moholy-Nagy missed the first International Congress of Independent Cinema in La Sarraz, Switzerland, in September 1929, even though he was a regular guest at La Sarraz. Just why he seems to have moved outside film cir-cles becomes clear only when we look more closely at the history of German avant-garde cinema.

Moholy-Nagy produced and directed his first film in 1929, probably in the summer months while on vacation in southern France. The date is im-portant for a number of reasons. In May of that year, he was one of the coor-ganizers of the *Film und Foto* exhibition in Stuttgart, Germany, an interna-tional exhibition that brought together avant-garde films and photography from Belgium, Holland, France, Czechoslovakia, the Soviet Union, and the United States. Moholy-Nagy was responsible for organizing some of the photographic exhibits, but it is very likely that he also participated in and was profoundly influenced by the film screenings, organized by the dadaist filmmaker Hans Richter. Among the many films shown at *Film und Foto* were Walter Ruttmann's *Berlin, Symphony of a City* (1926), Hans Richter's *Inflation* (1928), Viking Eggeling's *Diagonal—Symphony* (1925), Joris Iven's

De Brug (1928), and Dziga Vertov's *The Man with a Movie Camera* (1929). I mention these films because traces of them can be found in Moholy-Nagy's work. Moholy-Nagy's film *Ein Lichtspiel schwarz-weiß-grau* was shown in *Film and Foto* when it traveled to Paris in 1930. Ironically, *Film und Foto* was not so much an exhibition of things to come—at least as far as film was concerned—but rather a glance at the accomplishments of the silent cinema's avant-garde movements.[6]

The year 1929 marked a period of great turmoil in the film industry. While Moholy-Nagy was shooting his first independent silent film, the European film industry converted to sound. Within a year of *Film und Foto,* nearly 84 percent of all German cinemas switched to "talkies." The high cost of sound film production, the monopolization of sound-film patents by the German Tobis-Klangfilm A.G., and the rapid defection to the commercial film industry of former independents like Ruttmann, René Clair, and others led to a visible cutback in avant-garde film production. Apart from the independent feature *People on Sunday,* shot in the summer of 1929, avant-garde filmmaking and filmmakers gravitated toward private and government-sponsored projects. As Moholy-Nagy himself noted somewhat bitterly: "Most of the old avant-garde is gone, swallowed by industry or silenced by their own discouragement: René Clair, Picabia, Leger, Cavalcanti, Feyder, Renoir, Man Ray. I and perhaps Albrecht Viktor Blum and Hans Richter are the only ones left."[7]

Moholy-Nagy wrote a number of articles in which he denounced the commercial film industry's efforts to kill off the avant-garde, but they had little effect. In retrospect it seems that his silent, experimental shorts were simultaneously far ahead of their time (in terms of their aesthetics) and an anachronism (in terms of their technology). To the capitalist-oriented film industry of Weimar, able to maintain its commercial hegemony through monopolistic economic practice and government censorship, Moholy-Nagy's films could be of no interest whatsoever. As if this wasn't enough, Moholy-Nagy's last film in Germany, *Gypsies* (finished in 1933), faced the added restrictions of politically and racially motivated censorship, brought about by the institutionalization of the Nazi Propaganda Ministry under Joseph Goebbels. More than in any other art form, then, we can see that the reception and production of film, even for such independents as Moholy-Nagy, was and is dependent on the economic and political forces governing the production of culture.

Many writers have mistakenly described Moholy-Nagy's films as "mere documentaries."[8] Such labels have allowed them in some instances to downgrade Moholy-Nagy's films in favor of his allegedly more experimental (in a formalist sense) photography. In fact, Moholy-Nagy's films are all very much of a piece and in keeping with his theoretical writings and political sympathies. They give evidence of nothing less than a radical form of film syntax and design, while their formal composition relates directly to his other photographic work. Their perceptual "objectivity," created through the specific creative possibilities of the camera, is a far cry from the realistic conventions of documentary film practice. At the same time, their preoccupation with certain kinds of images consciously reveals both politically and socially concerned aspects of his films and a subconsciously motivated desire for order. His post-1933 films, on the other hand, are less personal (given his need to survive as an émigré), but nevertheless show his continuing concern with film experimentation.

László Moholy-Nagy was born in Bácsborsod, Hungary, on 20 July 1895. Growing up without a father, the boy and his brother moved in with their uncle, Dr. Gusztav Nagy, whose name they adopted.[9] The family had previously lived briefly in Moholy, later giving the artist the first part of his surname. After briefly studying law at the University of Budapest, Moholy-Nagy was drafted into the Austro-Hungarian Army and wounded in Italy during World War I. He began drawing while convalescing and eventually gave up law to become an artist in Szeged. Although he was probably not directly involved in the Hungarian Soviet Republic of Bela Kuhn in 1919, Moholy-Nagy does seem to have come under the political and aesthetic influence of the constructivist group MA, most of whose members were forced into exile when that government gave way to a fascist dictatorship. Moholy-Nagy followed them into exile by emigrating to Berlin in early 1920, which was at that time evolving into one of the most cosmopolitan cities in Europe. There he met and married Lucia Schultz in 1921. He attended the first dadaist congress in Berlin and became friends with such leading dadaists as Hannah Höch and Hans Richter. As the German representative of MA, Moholy-Nagy nurtured contacts with Van Doesburg and De Stijl in Holland, Karl Teige and the Czech Devĕstil group in Prague, and Alexander Rodčenko and the Soviet productivists in Moscow. Although as movements, constructivism (in its Soviet and Hungarian manifestations), dadaism, suprematism, productivism, and neoplasticism display somewhat different national and ideological characteristics, they did have much in common. In 1923 Moholy-Nagy joined the Bauhaus as the head of the metal workshop. He also taught the introductory course, which he had designed.

Sibyl Moholy-Nagy subtitled her biography about her husband *Experiment in Totality,* which is fitting, considering Moholy-Nagy's theory and practice in virtually every artistic medium—easel painting, photography, sculpture, architecture, typography, bookmaking, and film. A photo from those years shows Moholy-Nagy in his customary plumber's overalls. This working-class garb is symbolic of Moholy-Nagy's political and aesthetic concepts, as well as those of the manifold modernist isms defining European art in the 1920s. The notion of the suffering, romantic, intuitive nineteenth-century artist gave way to the idea of artist-as-technician. In numerous manifestos these new "artist-engineers" called for a proletarian, industrialized art that would deconstruct bourgeois aesthetics in favor of proletarian modes of communication. Art, if it was to be revolutionary, had to be both scientific and exact, the work of engineers rather than craftsmen. Moholy-Nagy's articles and manifestos in this period reflect his desire to politicize art through technology: "Technology knows no tradition and no class consciousness. Anyone can be master or slave to machine. Herein lies the roots of socialism and the final destruction of feudalism. The machine means the awakening of the proletariat."[10] Far from being intimidated by the loss of individuality in modern, industrial society, Moholy-Nagy hoped technology would actually liberate art and humanity. As a bourgeois intellectual with working-class, leftist sympathies, he still believed a revolution could be set in motion from within the structure of a class society. Following an idealistic set of scientific principles, he hoped to produce utilitarian works of art, intended for mass reception. It was this search for principles of aesthetic form, indivisibly connected to the ideological liberation of aesthetic production and reception, that guided Moholy-Nagy's experiments and teachings over the next thirteen years.

Photography and film, specifically the technical aspects of these media, were especially interesting to Moholy-Nagy and the modernist avant-garde. He and the Soviet productivists even rejected painting as an art form. He coined the phrase "the new vision" in connection with modernist photographic media, because the camera was deemed an expansion of human vision, a more veritable look at reality. Not that Moholy-Nagy thought the real world could ever be perceived apart from the distorting effects of ideology, but, in contrast to traditional painting, he believed photographic media to be less tainted by capitalism. "In the exact mechanical procedures of photography and the film we possess an expressional means for representation which works incomparably better than did the manual procedures of the representational paintings we have known hitherto."[11]

For Moholy-Nagy, the central manifestation of bourgeois ideology in traditional art was the use of central-perspective vistas and vanishing points. Renaissance perspective not only distorted objective space for the sake of a unified and monolithic "natural" vision of objects within a given frame, but also facilitated the promulgation of private ownership as a supposedly natural ordering of objects within reality. For example, landscape painting allowed landowners to survey their holdings. Since spatial relationships in art create a conceptually and ideologically filtered view, Moholy-Nagy's modernist approach theorized that the only way to liberate audience consciousness was through the use of multiple perspectives, whereby it was up to the viewer to construct an objective vision through the act of reception. While photography could destabilize the natural vision of traditional photography by using extreme camera angles, film could incorporate a multiplicity of perspectives. In writing of the new kinetic art, Moholy-Nagy notes, "The observer who—instead of meditating upon a static image and instead of immersing himself in it and only then becoming active—is forced almost to double his efforts immediately in order to be able simultaneously to comprehend and to participate in optical events."[12] In his later theoretical writings, Moholy-Nagy continually returned to the ever-expanding possibilities of the medium—not only sound films, but also color films, abstract films, three-dimensional films, multimedia productions, 360-degree film screens, and total film environments. While many of his ideas predate the experiments of the 1960s film avant-garde, one thing should be kept in mind: Moholy-Nagy's polemics were intended to be both politically and aesthetically radical. The film artist and the audience were meant to work hand in hand in these experiments, both contributing in equal measure to the liberation of consciousness.

This concept is central to Moholy-Nagy's theoretical and practical explorations of photography and film. In July 1922 he published his first theoretical ideas on the new media in "Prodktion-Reproduktion."[13] At the same time, he began making his first photograms (cameraless photographs) with his wife Lucia, apparently unaware of similar experiments by Christian Schad, Man Ray, and others.[14] In "Produktion-Reproduktion" Moholy-Nagy elaborates on his thesis that the mechanical media of sounding recording, photography, and film were particularly suited for experimentation in the industrial age. He makes it clear that these media are capable not merely of recording sound and image in the real world, but also of producing new synthetic auditory and visual sensation through direct manipulation of the medium: scratching directly on wax plates, making photograms, painting on film. Specifically, he focuses on the abstract films in production or recently screened by Viking Eggeling (*Diagonal—Symphony*, 1925), Hans Richter (*Rhythmus 21*, 1921), and Walter Ruttmann (*Opus I*, 1921). While these filmmakers were animating paintings, Moholy-Nagy hoped that light itself could be directly manipulated in film. According to Eleanor Hight, then,

Moholy's photogram series should be viewed "as an experimental step toward the creation of a new art form, the abstract film."[15]

Ten years later, Moholy-Nagy would attempt to put his theories into practice, not by creating abstract film images, however, but by creating synthetic
sounds through the medium of sound film. In *Tönendes ABC* (1932), he
demonstrates in front of a camera differences in sound produced by the arbitrary manipulation of the sound track. Like Rudolf Pfenninger in *Tönende
Schrift* (1929), Moholy-Nagy realized that the medium of optical sound allowed for the creation of sound through abstract drawings: he rephotographed the sound track as an abstract film image, thereby directly
demonstrating abstract sound without recourse to sound recording.

As early as 1921 he began working on a film script, "Dynamic of the Metropolis," which, though never produced, was published in his 1925 polemic
Painting, Photography, Film.[16] While obviously anticipating such city portraits as *Berlin, Symphony of a City, Rien que les heures* (1925), *The Man with
a Movie Camera*, and a number of other films in this genre, "Dynamic of the
Metropolis" seems more successful as what Moholy-Nagy calls "typo-
photo"[17] than it would have been as a film. The use of numerous kinds and
sizes of type, the constructivist ordering of geometric lines, and the dynamic
positioning of photographs and text within those lines make for an asyn-
chronic reception of images. As in his photomontages, Moholy-Nagy actually uses photographic images from other sources in the dynamic design of
his script. On the other hand, if a film script is to act as a blueprint for a film,
it must rely on a syntactical ordering of images and movements within time.
Thus, the usual argument that "Dynamic of the Metropolis" was not produced as a film because the film companies, for example, the Universum Film
Aktiengesellschaft (UFA), were not interested in the avant-garde experiments
seems only partially valid. Viking Eggeling, Walter Ruttmann, and others were
indeed funded by UFA. I would rather argue that in the early to mid-1920s,
Moholy-Nagy was still too caught up in researching two-dimensional, static
photographic media to comprehend truly the very different variables condi-
tioned by film syntax. Hight goes even further, arguing that despite his international reputation as a photographer and theorist, he still longed for
recognition as a painter.[18] At the same time, however, we can discover in
Moholy-Nagy's script some of the characteristic elements of his actual film
practice in the early 1930s. Especially important is his concept of film as a
non-narrative, visual experience that demands active rather than passive reception. In his introduction to the script, Moholy-Nagy writes: "The elements of the visual have not in this film an absolute logical connection with

one another; their photographic, visual relationships, nevertheless, make them knit together into a vital association of events in space and time and bring the viewer actively into the dynamic of the city."[19] As we will see, he followed through on exactly this principle in his later films.

Another film script has survived from the period between *Painting, Photography, Film* and his first film efforts in 1929. Inspired by a motif from Kurt Schwitter's short novel *August Bolte* and based on Moholy-Nagy's photomontage *Once a Chicken, Always a Chicken* (first published in the Hungarian arts journal *Telehor,* in 1936), the script consists of three parts.[20] The first part involves a massive invasion of anthropomorphic eggs into the streets of Berlin. Part two has a young woman chasing after a group of men, who disappear one after the other like so many little Indians. Part three mixes eggs, young women, and men in equal proportion. Whereas "Dynamic of the Metropolis" foreshadows the city symphonies, *Once a Chicken* clearly presages the absurdist-dadaist films of Hans Richter, especially *Ghosts before Breakfast,* but is also influenced by René Clair's *Entr'acte* (1924). Both films include anarchic chase sequences, lampooning Hollywood conventions, just as *Once a Chicken* offers a further permutation of the form. I suspect, however, that Moholy-Nagy's script and its technically complicated production setups would have demanded large capital investment, making the project unfeasible. Furthermore, the visual concept as realized in Moholy-Nagy's photomontage, which allegedly presents all of the film's scenes at once, seems untranslatable, because film is indeed a succession of images in time. In other words, filmic construction demands the creation of syntax instead of the photomontage's asynchronicity. Surprisingly, Moholy-Nagy overcame this very handicap once he started producing films.

If we look at Moholy-Nagy's bibliography, we can see that his interest in film-related media increased after he left the Bauhaus in early 1928. In that year, he published film reviews on three highly respected avant-garde feature films and a theoretical essay on sound films in *i10 International Revue*. He also presented a lecture, "Problems of the Modern Film," at the tenth Dresden Photo Week.[21] In another essay, Moholy-Nagy addressed for the first time the problems of sound film production, taking—in contrast to most intellectuals of the time—an optimistic view of the creative opportunities afforded by that medium.[22] A special issue of the German film trade journal *Filmtechnik* (25 May 1929), "Film und Foto," also included a reworking of some of Moholy-Nagy's film concepts as published in *Painting, Photography, Film*. Moholy-Nagy's interest in film at this time seemed logical, given his previous intense experimentation with photomontages. His theoretical essays on film expanded his own discourse on the aesthetics of light and space—two concepts essential to Moholy-Nagy's film practice. He wrote: "There is little in the current practice of film production to show that the essential medium of the film is light not pigment. Moreover the film today is exclusively confined to the projection of a sequence of 'stills' on a screen and it is apparently not generally realized that mobile spacial projection is the form of expression most appropriate to this medium."[23]

Moholy-Nagy, of course, overstated his case for the sake of polemics, since he must have realized that the mobile camera was in fact widely used, even in such commercial German films as *The Last Laugh* (1924) and *Variety* (1925). It might also be argued that German studio directors such as Fritz Lang and Paul Leni had already developed highly sophisticated lighting patterns in their films. Clearly, Moholy-Nagy was preparing the field for his own imminent film work.

Between 1929 and 1936, Moholy-Nagy produced seven films: *Impressionen vom alten Marseiller Hafen* (*Impressions of the Old Port of Marseilles,* 1929), also known as *Marseilles vieux port; Ein Lichtspiel schwarz-weiß-grau* (*A Light Play in Black-White-Gray,* 1930); *Berliner Still-Leben* (*Berlin Still Life,* 1932); *Großstadt Zigeuner* (*Gypsies,* 1932); *Architektenkongress Athen* (*Architects' Congress,* 1933); *The Life of a Lobster* (1935); and *The New Architecture at the London Zoo* (1936). I will discuss *A Light Play* first, because this film refers to Moholy-Nagy's previous experiments with his so-called light-space modulator, and then turn to his live-action films.

According to Moholy-Nagy's script, published in *Vision in Motion, A Light Play in Black-White-Gray* originally consisted of six parts. The first five demonstrated various kinds of natural and artificial light, the building of the light-space modulator, and the work in a film studio. However, only part six, which had the light-space modulator as its subject, was produced. Moholy-Nagy must have finished the film in 1930 shortly after his kinetic sculpture, *Light Prop,* was completed by the German electrical firm AEG. He noted: "The film demonstrates the refined values of the black-white-gray gradations of the phonogram (the cameraless photography) in continuous motion. . . . Through the systematic use of light and shadow in motion it tries to conquer the peculiar dimension of the film, the dimension of space time."[24] Just what Moholy-Nagy meant by "space time" is not easily explained. Space, according to modernist aesthetics, is no longer to be perceived as a fixed relationship consisting of three dimensions, but as the dynamic relationship of moving objects in time. Moholy-Nagy wrote in an article, "Space-Time Problems in Art": "By introducing consciously the elements of time and speed into our life, we add to the static experience a new, kinetic dimension."[25]

Film still from *Ein Lichtspiel schwarz-weiß-grau* (1930), directed by László Moholy-Nagy. Courtesy of Gerhard Ullmann, Munich Filmmuseum.

The concept of the light-space modulator, of course, is based on these very principles and central to Moholy-Nagy's concept of kinetic art. Some sources have described *A Light Play* as merely a documentary of the modulator, noting that it fails to create "cinematic space." In point of fact, Moholy-Nagy uses an array of specific filmic codes. *Light Prop* initially fulfilled the utilitarian purpose of creating theatrical set designs out of light for the stage. His film, however, shows more than just his modulator's manifold possibilities for manipulating artificial light in space. It uses the film medium to further abstract the kinds and degrees of light intensity, to change the very texture of light. Through multiple exposures, negative and positive images, reflected and direct light, close-ups of various moving parts, Moholy-Nagy creates an abstract film. These techniques and the film's synchronic construction through editing make *A Light Play* eminently filmic. On the other hand, Moholy-Nagy's intention to create space out of light seems to have been realized less satisfactorily. Given today's computer graphics, the film does not necessarily seem new, yet within its historical context, *A Light Play* was truly revolutionary, because it moved far beyond the abstract animation of Eggeling, Ruttmann, and Oskar Fischinger to create abstract movement through light.

According to Krisztina Passuth, the light-space modulator originally used colored lights, although it is not exactly clear if *A Light Play* was also conceived of as a color film, as has been alleged:[26] "The apparatus, 'light modulator' was built for colored lights. The apparatus used forty colored light bulbs, which was automated to allow for thirty light permutations, when the machine was used as the basis for *Ein Lichtspiel schwarz-weiß-grau*, although it was not the apparatus but rather its effects, its shadows, double exposures, and lighting effects which played the major role."[27]

Impressions of the Old Port of Marseilles, Moholy-Nagy's first film, is similar to his script for "Dynamic of the Metropolis" in that he rejects here the "day-in-the-life" narrative construction of such city films as *Berlin, Symphony of a City* and *The Man with a Movie Camera*. Instead, Moholy-Nagy's editing is based on non-narrative, associative principles. In this sense, his film seems more strongly influenced by Joris Ivens's impressionistic *Rain* (1928), especially in its attempt to capture the ambience of a particular place, and by Alex Strasser's *Berlin from Below* (1928), with its oblique, extreme low-angle compositions. It can also be compared to Jean Vigo's *A propos de Nice,* although the latter film was probably completed after Moholy-Nagy's. However, according to his own statements, Moholy-Nagy's impressionistic concept was as much a matter of limited raw film stock as of style: "I had a limited amount of material (300 meters) and thought it useless to try to present such a huge city in so few meters of film. So I consciously chose a small section of this huge city, in particular a part that was unknown, because of its sad social conditions, its poverty, and its dangerous streets, the Vieux port."[28]

In terms of composition, Moholy-Nagy was working out many of the problems confronting him in his photographic work. One sequence in *Impressions,* in particular, refers us back to his photographs of the Eiffel Tower (1925) and the Berlin Radio Tower (1928). Consider the extreme high angles taken from the Pont Transbordeur, the bridge over Marseilles harbor, of pilings and sailboats along the docks and the extreme low-angle shots looking up at the bridge. We can find almost identical images in his photographic work, almost as if he worked with a film camera in one hand and a still camera in the other. Similarly, there are film images and photographs taken through an iron lattice, looking down on the street below. Oblique angles serve the same purpose here as in his photographs. Moholy-Nagy notes:

> The secret of their effect is that the photographic camera reproduces the purely optical image and therefore shows the optically true distortions, deformations, foreshortening etc.; whereas the eye together with our intellectual experience supplants perceived optical phenomena by means of association and formally and spatially creates a conceptual image. Thus, in the photographic camera we have the most reliable aid to a beginning of objective vision.[29]

These bird's-eye and worm's-eye views were, according to him, a more objective mode of representing reality than the artificially constructed normalcy of central perspectives. On film, however, Moholy-Nagy could take this logic one step farther because of the additional element of movement. Time and again he either moved the camera, revealing a different perspective or new subject matter, or captured movement within the frame. The bridge sequence mentioned above is especially revealing in this sense, since his close view of various moving parts creates a continual shift of the image's visual planes, which in turn forces the viewer to constantly revise his spatial perception of the relationship of objects within the frame. Here, then, Moholy-Nagy achieved that very quality missing in *A Light Play,* namely the creation of space through kinetic movement. This particular sequence is undoubtedly influenced by Joris Ivens's short documentary *De Brug* (1928), which includes an almost identical scene. The Pont Transbordeur in Marseilles was a favorite visual motif for a number of new realist photographers, including Herbert Bayer, Alex Strasser, Sigfried Giedion, Florence Henri, and Germaine Krull.

Film still from *Impressions of the Old Port of Marseilles* (1929), directed by László Moholy-Nagy. Courtesy of Gerhard Ullmann, Munich Filmmuseum.

According to Sibyl Moholy-Nagy, another formal element emphasized by *Impressions of the Old Port of Marseilles* is light-dark contrasts within the image.[30] We can again see Moholy-Nagy's preoccupation with abstract light in the light-space modulator, here translated into light compositions in quasi-documentary images. There are continual contrasts within individual shots between dark interiors and over-lighted exteriors, between sunlit squares and shadowy alleys, between the silhouettes of working men and the white light of molten iron. In these images Moholy-Nagy was pushing to the limit the reproductive capabilities of the medium in an effort to explore the purely technical limitations of film emulsion. At the same time, the light-dark contrasts (often from shot to shot) can sometimes be read ideologically, whereby darkness signifies the poverty, filth, and exploitation of Marseilles's slums, while light heralds the new architecture and society envisioned by the Bauhaus. That Moholy-Nagy's intentions were specifically political is indicated by his choice of subject matter—the slums of Marseilles—and the note he typed at the beginning of the film: "All day long in mud and *schmutz,* deep social misery, all the glitter of the boulevards can't cover that up." To what degree Moholy-Nagy considered film to be a social and political medium is stated in *Vision in Motion:* "In our epoch of political and economical struggle, the film as a record of facts, as reportage, has become an educational and propaganda medium of first importance."[31]

Both *A Light Play* and *Impressions* were first exhibited publically on 4 March 1932 at the Kamera cinema in Berlin. Moholy-Nagy himself introduced the films, after which William Wyler's Hollywood masterpiece *Hell's Heroes* (1929) was shown as the feature presentation. The cinema theater also presented a little exhibition of Moholy-Nagy's work.[32] Significantly, numerous Berlin papers mentioned the films in their reviews of the event. Neither film was greeted with raves, although both were thought to be interesting experiments, each different in its own way. A positive review appeared in the film industry weekly *Die Licht-Bild-Bühne,* where the reviewer appreciated the formal experiment in the abstract film and the new vision of the documentary.[33]

The social concern discovered by a number of critics[34] in *Impressions* is even more evident in Moholy-Nagy's 1932 production, *Berlin Still Life,* shot mostly in the slums of Berlin's working-class district, Wedding. The film's images are strongly reminiscent of other leftist films made during the Weimar Republic, for example, *Mother Krausen's Trip to Happiness* (1929) and *How the Berlin Worker Lives* (1930). Moholy-Nagy's pan shots of stark tenement walls, an image of a bird cage outside an apartment window, and a scene of an old woman being evicted from her dwelling are in fact highly emblematic, having been used in a number of other films as significations of poverty and imprisonment.[35]

According to Sibyl Moholy-Nagy, this social concern mitigates the whole visual design of the film, which is based on a horizontal and vertical organization of surface planes:

> Like the backdrops on an eerie stage, the shoddy tenements rise up between man and man, leading into the depths of ever increasing misery. In a human chaos of decay and disorder, the clean functional forms of machinery and the pleasant patterns of tracks and pavements acquire a ridiculous precision. Motion and counter-motion of men and vehicles are deprived of any sensible direction by the towering blackness of backyard walls and defaced fences, symbolizing more powerfully than direct action the grim atmosphere of economic depression and political defeatism.[36]

While Sibyl Moholy-Nagy's description seems to make sense in terms of the film's total impression, I think it misreads Moholy-Nagy's editing structure. The film begins with an extreme high-angle view from the balcony of a middle-class apartment house, recalling his well-known balcony photographs. We can assume the balcony and its view might be from Moholy-Nagy's own flat. In the following sequence, we see street scenes, moving-camera shots taken from a trolley, construction workers, parks, and so on. Only then do we enter the slums of Berlin, as signified by the eviction scene and a characteristic tenement entrance way. The film's syntax can thus be interpreted as a journey into the slums, as a bourgeois artist's view of poverty, perceived from the outside. As in *Impressions of the Old Port of Marseilles,* social criticism is often reduced to an impressionistic, tourist perspective of class conflict, despite Moholy-Nagy's undeniably good intentions. This view searches out the quaint and pictorial—such as the highly symbolic mechanical birds in the film's last image. Moreover, Moholy-Nagy concentrates on texture, surface, and pattern. In both his Bauhaus courses and in his book *Painting, Photography, Film,* he discusses the importance of these formal elements in aesthetic creation. In *Berlin Still Life,* he intercuts numerous shots of trolley tracks, sidewalk and street pavements (each with a different cobblestone design), extreme perspectives of fountains and umbrellas. In each case it is the texture or structure of the material that catches the audience's interest; pictorial composition rather than iconographic content prevails. The juxtaposition of images or objects moving in opposite directions creates kinetic movement at an abstract level but hardly contributes to an understanding of the social problems supposedly central to Moholy-Nagy's intentions.

Moholy-Nagy's images of the slums of Marseilles and Berlin never investigate the sociopolitical and economic conflicts that created those conditions. Unlike Piel Jützi's *Mutter Krausens fahrt ins Glück* (1929) or Slatan Düdow's *Wie der Berliner Arbeiter lebt* (1930), Moholy-Nagy's films fail to point a finger at capitalism's culpability, nor do they suggest to the working class a productive course of action, for example, by joining the political left. Moholy-Nagy's belief that radical aesthetic form and the accompanying objective modes of reception would automatically bring about a liberation of consciousness ignored the underdevelopment of class consciousness at that time. Not surprisingly, the above-mentioned workers' films successfully fused experimental and liberating form with an unambiguous political message by clearly defining the sources of social evil and their eradication.

Impressions and *Berlin Still Life*, on the other hand, are very much constructivist works in that their vision of human problems is essentially abstract. Moholy-Nagy's last film in Germany, *Gypsies*, seems more personal, allowing the camera to approach its subject much more intimately, while simultaneously focusing attention on another social evil. The film was shot in April 1932 with the help of Hellmuth Brandis and Sibyl Moholy-Nagy. Moholy-Nagy's interest in Gypsies goes back to his childhood in Hungary and is expressed in a brief scene in *Impressions*, where we see a horse-drawn Gypsy wagon. The film's German title, which translates as "urban Gypsies," ironically captures the theme and tenor of the film, namely the modern plight of a people romantically associated with the pastorialism of a bygone age, who have been forced into the role of social outcasts by society. Sibyl Moholy-Nagy writes: "It was almost too late to record this ancient nomadic culture. Automobile and radio had reduced the horse-traders and fiddlers to utter poverty, and the still hypothetical race laws of the National Socialists were poised to exterminate the 'non-Aryans' in Germany the day the Republic fell."[37]

There is a mood of somber nostalgia in *Gypsies*, making the film more accessible than Moholy-Nagy's earlier work. At the same time, his hand-held camera documents life in the Gypsy camp in a way that imbues the film with a degree of spontaneity uncommon to films of the period. His camera work and editing, specifically his use of jump cuts, presage cinema verité techniques of the 1960s.

One scene in particular illustrates Moholy-Nagy's expressive application of a hand-held camera, where visual effect places the audience in the position of a participant in the action. In the scene, the Gypsies are seen dancing, surrounded by wagons and children. The camera literally dances and swirls among them, its angle of vision sometimes slightly below, sometimes above, the dancers, one moment in long-shot, the next in close-up. The action and camera movement preclude an evenly lighted and continuously focused image, which is exactly Moholy-Nagy's intention. "Camera truth," according to Moholy-Nagy, implied capturing movement, form, and light as constantly shifting and changing variables, rather than as static compositions. Sibyl Moholy-Nagy quotes her husband on this point: "There is an interplay of advancing and receding form in every movement—the unit that moves and the unit remaining static. One of them is always 'out of focus.' And from the corners of our eyes we are conscious of shadowy objects and anticipated faces. The invariably sharp focus of the commercial cinema takes none of this into account. Vision becomes two dimensional and therefore uninteresting."[38]

Moholy-Nagy's hand-held camera thus intuitively achieves two important goals. First, it captures the immediacy of the situation much better than a static composition would have by heightening our awareness of the way we actually perceive reality. At the same time, the camera's movement, the continual shift in focus, the contrasts in light and dark, remind the viewer that this is indeed film and not reality. Such a self-conscious mode is of course *de rigueur* in modernist film aesthetics, but it was extremely rare at this point in film history. Only Dziga Vertov, as I have argued elsewhere, attempted a similar "perceptual realism," which constantly positioned the viewer's gaze within the context of the film viewing experience.[39]

Moholy-Nagy's film syntax further deconstructs any illusion of reality to which the viewer might succumb. For example, the scene showing various Gypsies attempting to sell goods on the street to stodgy German burghers is actually a montage of a number of different scenes. Here, then, the viewer is made aware of the fact that the action was artificially constructed out of heterogeneous spatial and temporal elements. The scene's specificity is thus generalized to make a statement about the uncomfortable relationship between the Gypsies and the society around them. Furthermore, continuous action is interrupted through jump cuts, a device that would not come into general use until the age of Godard. In fact, Moholy-Nagy's sense of rhythm and syntax in all of his films is totally unconventional and—to my knowledge—without precedent. In keeping with his modernist and revolutionary aesthetics, the audience is actively engaged in the process of reception, which in turn becomes an act of liberation. Moholy-Nagy achieves this not only through photographic elements, that is, the use of extreme perspectives, but also by discovering specifically cinematic devices. Like his earlier films, though, *Gypsies* fails to deliver a critique of class society. Worse, his images of wildly dancing Gypsies reinforce bourgeois stereotypes concerning their supposedly uninhibited nature.

Film still from *Gypsies* (1932), directed by László Moholy-Nagy. Courtesy of Gerhard Ullmann, Munich Filmmuseum.

Apart from Moholy-Nagy's formal and sociopolitical concerns, there also seems to be a more private element in the films, which is evident in only a few photographs (at least in the 1920s) and may be related to subconscious fascination. Given the linear geometry of Moholy-Nagy's constructivist design, his leftist sympathies only partially explain his choice of subjects such as the slums of Marseilles and Berlin. Although his view of the Gypsies may be more romantic, they too are perceived in the eyes of the bourgeois society as socially marginal, the flotsam of the *Lumpenproletariat*. The dark, narrow, filthy streets of Marseilles, the dirty, enclosed courtyards of Berlin, the loose array of Gypsy wagons present us with helter-skelter architecture, which in turn could be perceived as a trope for poverty, class conflict, and social upheaval. Yet, here we have Moholy-Nagy pointing his camera at these realities and finding—that is, constructing—geometric order through compositional design. Can it be that we are perceiving more than just the constructivist urge to create a new ideal reality?

It is at this point that we need to turn to a Freudian psychoanalytic paradigm for at least a partial explanation. Sigmund Freud wrote in *New Introductory Lectures on Psychoanalysis:*

> We have been made aware of a triad of characteristics which are almost always to be found together: orderliness, parsimoniousness, and obstinacy, and we have concluded from the analysis of persons possessing them that these characteristics proceed from the dissipation of their anal-eroticism and its employment in other ways. Where this remarkable combination is to be found, therefore, we speak of an 'anal character,' and in a sense contrast it with unmodified anal-eroticism.[40]

According to Freud, then, the overpowering wish for orderliness and cleanliness may be a reaction to a fascination with body excrement and uncleanliness in general. Moholy-Nagy himself delivers the clue that allows us to make the connection between subconscious elements in his film work and Freud's concept of an anal personality. In *Impressions of the Old Port of Marseilles*, he presents us with a shot of a little boy defecating on a street corner, while his mother looks on approvingly. The shot can be read as a perfect trope for the "anal phase" as described by Freud: having overcome the oral phase of sexual development, a child's interest turns to his or her own genitals, to bodily functions. At the same time, the child understands that the ability to master those functions influences the degree of affection he or she receives from the mother. Were this the only shot of this nature in the film, it would be easy to counter that this Freudian analysis of Moholy-Nagy is an overinterpretation. But, in fact, *Impressions, Berlin,* and *Gypsies* are filled

Film still from *Berlin Still Life* (1930), directed by László Moholy-Nagy. Courtesy of Gerhard Ullmann, Munich Filmmuseum.

Film still from *Impressions of the Old Port of Marseilles* (1929), directed by László Moholy-Nagy. Courtesy of Gerhard Ullmann, Munich Filmmuseum.

with images of refuse, sewers, and garbage. One of his most well-known photographs, "Rinnstein" ("The Gutter," 1925), already demonstrates his penchant for turning images of human waste into abstract formal designs. In some cases these images, often in extreme close-up, may be discussed in terms of Moholy-Nagy's concept of texture and surface quality, but the sheer number of shots in all three films leads us at least to consider a Freudian interpretation. If we accept his fascination with refuse as a manifestation of his anal personality, we can then also hypothesize that his urge to construct the world in terms of neatly defined circles, lines, and squares is partially founded in this aspect of his psychic makeup.

If nothing else, this element in Moholy-Nagy's film work indicates that his films were more than "mere documentaries" or formalist exercises. They were highly personal expressions in which Moholy-Nagy attempted aesthetically to shape the preoccupations of his social, political, and private-psychological personas.

With the advent of Adolf Hitler in January 1933, Moholy-Nagy's days in Germany as a "degenerate artist" were numbered, although he apparently did try to join the Reichskulturkammer, the Nazi Chamber of Culture, in 1934.[41] According to Sybil Moholy-Nagy, *Gypsies* was banned because Moholy-Nagy was not in the Kulturkammer and because it showed Germany in an unfavorable light.[42] While still living in Germany, Moholy-Nagy apparently traveled to Athens in August 1933 to attend an architecture conference. A short documentary was the result: *Architects' Congress* (1933).[43] In 1934 Moholy-Nagy emigrated to Amsterdam, and in 1935 to Great Britain, where he worked as a designer.

Architects' Congress is characterized by Moholy-Nagy in the film credits as a "diary film,"[44] documenting a journey to the Fourth Congres International d'Architecture Moderne (CIAM),[45] and it is indeed shot in the style of an amateur travelogue.[46] The film opens in Marseilles with shots from Moholy-Nagy's first film, *Impressions,* then continues on a cruise ship to Athens. A large number of the delegates to the congress were on board, including Le Corbusier (Paris), Van Aesteren (Amsterdam), Siegfried Giedion (Zürich), José Maria Sert (Barcelona), and Bodoni (Milano), all of whom apparently gave informal seminars on deck to their colleagues. Other delegates are seen sitting in the sun. The trip continues through the straits of Corinth, which Moholy-Nagy filmed at great length, then on to Athens. Relatively little time is taken up with the actual CIAM congress except for a few welcoming speeches and some field trips to sites in Athens of interest to architects (the Acropolis and a new reservoir). Then the delegates board the cruise ship again for a journey to several Greek Islands before returning to Marseilles.

The film's most interesting feature, other than providing a visual record of many of Europe's greatest architects, is Moholy-Nagy's continued use of hand-held camera techniques (panning and tilting frequently) and extreme camera angles, reminding us of *Gypsies*, as do the shots of Gypsy musicians on the Marseilles pier. Moholy-Nagy's use of the hand-held camera explicitly underscores his "amateur" aesthetic and his belief in the amateur's "contribution to the art of film": "The film was made under typical amateur conditions, with a hand camera devoid of tripod, with very limited quantity of film stock . . . with no prepared scenario or pre-determined order of shots, but was taken when and where occasion offered."[47] Such a link between amateurism and avant-garde would of course be exploited even further by Jonas Mekas in his diary films of the 1950s and 1960s.

Once in England, Moholy-Nagy was hired by Alexander Korda, the Hungarian-British film producer, to make a silent fifteen-minute documentary, *The Life of a Lobster* (1935). The film opens with lobster fisherman off the coast of Sussex weaving lobster pots, then presents the birth and growth of lobsters with underwater and microscopic footage. The last portion of the film shows lobster fishermen at sea and returning to port when a storm approaches. The documentary is relatively conventional, although some of the high-angle shots of fishermen and a closing animated montage of a lobster cutting its way through a restaurant menu show the Moholy-Nagy touch. Moholy-Nagy also worked as a consultant for Korda on the science fiction film *Things to Come* (1936), designing some of the sets for Everytown in 2036. However, neither the designs nor the animated film sequence Moholy-Nagy may have worked on were used in the final film.[48]

Finally, he made another short, silent documentary in Britain shortly before emigrating to the United States in 1937, where he became head of the "New Bauhaus" at the Illinois Institute of Design in Chicago. *New Architecture at the London Zoo* (1936) was produced for the Museum of Modern Art (New York), the Architecture Department of Harvard University, and the Zoological Society of London, and premiered at MOMA in February 1938, in conjunction with an architecture exhibition. The film highlighted the work of the group TECTON, founded by Bertold Lubetkin, which had built several buildings for the London Zoo, including the gorilla house, the giraffe house, the new restaurant, and the penguin pond, the latter showing the influence of the Russian constructivists.

Like *Impressions, New Architecture* opens with a map of central London, panning to the location of the Whipsnade Zoo. Likewise, a sequence demonstrating the motorized, movable walls and roof of the gorilla house remind one of the bridge-raising sequence in *Impressions*. But Moholy-Nagy seems

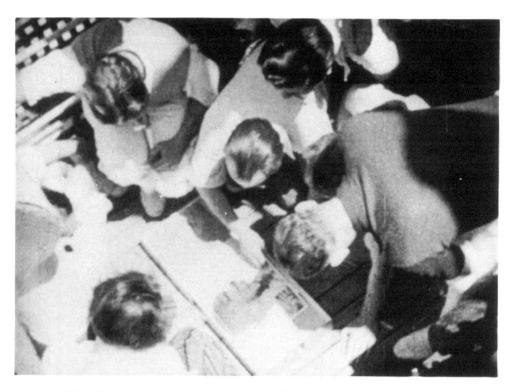

Film still from *Architects' Congress* (1933), directed by László Moholy-Nagy. Courtesy of Gerhard Ullmann, Munich Filmmuseum.

Film still from *New Architecture at the London Zoo* (1938), directed by László Moholy-Nagy. Courtesy of Gerhard Ullmann, Munich Filmmuseum.

to have had the most fun with the penguin pond sequence at the end of the film, panning and swirling the camera at extreme angles to capture the elliptical curves of the penguin ramps, while visitors peer down from above.

At the Illinois Institute of Design (IID), Moholy-Nagy shot at least seven "amateur" films between 1940 and roughly 1945. For the first time, he used the new Eastman Kodak 16mm Kodachrome film stock, although one film was shot on black and white 16mm stock. These films were only recently discovered when they were donated to the Chicago Historical Society.[49] From the evidence of their titles, they document Moholy-Nagy's work with his students at IID: *Children's Workshop* (1940), *Work of Camoflague Class* [sic] (1942), *Student Exhibition #1* (1944), *Students Working in Photo Room* (1945), and others. Since these films ended up in the dumpster, it must still be ascertained whether Moholy-Nagy meant them to be any thing other than simple visual records of his students' work.

In conclusion, then, we can see that despite Moholy-Nagy's undeniably good intentions as a politically committed leftist intellectual and artist, he remained trapped to a certain extent by perceptions predicated on bourgeois ideology. While being aware of and concerned about the social evils depicted in his films, Moholy-Nagy's view remained essentially aesthetic, at best failing to define the origins of the class conflicts presented in his material, at worst unconsciously reproducing some of the very prejudices of bourgeois society that he is attacking. Like many of his constructivist colleagues from the middle class, Moholy-Nagy idealistically believed that the artist could use revolutionary aesthetics as a weapon against the status quo. Avant-garde film forms were thought to be a priori revolutionary, because they fostered a new vision in the viewer. Moholy's vision was in this sense utopian, since experience has shown that without a change in the economic forces governing society, the reception of such art is either impossible (censorship) or perverted by the context of reception.

At the same time, we can see that Moholy-Nagy's films were modest exercises, indeed. Isolated from both the professional film industry and those avant-garde filmmakers attempting to professionalize their craft, Moholy thought of his work as *amateur,* in the French sense of the word: he was a lover, an aesthetic generalist who sought to experiment in numerous visual media. Unfortunately, like so many artists of his generation, Moholy-Nagy's exile from Germany took its toll on his psychic energy. Not until he became established at the "Bauhaus in exile" at the Illinois Institute of Technology in the 1940s could he again think about experimental forms. But by then painting had returned to the forefront of his aesthetic concerns.

If in Moholy-Nagy's late film work (as seen in *Architects' Congress* and the IIT films) we can see a turning away from the political to the personal, then it is only predicting a development that was to characterize much modernist art in the post–World War II period. Indeed, photography and film avant-garde trends in the late 1940s and 1950s can be characterized in terms of a movement away from the the politicized art of the war, that is, as a reaction to "propaganda" in art and as a flight into subjectivity. The photography and film work of Helen Levitt is typical of the sea change at work in American modernist art. Like many other filmmakers, Levitt had learned her craft as a documentarist working on government-sponsored films. As a woman photographer and filmmaker, though, her concerns gravitated elsewhere.

6 Helen Levitt

SEEING WITH ONE'S OWN EYES

Helen Levitt's photographs move, even as they freeze time and action. Levitt's compositions continuously spill beyond the borders of the frame, as if the photograph's two-dimensional space is incapable of enclosing its people and environments. Unlike the photographs of her mentor, Walker Evans, which are classically composed, deliberate, metaphorical studies of their subjects, Levitt's images revel in their own spontaneity. Whereas Evans's sharecroppers look directly into the camera, photographer and subject conspiring in the making of a static portrait, Levitt's playing children, gossiping housewives, curious grandparents, and loitering young toughs barely acknowledge the camera before fleeing beyond its intruding gaze.

As a "street photographer" before the term had been invented, Levitt has claimed to be attempting to capture life as she found it. Her subjects are ordinary people, doing nothing in particular, behaving naturally, without an awareness of being watched or photographed, without the artifice that comes with the sophisticated knowledge of the camera's capabilities to transform life into art or celebration. The necessary requirement for such imagery is the photographer's ability to blend into the environment, to blend into the fabric of life around her, to become invisible. Intensely aware of her intrusion into the personal, albeit public spaces of strangers, of a neighborhood not her own, Levitt strove for her own invisibility by using a 35mm miniature camera and a right-angle viewfinder, which allowed her to photograph persons and objects she was not pointing at with her camera.

But there is paradox in her technique. Her off-the-cuff, one-quick-shot aesthetic seemingly guarantees "objectivity" yet ironically masks a subjectivity all its own, leaving the gaze firmly in control of the photographer, without allowing the subject to return or influence it. Thus, the ephemeral quality of those moments of action, chemically bound to paper, reflect a deeper agenda, that of a photographer looking, and documenting her own subjectivity. What we see in Helen Levitt's photographs are not only real people in real places leading everyday lives, but also the codification of the photographer's vision, reflecting personal desires and obsessions. Unlike many photographers of her generation, Levitt turned away from the tyranny of objectivity, which itself was a necessary tool in the social, political, and propagandistic utilization of images (in the 1930s and 1940s), in order to find herself.

This subjectivity becomes even more apparent in Levitt's filmmaking, for example, *In the Street* (1945–46), undoubtably her most personal film. In its use of a hand-held camera and nonlinear editing, *In the Street,* like a number of Levitt's later films, foreshadows the cinema verité aesthetic of the 1960s, but with a difference. If cinema verité is a technique for creating documentary objectivity, then Levitt's purpose is to visualize her own inner states, as well as those of some of her protagonists. In this sense, Levitt as a filmmaker is very much ahead of her time, in terms of her technique, but also leading the way into an era (the 1950s) that eschewed the politicized social agendas of the 1930s and 1940s to discover the personal.

Like many women of her generation, Helen Levitt has played down her role in the *his*tory of photography and film. Similar to many women working in film and photography, her contributions to these media have remained hidden for years to all but a few aficionados, while her more famous male colleagues—Walker Evans, James Agee, Ben Maddow—garnered attention in museums and academic publications. Thanks to a major exhibition mounted by the San Francisco Museum of Modern Art and Metropolitan Museum of Art, Levitt's photography has now been rediscovered.[1] The authors of the exhibition, Sandra S. Phillips and Maria Morris Hambourg, have done an admirable job reconstructing Levitt's biography, tracing her influences, and contextualizing her photographic work within the social and political currents of the period. Understandably, given their focus, they were less interested in Levitt's film activities. They see Levitt as essentially a film amateur and were thus amenable to accepting Levitt's own negative evaluation of her later "professional" films.[2] Her film work therefore remains for the most part an unknown quantity.

In this respect, Levitt has been treated by film historians no differently from a host of other women involved in documentary and avant-garde film production, including Sarah Arledge, Elaine Basil, Mary Ellen Bute,[3] Mary Darling, Helen Grayson, Hilda Gruenberg, Mary Losey Field, Marie Menken, Helen van Dongen, and Hannah Cheney Williams. All of them, as well as others, have remained invisible in the standard documentary and avant-garde film histories. Lauren Rabinovitz's book, *Points of Resistance: Women, Power and Politics in the New York Avant-Garde Cinema, 1943–71,* begins to rectify this situation, but Rabinovitz concentrates on those women film-makers who have already entered the canon to a certain extent: Maya Deren, Shirley Clark, and others.[4]

This critical neglect can be traced to several factors. First, an institutional history of avant-garde and documentary film practice, especially for the post–World War II period, has yet to be written. Those histories that have been published have until recently focused either on the "golden age" of American government-sponsored documentary in the 1930s (with exten-sions into the World War II propaganda work for the Allied cause) or on the personalities of the post–World War II avant-garde, the latter histories rarely rising above hagiography. The active New York documentary community of the 1950s, including such filmmakers as Henwar Rodakiewicz, Mary Losey Field, Willard Van Dyke, Lewis Jacobs, Julian Bryan, Helen Greyson, Irving Lerner, Sidney Meyers, and Leo Hurwitz, has yet to be treated in a serious history. These filmmakers have fallen through a crack in documentary film history between *Why We Fight* and cinema verité, possibly because these "leftists"—many of them holdovers from the Film and Photo League of the 1930s—were out of step with the cold war mentality of the 1950s.

More to the point, though, these filmmakers have not fit into aesthetically based film histories, which have focused on the cinematic innovation of in-dividual film artists. In fact, the valorization of the independent filmmaker, with all the romantic notions of being an artist such an inscription entails, has always been central to traditional avant-garde and independent film his-tories. As Peter Lehman has pointedly noted, the history of the avant-garde as imagined by P. Adams Sitney and the Anthology Film Archives offers "at best a great man theory of the avant-garde to sit alongside the great man theory of the unnamed darkness," that is, commercial cinema.[5] As the quote indicates, this history is indeed a *his*tory, documenting a boy's club.

Finally, given women's traditional role in society, it is not surprising that Levitt, like most of her female contemporaries working outside of Holly-wood cinema, rarely worked independently of men or as the controlling force within a film production. Rather, she functioned in various capacities behind the scenes, often without credit, offering her creative input but just as often deferring to the men who were seemingly in control of the project.

Even in the films of the politically committed filmmakers of the Left, women were relegated to positions as production assistants and editors, positions defined as "for women." As the result, the creative work of many women has remained invisible or disappeared with time.

The first step in any film historical research, then, is necessarily to produce a credible filmography, a task that remains fraught with difficulties. This chapter on Helen Levitt's films is as much a work of archeology as it is an analysis of a film career. Given her "subordinate" role in many of the films she participated in—even *In the Street* is ostensibly a collaborative effort— an analysis of Levitt's films is a discourse on possibilities as much as realities, on a Helen Levitt metafilm, composed of moments in other people's films. Levitt has not made the task any easier by disowning all of her film work other than *In the Street*.[6] Second, it is an attempt to analyze Levitt's films as avant-garde, rather than amateur, thus removing the pejorative connotations associated with the latter term.

Her film output, as measured by credited film work, is slim indeed. After making *In the Street*, Levitt collaborated with Sidney Meyers and Janice Loeb on *The Quiet One* (1948), where she received co-credits as writer, editor, and "documentary photographer." She worked as producer with director Ben Maddow on *The Steps of Age* (1950). She directed a short documentary, *Another Light* (1952). She received a credit as a cameraperson on *The Savage Eye* (1959), directed by Meyers from a script by Maddow and produced by Joseph Strick; and as an assistant director for Strick's *The Balcony* (1963), based on Jean Genet's play.[7] Finally, she was producer on Maddow's film, *An Affair of the Skin* (1963).

Born in Bensonhurst, New York, on 31 August 1913, Helen Levitt grew up in an Italian-Jewish neighborhood among immigrants like her Russian-Jewish parents. In the nonsecular household, Levitt learned to enjoy literature, music, and the Saturday movie matinees, especially Charlie Chaplin, Buster Keaton, and Pearl White serials. Despite her appetite for learning, she dropped out of New Utrecht High School in 1930, her senior year, but continued her education as an autodidact. She started working for a professional portrait photographer, J. Florian Mitchell, in the Bronx, learning darkroom techniques.[8] While continuing her apprenticeship, she began visiting Film and Photo League screenings of foreign films at the New School for Social Research, where in the course of 1934–35 she met such filmmakers as Sidney Meyers (also known as Robert Stebbins), Ben Maddow, Willard Van Dyke, and Leo Hurwitz. Maria Hambourg notes that Levitt was particularly impressed with Dziga Vertov's *Man with a Movie Camera* (1929), not because of its technical camera tricks, but because "Levitt was struck by Vertov's close shots of real people moving about the city unaware of him."[9] Aside from speaking volumes about Levitt's own soon-to-emerge photographic predilections, it is worth noting that Vertov is considered a predecessor and spiritual father to cinema verité, which Levitt's films would also foreshadow.

Influenced by Henri Cartier-Bresson, whom she met at Willard Van Dyke's apartment in 1935, Levitt purchased a 35mm Leica camera in 1936 and began taking her own pictures. Two years later she visited Walker Evans (and met writer James Agee), another photographer with whom she felt an aesthetic kinship, occasionally using his darkroom and becoming his assistant while he prepared his *American Photographs* exhibition at the Museum of Modern Art.[10] According to Maria Morris Hambourg, Levitt's mature work as a photographer begins with this period. By 1940, though, *PM* reported in a story accompanying Levitt's photographs, "Her big ambition is to direct a movie."[11]

At the beginning of 1942, Levitt was hired by Luis Buñuel as an apprentice cutter to Helen van Dongen, the Dutch émigré editor of *The Spanish Earth* and many other well-known 1930s documentaries. Van Dongen was working for the Motion Picture Division of the Coordinator of Inter-American Affairs (CIAA), headquartered at the Museum of Modern Art, New York, under the direction of MOMA's film library president, John Hay Whitney.[12] The CIAA's film section at 1600 Broadway had been set up by Nelson A. Rockefeller in January 1941 to distribute Spanish-language versions of American-made, commercial and nontheatrical, documentary, industrial, and medical films in Latin America.[13] Once the United States entered World War II, the CIAA Film Section's mission was expanded to include the distribution of 16mm documentary films about Latin America to nontheatrical venues such as universities, schools, and libraries, as well as to produce documentaries.[14] Levitt had met Buñuel after he saw some of her photographs through her close friend Janice Loeb, who in turn was a friend of Alfred Barr's wife.[15] Buñuel worked at CIAA from May 1941 to June 1943, when he resigned after a story in *Motion Picture Herald* identified him as "the atheist who had directed *L'Age D'Or*."[16] At CIAA Levitt learned the techniques of film splicing and editing, while generally assisting van Dongen prepare distribution prints. It is likely, however, that Levitt had left CIAA before the motion picture unit actually began producing films under the directorship of Julien Bryan.

After leaving CIAA, Levitt was hired to research and edit a short compilation film, *Here Is China* (1943), put together from commercial stock-shot and newsreel footage, which Levitt culled from various sources. By April

1943 she was working for Irving Lerner, who headed the editing department at the Film Division of the Office of War Information (OWI) in New York. There she worked as an assistant editor for Henwar Rodakiewicz and began learning about camera work. At first she was not very happy. In April she wrote to a friend: "I'm writing this in the cutting room. I'm working with the O.W.I. film unit. It's all right as jobs go, but I do hate to work—can't get enough sleep."[17] OWI's Film Division was producing war propaganda shorts for civilian use. After Congress defunded the domestic branch of OWI in the summer of 1943, these films were mostly available to foreign audiences only. The Film Division gathered together many of New York's best-known documentary filmmakers, including Willard Van Dyke, Ben Maddow, Sidney Meyers, Helen Grayson, Irving Lerner, Joseph Krumgold, Jules Bucher, Irving Jacoby, and Alexander Hammid. Unfortunately, because of the nature of this government work, filmmakers worked without credit, making it extremely difficult to reconstruct production histories. The only film Levitt will admit to working on at OWI is Rodakiewicz's *The Capital Story* (1945), although she did apparently warm up to her job. In September 1943, she wrote: "My work at OWI is much better than it used to be. I'm learning to be a cameraman. Everyone is swell to me and lets me do what I please—more or less. So that part of my life is all right."[18]

While at OWI in 1944–45, Levitt began her own first efforts at filmmaking, probably utilizing a standard-issue U.S. Signal Corps Bell & Howell 16mm camera.[19] Levitt and her friend, Janice Loeb, shot footage of three Sinti boys playing on a stretch of river in the East Bronx, and a parade in Yorkville.[20] A finished film was, however, never completed.

Financed by Janice Loeb, *In the Street*, a sixteen-minute short film, was shot on and off in 1945 and 1946 by Levitt and Loeb but not released until 1952, when it was picked up for nontheatrical distribution.[21] Loeb had her own Kodak Cine K 16mm camera, and Levitt bought a Kodak Cine B camera for nine dollars. Initially they just shot 100-foot reels for fun, screening them for friends. When Levitt was housebound for an extended period due to illness, she cut the film, using an old projector as her editor. She screened the film under the title *I Hate 104th Street* in Provincetown, Massachusetts, in the summer of 1947. Later she took out the film's first shot (an image of a chalk drawing: "I hate 104th Street") and recut the film slightly, using professional editing equipment.

Levitt had initially asked James Agee about making a film, and together they spent two days shooting around Spanish Harlem. It was, in fact, a project that developed directly out of an aborted book with James Agee, *A Way of Seeing*,[22] which gathered together a selection of photos of New York street life taken by Levitt since 1939. Conceived of as an urban counterpart to *Let Us Now Praise Famous Men*, the book Agee had published with Walker Evans, *A Way of Seeing* was not published until 1965, because the project had to be shelved in 1948 when one of the publisher's owners died.[23] In his 1946 introduction, Agee wrote that these photographs were not "intended as social or psychological document(s)," but rather could "best be described as lyrical photographs."[24]

Shot in Harlem and other working-class neighborhoods, Levitt's photographs are momentary glimpses of human beings, black, white, Hispanic, interacting in the street, in the public places tenement dwellers use for socializing. Significantly, more than two-thirds of the photographs portray children at play or with their parents and traces of their play (chalk drawings), betraying Levitt's obsession with children and their forms of social interaction. Of particular interest is the number of images of children in costume or masks, children hiding their identities, children "making believe," children fantasizing a particular kind of freedom. It is an obsession that would appear again and again in the films she later produced.

Children and adults are caught in the act, seldom aware that they are the object of the photographer's gaze. With her right-angle viewfinder, Levitt remains invisible, voyeuristically participating in the life she documents, yet never actually a part of it. The book's title, *A Way of Seeing*, thus becomes doubly revealing, emphasizing the photographer's subjectivity and scopophilic impulse. Likewise, *In the Street* begins with Agee's unconscious recognition of the filmmaker's look. An intertitle reads: "In the streets of the poor quarters of great cities are, above all, a theater and a battleground. There, unaware and unnoticed, every human being is a poet, a masker, a warrior, a dancer: and in his innocent artistry he projects, against the turmoil of the street, an image of human existence. The attempt in this short film is to capture this image." "Unaware and unnoticed," the people in the film become objects of the cameraperson's gaze. This subjectivity is further emphasized by the cinematography. Eschewing a tripod, which was considered *de rigueur* at this time for steady professional filmmaking, Levitt and Loeb work almost exclusively with a hand-held camera, which is indeed constantly moving, panning, tilting, reframing, keeping moving objects in frame, searching out new material. Moreover, the camera's nervous gaze is accentuated by jump cuts, which break up the action.

Far from being "amateur," such formal devices and techniques had rare precedents in Dziga Vertov's films but, more importantly, foreshadow the cinema verité styles of the 1960s, as practiced by Jean Rouch (in France) and Richard Leacock, Frederick Wiseman, D. A. Pennebaker, and the Maysles

Frame enlargement from *In the Street* (1952), directed by Helen Levitt.

brothers (in the United States).[25] Like the cinema verité filmmakers, Levitt and Loeb allow their subjects "to play out" their emotions without directorial intervention, thus ideally allowing for the documentation of "life as it is." The images are held almost exclusively in medium- and long-shot, signifying not only the filmmaker's distance from the objects of their gaze, but also discouraging any identification on the part of the spectator. The crucial difference between *In the Street* and films such as *Primary* (1960) and *Showman* (1962) is that the former is constructed of short shots, rather than long takes, since the "actors" are not necessarily willing participants. Indeed, at 120 shots in sixteen minutes, the average shot length is a mere eight seconds. Such an average shot length indicates that Levitt's intention is not to produce an "objective" documentary in which the camera passively observes action for minutes at a time, but rather a lyrical, subjective meditation, proper to avant-garde film forms.

In the Street's overall editing structure is also indicative of its experimental form. Completely avoiding any "narrative" design, the film's syntactical construction seems serendipitous, its placement of shots and sequences random, almost haphazard. With the exception of a few sequences in which children are seen playing, most of the film's individual images could also function as stills with little syntactical connection to each other, at least as far as the building up of sequences is concerned. Even sequences that imply a unity of time and place, for example, the chalk fight or the Halloween night, are broken up into individual shots, with cut-aways to other times and places. These sequences are only read (or reconstructed) as sequences in the mind of the viewer after reception, fostering a sense of the immediate and the fortuitous. The fragmented quality of the editing results in an avant-garde film that stands in opposition to classical aesthetics, privileging heterogeneity over unity, polyphony over harmony.

In keeping with the film's introductory remarks, *In the Street* also rarely focuses on architecture, other than as a spatial environment in which human activity occurs. Time and again the film recalls images from Levitt's book, *A Way of Seeing*: a woman with a baby carriage, a couple standing in a doorway, an open fire hydrant, an old women hanging out on the stoop, a grandfather with his grandchild, and the ubiquitous children.[26] Indeed, as in *A Way of Seeing*, the focus in *In the Street* is again on children: of 120 shots, no less than 84 involve children (66 percent, the same proportion as in the book). Children playing and adults observing are the two poles that make up the film. Levitt avoids seeking out other more private human activities such as eating, sleeping, working, reading, going to church, making love. Instead, the street becomes a space for social and leisure time activity.

While the parents and other adults are generally seen in passive states, the children are seen playing, fighting, standing around, dancing, observing, crying, mugging (for the camera). Portions of the film have been shot around Halloween, because there are numerous children seen in costumes, for example, a little girl in a devil's costume, another wearing her mother's clothes, a boy with a beard drawn of charcoal, two girls dressed as Gypsies exchanging candy, a child dressed as a ghoul. In three other sequences, we see a group of boys "jousting" with chalk-filled socks, their home-made weapons. The exuberance of the children, the energy of their play, the sheer speed of their movement, the quiet exchange of the girls, and the wild competition of the boys gives the film much of its own energy. Such "make-believe" stands in stark contrast to the children's lack of material wealth. They are visibly poor, many of them in rags, some with dirty, neglected faces. City streets filled with traffic, and abandoned lots paved with the detritus of torn-down tenements are their playgrounds; paper masks and socks filled with chalk their toys. Yet the children seem oblivious to the squalor around them, at least in those moments of intense activity. Even when they look directly at the camera, these children remain curious, unselfconscious participants, unashamed of their ragged clothing and squalid surroundings.

As Sandra Phillips comments on the photographer's 1939 image of three children in Halloween costume, "Levitt was singularly devoted to the play of children in the street, especially during these early years."[27] Phillips connects this interest in children's play to surrealist tendencies and the emerging psychology of children as prerational, even primitive beings.

Given the prevalence of Halloween masks and costumes, and images of fantasy and child's play in In the Street, as well as in subsequent films, I would like to explore Levitt's images in relation to the concept of the carnivalesque. Developed by Soviet linguist and philologist Mikhail Bakhtin, the theory of the carnivalesque in literature and the arts has recently been fruitfully applied to culture and film by critics such as Julia Kristeva and Robert Stam.[28] In Rabelais and His World, Bakhtin discusses carnival as a "popular-festive" manifestation of folk culture, during which all social norms are overturned, the hierarchies of church and state are abolished, and rational order gives way to a free play of fantasy through impersonation, parody, and costume. Bakhtin notes: "Life was presented as a miniature play (translated into the language of traditional symbols), a play without foot lights. At the same time, games drew the players out of the bounds of everyday life, liberated them from the usual laws and regulations, and replaced established conventions by other lighter conventionalities."[29]

Frame enlargement from *In the Street* (1952), directed by Helen Levitt.

Halloween is a modern remnant of the medieval carnival of Rabelais' world, but maybe more importantly, Levitt's images of children, uninhibited, acting out of their desires through costume, makeup, and mask, signify in the Bakhtinian sense both their freedom from the constraints of socialization and the loss experienced by adults who can now "observe," but no longer participate. Indeed, Levitt shot footage on two consecutive Halloweens "because she liked the material," certainly indicating that the images of costumed children were not serendipitous.

In the Street's chalk battle, which may be the film's only concrete "narrative" moment, takes on added significance in the light of Bakhtin's concept of games and the carnivalesque. Involving numerous boys, some in costumes with capes flying, the "battle" consists of the participants trying to mark their enemies' backs by hitting them with chalk-filled socks. Like the Roman and medieval carnivals described by Bakhtin, the chalk fight acts out its drama in the street for an observing public. Indeed, the boys are not only aware of the nature of the game, they are intensely conscious of their audience, especially the girls for whom they are "performing." In Bakhtinian terms, these carnivalesque images signify the uncrowning of the old and crowning of the new, death, rebirth, and renewal. The children playing and adults watching form a carnivalesque unity, "not merely a crowd," but a people "organized in their own way . . . outside of and contrary to all existing forms of coercive socioeconomic and political organization."[30] Levitt's gaze on their unconsciously symbolic play, her documentation of this free "gay time," acknowledges her own desire to return to a childhood state, free from the constraints of social organization.

Bakhtin's concept of the carnivalesque also gives us the key to *In the Street*'s editing structure and lack of classical aesthetic norms. According to Robert Stam, "Art becomes carnivalized in those texts which productively deploy traces, whether absorbed directly, indirectly, or through intermediate links, of carnivalistic folk culture."[31] The carnivalesque in cinema is therefore not limited to thematic visualizations of carnivalesque culture, but must be expanded to encompass carnivalesque textual forms, including American avant-garde films that eschew psychological verisimilitude, deny conventional audience identification, and "foster 'antigrammaticality,' carnivalizing film on a purely formal level."[32] Carnivalesque imagery appears again and again in Helen Levitt's later film work, but only as isolated moments, not the complete aesthetic position articulated in *In the Street:* at no other time would she have as much control over a project as she did with *In the Street.* Small wonder that it is the only film whose authorship she will acknowledge.

After completing *In the Street,* Loeb and Levitt tried to shoot a lyrical documentary on the outskirts of the city using the newly available Kodachrome 16mm film stock but abandoned their effort when they were unhappy with the color prints they received from the lab. Instead, they decided to make a film about a school for delinquent boys, which could be used for development purposes. The original idea may have resulted from Loeb's great admiration for the classic French film, *Poil de carotte* (1932).[33] According to Loeb, the production began much like *In the Street:* "We started by buying a camera and taking pictures in East Harlem. We shot some pictures in the streets, then suddenly thought we should photograph a child. We visited a home for delinquent children, but they were too tough for us to manage."[34] After developing a script about a fictional young boy by reading numerous case studies (all of which they thought unsuitable) in the offices of Wiltwyck School for Boys in Esopus, New York, Levitt and Loeb brought in Sidney Meyers to direct and Richard Bagley as cinematographer, with Levitt handling a second camera. Financed by Loeb, who was independently wealthy, *The Quiet One* cost $28,000.

The Quiet One concerns a troubled, virtually mute, young black boy, abandoned by his parents and living with an overworked and unsympathetic grandmother. He is sent to a school for mentally disturbed juvenile delinquents, where he slowly recovers from his childhood traumas. A one-hour docudrama shot between 1946 and 1948 on location at Wiltwyck and in New York, the film utilized mostly nonprofessional actors, including the children and staff from Wiltwyck, and the young boy, twelve-year-old Donald Thompson, who was found in East Harlem through a black friend of Levitt's.[35] Shooting in Harlem, the film company was apparently harassed by the police, who instructed the film crew to "move on." Sidney Meyers played the role of the psychologist, while the boy's mother and grandmother were professional actresses from the American Negro Theatre, Estelle Evans and Sadie Stockton. While presenting the Wiltwyck School in a positive light, the producers "wanted to do away with the stereotyped approach of courts, judges, and lecturers."[36]

Although *The Quiet One* also encountered problems finding a distributor, it was eventually picked up by Joseph Burstyn, who blew up the 16mm original to 35mm for theatrical release, opening in New York at the Little Carnegie in February 1949. According to statements by Loeb and Levitt, the film had never been intended for theatrical distribution but took off after winning prizes at the Venice and Edinburgh Film Festivals in 1948.[37] Only then did Loeb, Levitt, Meyers, and William Levitt (Helen's brother) found Film Documents, Inc., as their production company.[38]

The Quiet One was nominated for an Oscar for best documentary of 1948, while Levitt, Loeb, and Meyers were nominated a year later by the Academy for best script and story. It garnered excellent reviews in the mainstream press. In the *New York Times,* Bosley Crowther compared the film to recent Italian neorealist films, especially Vittorio De Sica's *Shoeshine,* calling it a masterpiece equal to that film and complimenting it on its unsentimental view and "far from happy end."[39] Walter Rosenblum gave the film a glowing review in *Photo Notes,* stating: "THE QUIET ONE rescues the documentary film from the hollow shell that Hollywood was forcing it into."[40] The film was chosen as one of the ten best for 1949 by the National Board of Review and received a Page One Award from the *Boston Globe.*

As a documentary structured around fictionalized events, *The Quiet One* was ground-breaking, indeed. The film's completely understated handling of race was also to its credit: unlike Hollywood's one-dimensional, stereotypical view of minorities, it presented a very realistic and accurate image of family relations in the black community, without ever making race an overt issue. From Levitt's point of view, though, the film had its deficits. While Levitt's earlier photographs and film avoided psychology or psychological readings like the plague, *The Quiet One* is filled with pop child psychology, which may explain Levitt's antipathy to the film. Beginning with a male psychologist who in a voice-over narrates the case, the film's oedipal climax comes when Donald is able to symbolically confront his "lost" father (seen in a photograph with the family at the seashore) and relinquish his emotional demands on a surrogate father (a school counselor).[41]

Nevertheless, the film does include quite a few moments with clear evidence of Levitt's participation: she was responsible for much of the outdoor cinematography, including the picnic scenes at Wiltwyck. The early scenes, in particular, in which the truant boy is seen aimlessly wandering about Harlem, reprises images from *In the Street,* especially in terms of their ability to recreate Donald's disturbed subjectivity. One of these sequences even makes do without the otherwise omnipotent and controlling narration (written by James Agee, narrated by Gary Merrill), while the camera gazes on early morning street scenes: old women gossiping, a family sitting on an urban stoop, a pregnant Italian woman, a man with a chicken, a boy leading a blind man. Interestingly, these scenes are mostly of adults observed by a child. Like the invisible observer in the former film, the boy is disconnected from the life around him, observing it without participating in it. The carnivalesque aspects of childhood are recalled in a scene at Wiltwyck, when a boy makes and wears a paper mask, as well as in numerous other scenes, where the boys are seen playing, chasing butterflies, and fishing.

Frame enlargement from *The Quiet One* (1948), directed by Sidney Meyers.

Frame enlargement from *The Quiet One* (1948), directed by Sidney
Meyers.

After the relative success of *The Quiet One,* the Film Documents crew had big plans for future productions. The *New York Times* reported that the team was working on a film production about marriage and society, which had a projected budget of $100,000 and was to be filmed in 35mm, again directed by Meyers.[42] Both Levitt and Loeb had been terribly impressed with *Brief Encounter* and were looking to make a similar film. They asked Agee to write a script with a working title, "Bigger Than We Are," but abandoned the project when it told the illicit love story from a man's point of view. Another aborted project was to adapt Carson McCuller's *The Heart Is a Lonely Hunter* with a virtually unknown actor named Marlon Brando, who had been impressed by *The Quiet One.*[43] Instead, Film Documents produced several modest projects, more in keeping with Levitt's personal aesthetics, but also a natural follow-up to the social concerns of *The Quiet One.*

Shot in 35mm, *The Steps of Age* (1950) is a twenty-four-minute film dealing with the psychological trauma of an elderly woman, Mrs. Potter, who has lost her husband and, consequently, her purpose in life. It was produced by Helen Levitt for the Mental Health Film Board, which had been established in 1949 to develop a continuing series of mental health films, and distributed by the International Film Bureau. Directed and written by Ben Maddow, the film received excellent reviews. The *Los Angeles Times* wrote: "Although it ends with a question mark, the film is so memorable in treatment and technique that it would rank even by theater standards as a little masterpiece." The *Saturday Review* noted: "There will be a few tears shed in the audience, too, I suspect, for this is a remarkably touching story."[44]

The film's central metaphor, the stairs of life, become a narrative device: the female protagonist is seen walking up some stairs near her daughter's home, while images and flashbacks are intercut in a stream-of-consciousness fashion and her own inner voice narrates the film. Her crisis arises when her husband dies, having lost the will to live after being forcibly retired from his industrial job.

As a documentary drama, *The Steps of Age* is particularly strong in developing female subjectivity through a female voice in connection with less overt narrative devices. For example, one of the film's most striking scenes involves a group of children running down the stairs as Mrs. Potter walks up: a scene that unobtrusively leads to the protagonist's realization that life is worth living for her own children and grandchildren. The film constantly refers to other phases of life, as when her daughter throws a costume party for her and her husband's friends. The adults in costumes, drinking and smoking, again remind us of the carnivalesque aspects of Levitt's work. Like *The Quiet One, The Steps of Age* ends hopefully but inconclusively when the

Frame enlargement from *The Steps of Age* (1950), directed by Ben Maddow.

mother returns to her daughter's home, from which she had fled in disgust. Given the film's positive themes, it is not surprising that it was picked up for distribution by the National Association for Mental Health.

Helen Levitt's next project for Film Documents was *Another Light* (1952), a film she both directed and edited, while Richard Leacock was hired as a cameraman. Produced in Paramus, New Jersey, the short documentary concerned the local hospital, urging community support for health care. Once that film was completed, Film Documents broke apart, ostensibly because Janice Loeb had married William Levitt and went off to have children, but also because of Helen Levitt's chronic health problems.[45]

For the next several years, Levitt was to continue work as a filmmaker, but it has not been possible to establish any credits for this period. In 1959 she received a Guggenheim Fellowship and returned to photography after a decade's absence.

Previously Levitt had been involved in the production of *The Savage Eye* (1960). Her contribution to this fiction feature is at first glance difficult to ascertain. In the main, *The Savage Eye* was a collaboration between Meyers, Ben Maddow, and Joseph Strick. Levitt was one of several cinematographers, including Jack Couffer and Haskell Wexler. In the film a woman, Judith McGuire, goes to Los Angeles to wait out her divorce and must confront the loneliness of an impersonal city. She throws herself into the seedier side of L.A. life, searching for any distraction to relieve her boredom, before an auto accident allows her to recognize the positive sides of humanity. Two stream-of-consciousness narrators dominate the sound track: Judith and a male angel/poet, who carry on a dialogue about what she sees and experiences.[46]

According to Levitt's own statements, very little of the material she shot was used in *The Savage Eye*'s final version, which was produced on weekends from 1956 to 1959. Costing approximately $65,000,[47] the film took the Edinburgh Film Festival by storm in 1959, winning First Prize, as well as a special jury prize out of competition at the Venice Film Festival, the Robert Flaherty Award of the British Film Academy, and a prize at the Mannheim Film Festival.[48] "She [Levitt] mainly recollects going around with Strick and filming 'everything that appealed to us,' including 'a lot of oil pumps and places in Venice' and the dinosaurs in the La Brea Tar Pits."[49] In point of fact, the Levitt material is relatively easy to identify, since it is characterized by the same "in the street" look of her first film. It constitutes a not insubstantial portion of *The Savage Eye*.

Interestingly, especially in reference to *In the Street*, the two major sequences of Levitt's imagery are framed within the narrative by woman's subjectivity and her gaze. The first sequence follows the morning after Judith's arrival, while the angel quizzes her about her life: oil derricks, an old woman gazing into the distance, the freeway, an auto junkyard. It is a topographical exploration by the female protagonist, marked as her subjective view. The second, much longer sequence is even more clearly defined as significations of her subjectivity, since this sequence of close to thirty shots cut away from Judith musing in a bar: "A penny for your thoughts," asks the angel before the sequence begins. The images are her observations of the street, held mostly in long and medium shots: mannequins in shop windows, people standing in line, a woman on a treadmill in a Venice amusement park, old men and women sitting on benches watching, a Jehovah's Witness selling the *Watchtower,* city dwellers walking down the street, old people watching from behind windows. In contrast to other sequences, where Judith actually appears in the physical space of the scene, she remains invisible in the "Levitt sequences," reinforcing the sense that these are reflections of her subjectivity; they are people and events she has looked at without engaging them. Furthermore, unlike other sequences in the film, these two sequences also have an almost random editing structure, recalling Levitt's earlier work.

In the middle of the second sequence, a shot of a huge eye functions as a perfect metaphor not only for her gaze and subjectivity, but also for the film as a whole. Indeed, virtually every other sustained sequence in the film thematizes either directly or indirectly the voyeuristic desires of the subject: the airport opening, the wrestling match, the striptease, the New Year's Eve party, the accidents, the transvestite ball, and the Pentecostal church scene, which includes cut-away shots by Levitt.[50] Given the cynical gloom of much of the film, it is surprising that it ends with a short sequence filled with hope, images certainly photographed by Levitt: a doll in the surf, a little girl running with a parasol, a boy playing with a ball—children on the beach at Venice—images of innocence and freedom.

Levitt's next project, Joseph Strick's *The Balcony,* took her back to her beginnings as an apprentice editor of stock footage. Strick, who directed Genet's play on a large movie studio set from a script by Ben Maddow, shot the film at the KTTV studios in Los Angeles for approximately $150,000. It starred Shelly Winters, Peter Falk, Lee Grant, Ruby Dee, and Leonard Nimoy.[51] The film, like the play before it, caused an instant scandal and was banned in Texas, Atlanta, Italy, and numerous other places due to its "blasphemous" content. The press reviewed the film positively, as they had *The Savage Eye,* respecting its European flavor and seriousness,[52] but according to Levitt her role in its production was no more than that of a "film researcher."

In fact, Levitt, as "director's assistant," was responsible for the montage sequences that pepper the film and open up to historical reality the play's

Film still from *The Savage Eye* (1959), directed by Ben Maddow, Joseph Strick, and Sidney Meyers. Courtesy of Film Stills Library, Museum of Modern Art.

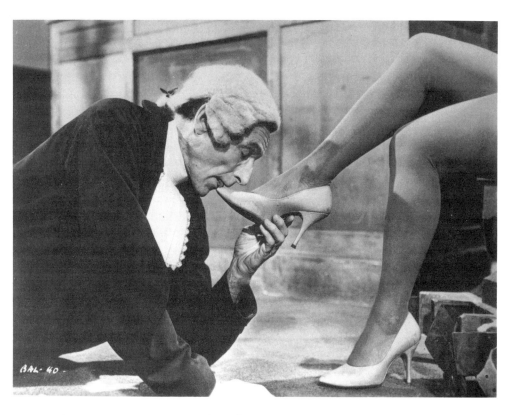

Film still from *The Balcony* (1964), directed by Joseph Strick. Courtesy of Film Stills Library, Museum of Modern Art.

theatrical insularity. In the title-credits montage of street fighting, as well as in later sequences, Levitt used not only stock shots and newsreels, but also some footage of burning garbage and burnt-out buildings she shot in the New Jersey flats. While the brothel called The Balcony is a world of illusion, of costumes and fake sets, allowing clients to make believe they are whoever they wish to be, Levitt's documentary shots interpolate images of street riots, cheering crowds, and the devastation caused by war and revolution—the very reality the patrons are escaping. According to Genet, though, this dichotomy between fiction and newsreel, theater and life is a false one, since it is the illusions and desires of the individual that are the stuff of political revolutions.

Levitt's last major film credit was as a producer in *An Affair of the Skin* (1963), an independently produced fiction feature, written and directed by Ben Maddow. The film's narrative involves the intertwining sexual relationships of five New Yorkers: a couple, Allen and Katherine, whose marriage is on the rocks; Veronica (a fashion model); Max (a real estate dealer); and Janice (a woman photographer). Allen falls in love with Veronica but is unable to leave his wife, forcing Veronica to accept a proposal of marriage from Max, who in turn is attempting to bring Janice and Allen together. After Katherine attempts suicide, Allen returns to the marital fold.

Overscripted and consciously based on "adult" European models of realistic, sexual (melo)drama, Maddow's film was generally not well-received. Eugene Archer in the *New York Times* noted that "pretentiousness is the order of the day," calling the story thin and the film's pacing "slow enough to overemphasize every syllable in the script."[53] Other critics concurred, although Arthur Knight praised performances by Viveca Lindfors, Herbert Berghof, and Diana Sands, and called the film's European flavor "constantly fresh and challenging."[54]

While Levitt seems to have contributed very little to the film's overall conception and design, she is very much a part of the picture through the character of Janice,[55] who seems to have been written as an "homage" to Levitt. The fictional Janice says: "You know when people begin to look at my work, I begin to hate them. I mean the prints. I also mean the people." Such a statement recalls Levitt, who is reticent to the point of self-effacement about her photographic work.[56] Early in the film Janice goes to the fruit and vegetable market, then to Harlem with her Leica camera. She spends as much time standing and watching her environment, searching out motifs, as she does photographing. She walks through an abandoned lot, photographing schoolchildren playing, a scene that recalls Levitt shooting *In the Street*. Back at her loft, she looks at a photo (seen in the film in close-up) of a young girl, a photo obviously made by Levitt in the late 1930s or early 1940s. At various moments in the film, eight of Janice's, that is, Helen Levitt's photos are shown, including six published in *A Way of Seeing*.[57] They are images of black and white children playing, of pregnant and aging mothers, ostensibly made by a woman photographer who avoids personal relationships, who lives only for her art. Like Levitt, who at one time wanted to become a painter, Janice regrets that she is not Michelangelo but nevertheless views her photographs as reflections of her own subjectivity. "All I have in a funny way are pictures of me," Janice says.

Ironically, a few years before this film, Levitt returned to her first love, photography, for the first time since the 1940s. There she could give her subjectivity the free rein denied her in the filmmaking process. Yet, in an era when men controlled the production of moving images, when subjectivity in the cinema was defined by the male gaze, Helen Levitt was a rarity. She was an independent woman who at least attempted to document her own subjectivity, even when she had to subordinate her work to the desires of others. That we are able to reconstruct that subjectivity and its fascination with the carnivalesque is to Levitt's continuing credit.

Subjectivity is also central to the work of the photographer/filmmaker Robert Frank. Emigrating to the United States from his native Switzerland in the 1940s, Frank was catapulted into the forefront of American photographers with his book *The Americans*, which literally established a whole new photographic genre, "street photography." With his first film, *Pull My Daisy* (1959), Frank established himself as a major figure in the film avant-garde. Over the next forty years, Frank's film career has had its ups and downs, but he has consistently striven to create a personal narrative, reflecting his male subjectivity.

7 Robert Frank

DADDY SEARCHING FOR THE TRUTH

There is a scene in Robert Frank's film *About Me: A Musical* (1971) when Frank goes home: "Heim nach Zuri," as one would say in Swiss-German dialect. It begins when the actress playing Frank's alter ego says her mother is blind. Cut to the camera moving rapidly into a room, past the mother whose back is turned, then tracking into the corner of the room, where it stops for a second before slowly panning over walls covered with paintings and family photographs. The camera pauses again briefly to show us Mom full-face before it roars into the living room, where Dad is peering into a stereo viewer. After seeing a close-up of Robert as a child through the stereoscope, we cut back to the artist, repeating: "My mother is blind. I went to visit her." The scene seems ripe with meaning, both in its conscious visual construction, a seemingly perfect metonymy for the real world, and in its unconscious revelation of an artist whose view through the lens of a camera allows him to remain distant and abstract, even in moments of intense oedipal conflict.

The camera in this particular scene is never a mere silent observer or an objective recorder from a distance or close up, but rather always a moving, roving, subjective participant, which through the very recognition of its own subjectivity gives credence to the reality of the image. Frank's very denial of classical film practice, the off-the-cuff aesthetics of his film technique, are a function of a style of cinema that seeks to communicate its honesty, the sincerity of the feelings it seemingly captures, the truth of its personal reality. Yet this apparent closeness to "reality" is deceptive.

Robert comes home: "kommt Heim nach Zuri." The camera allows only a brief glimpse of the mother before swishing into the next room. The father doesn't acknowledge the camera's, that is, his son's presence, but instead keeps flipping through the stereo views. On the sound track we've been hearing the clicking of the stereo viewer all along, the mother's words spoken, but not heard. Thus, it is the father, not the mother, who defines the scene through his presence on the sound track.

Frank's mother looks down and away from the camera's gaze, somewhat bewildered, blind we are told, but also made mute by the artist. Her silence, a function of nonsynchronous sound, symbolically mirrors her lack and subservience to the father. Frank's father's face is hidden by the stereo viewer. Neither mother nor father ever exchange glances or even acknowledge their son's presence. No one really connects, no emotions are communicated. The scene reveals an obsession with images, both in its positioning of the camera as a surrogate for the son and in its stubborn gaze on other images: the paintings and family shots on the walls, the stereoscopic views. The father, like the son, is entranced by images. According to Philip Brookman: "His father photographed the family constantly with a stereo camera. The glass plates he made could be viewed on a special viewer at their home. There were pictures of the immediate family as well as aunts, uncles, and relatives from Germany who posed stiffly for the camera."[1]

There is the implication in Frank's work that to make images is to gain knowledge, and, by extension, power: power over memory, power over history. Here we have father and son in competition as makers of images, as arbitrators of family history and memory, while the silent mother is blind to their labor. In later films, Frank's own children will demonstrate a similar blindness to images, thus resisting their power, the way Frank resists and is fascinated by his own father's power.

Suddenly, the camera switches to the father's point of view as he gazes into the black box. At first out of focus, the image slowly sharpens into an iris, revealing a boy, while on the sound track we hear Frank in guttural Swiss-German: "Das bin ich. Das bin ich, wann ich auf dem Balkon sitz." (That's me, that's me sitting on the balcony.) The father barely manages a grunt. As in so many other moments between fathers and children in Frank's other films, the only communication occurs through the narrativization of images. Little Robert on the balcony in Zürich: by means of a simple edit the father, peering, becomes the son, both subject and object, just as Robert Frank will continually attempt to trade places with his own son (and daughter), hoping to communicate from the opposite side of the camera.

Frank's films, like his photographs, but in a more direct and personal sense, continually decry the intolerable schism between the outside world—

the physical realm of real life, that portion of the universe which is beholden to the physics of light, optics and photochemistry—and the inner world of the spirit, of human emotions. Frank keeps hoping that there is a connection, that the meaning of images can be read as semaphore of the soul. At the same time, he documents their failure to communicate, their opacity when the concerns of the father are to be articulated to the offspring. Frank's desire that photographic images function as memory is continually thwarted, because the past is a foreign place, because the father's narrative of history is perceived by the son as a means of controlling the present, of defining power relations.

In all of his film work, Robert Frank, the artist, the husband, the father, is the subject. Although he never appears in the scene, he is omnipresent through the surrogate, the camera eye. A number of critics have remarked on the "rather self-obsessed group of autobiographical films."[2] But are they? Are we getting the real Robert Frank, or only his image? A screen persona, an aesthetic construction, a fetish? Frank remains an enigma, an image, undecodable, forever trapped on the other side of the lens. He resists interpretation, definitions crowd him, like just so many armored tank traps at the Swiss border in 1940. "It's the misinformation that is important," Frank once said in reference to Brookman's biographical video on Frank, *Fire in the East: A Portrait of Robert Frank* (1986).[3] For all their autobiography, Frank's films are not consciously revealing. He keeps the audience at a distance, just as he uses the camera to keep his distance from those around him. Being close and yet keeping distance is the key to Frank's voyeuristic gaze, as Christian Metz has pointed out: "The voyeur is careful to maintain a gulf, an empty space between the object and the eye, the object and his own body: his look fastens the object at the right distance."[4]

Referring to Frank, Jonas Mekas once asked: "Where does this morbidness come from? From this world, you fool."[5] But it is not the world, rather an obsession with images of the world, silent, incommunicado, that gives his films their nihilistic tinge. In *Home Improvements* (1985), while his camera is pointed at a window of his house, allowing him to film his reflection filming the artist, Frank notes: "I'm always doing the same images. I'm always looking outside, trying to look inside. Trying to tell something that is true. But maybe nothing is true. Except what's out there. And what's out there is always different."

As he speaks, the camera pans away from the window to a completely empty landscape, then to a barren, wintry shot of the same scene: inside/outside, a world of reflections in which everything is an illusion, because emotions are by definition as fleeting as the images that supposedly capture them. Inside/outside, Frank positions himself as subject in a voyeuristic spectacle, where his desire depends on the continual pursuit of an absent object, the camera a permanent barrier between himself and the object. In the newest, as yet unpublished edition of *The Lines in My Hand,* Frank writes under a frame enlargement of himself holding the camera from *Home Improvements,* "Daddy looking for the truth": again, the narrative of the father whose history presents a world full of emptiness. Nietzsche died a madman in Switzerland; Frank escaped its borders, but he took his darkness with him.

In talking about Robert Frank, Jonas Mekas once asked with Nietzsche: "Gibt es ein Pessimismus der Staerke?" (Is there a pessimism of strength?).[6] Interestingly, Mekas mistranslates or misinterprets the quote to postulate a pessimism of self-knowledge, giving Frank's pessimism an emancipatory quality, which Mekas undoubtably desired to see. The question here will be whether in fact Frank's films allow the subject access to such knowledge, or whether it is really a Nietzschean pessimism of strength, of denial.

Robert Frank's contribution to photography in the mid-twentieth century is unquestionable. His book *The Americans* is probably the single most important American photography book of the post–World War II period. Frank's photography has spawned numerous disciples, as well as a rich critical literature.[7] However, at the very moment Frank achieved the status of a "star," he gave up photography to become a filmmaker. After roughly fifteen years as a photographer, he has spent the last thirty-five years as a filmmaker. He has continued to photograph sporadically. In relation to his stature as a photographer, Frank's film oeuvre received until the late 1980s minimal attention from film critics, historians, and the viewing public. In fact, for years Frank's critical reputation as a filmmaker rested more or less on one film, *Pull My Daisy,*[8] and on the legend of a second, his banned *Cocksucker Blues* (1972).[9] This chapter will focus on Frank's more personal films and autobiographical moments in others, rather than his oeuvre in its totality.

The only serious production history of any of Frank's films is Blaine Allan's exact historical reconstruction of events in "The Making (and Unmaking) of *Pull My Daisy.*" Quoting from an article by Alfred Leslie,[10] Allan demonstrates both the close and well-organized collaboration between the artists making the film—hardly any off-the-cuff improvisation—and their outright commercial intentions.[11]

The spontaneity attributed to *Pull My Daisy* for the past thirty years is a legend, constructed and maintained—just as Frank's artistic persona in his later films is as much a product of narrative as it is of lived experience. Yet, as the scene in Zürich from *About Me* demonstrates, Frank's films, against his conscious intentions, slip from their maker's hands onto the screen, re-

vealing a disturbing vision filled with oedipal complications in the gaps between intentions and perceptions.

Robert Frank was born in Zürich on 9 November 1924 of German-Jewish
parentage and grew up in an environment of cultured, middle-class values.
According to William Johnson, "There are hints from Robert that his father
ran the type of rigid, authoritarian household not uncommon to that generation."[12] After dropping out of school in 1940, Frank apprenticed with a
photographer, a move that was probably not completely sanctioned by his
parents. He noted in an interview: "Early on I made decisions based on negative feelings. I didn't know exactly what I wanted but I sure knew what I
didn't want. I didn't want to be part of the smallness of Switzerland. Switzerland was a very traditional place where you were expected to do what your
father did—follow some sort of directions that were laid down. I didn't want
the restrictions of life that my parents had, their concerns about money and
respectability and all."[13]

Yet, the normality of Frank's privileged youth was deceptive, too, a fact
that did not escape Frank or his German father. Frank did not become a
Swiss citizen until 1945,[14] so that deportation to Nazi Germany was certainly
a possibility. Living in such a situation must have made the teenage Robert
feel trapped. He later noted: "It was an unforgettable situation. I watched the
grown-ups decide what to do—when to change your name, whatever. It's on
the radio every day. You hear that guy [Hitler] talking—threatening—curs-
ing the Jews. It's forever in your mind—like a smell, the voice of that man—
of Göring, of Goebbels—these were evil characters."[15]

After several apprenticeships with various photographers and brief military service, Frank arrived in New York in March 1947, where he got a job
shooting fashion for *Harper's Bazaar*.[16] In 1951 his son Pablo was born.
Throughout the 1950s Frank's reputation continued to grow as a freelance
photographer, and in 1955 he received a Guggenheim Fellowship to create a
portrait of the United States, resulting in *The Americans*.

In 1958 Frank made his first film, a collaborative effort with the painter
Alfred Leslie. According to Leslie,[17] *Pull My Daisy* was part of a trilogy, which
also included *The Sin of Jesus* and *Mr. Z* (unproduced). While appearing
spontaneous, the film was indeed highly scripted, based on the third act of a
Jack Kerouac play, *The Beat Generation*—the retelling of an episode that occurred in the home of Neal and Carolyn Cassady. Kerouac, Allen Ginsberg,
and Peter Orlovsky meet a member of the clergy, his mother, and his aunt.
The incident could have appeared in Kerouac's *On the Road*, but didn't.[18]
The actual production, while giving the actors (and nonactors) a degree of
improvisational freedom, also involved shooting up to three takes per shot,

so that Frank and Leslie would have enough choices in the editing process. The legendary voice-over narration, supposedly composed and recorded spontaneously by Kerouac during his first viewing of the film, turns out to have been constructed by Leslie, Frank, and the sound engineers out of at least three different takes.[19] When confronted with this interpretation, Frank still maintains the film was improvised.[20]

That the film is highly structured in terms of its formal design has not been commented on heretofore. The first scene is a good example. After slowly panning along a semidark and barren wall behind the film's credits, the film cuts to an overhead shot of the kitchen table, a chair and sofa, which form a circle, triangle, and square. This homage to constructivism continues through the following six shots, including Kerouac's famous "early morning in the universe" sequence, in which Frank breaks the compositional frame into highly contrasting, geometric spaces of light and dark.

Later in a long sequence, the camera slowly completes a 360-degree pan shot, interrupted four times by visual reveries of different characters, while Kerouac's monologue flows uninterrupted on the sound track. Originally in one continuous take, the scene now juxtaposes the objective pan of the camera—a representation of the outside world—with internal images, subjective memories of the persons in the frame. In the case of the Carolyn Cassady character, she imagines slapping her husband: Neal Cassady was living with another woman at the time of the original episode.[21] Though interesting, the formal experiment ultimately doesn't work, because the filmic convention utilized here by the filmmakers to denote interior monologue predicates character psychology and audience identification, elements proper to classical Hollywood narrative, rather than its antithesis.

In another sequence, the filmmakers cut between extreme close-ups of objects and long shots of the poets blowing a jazz tune. The rhythm of spatial perception from details to the whole functions as an experiment in filmic editing possibilities but also relates closely to the conceptualization of jazz music, its interplay of structure and improvisation, musical details related to a whole. Thanks to the intensive participation of David Anram, jazz is in fact an important element in the film's effect, as well as a metaphor for the film's overall design.

Robert Frank's composition of shots defies the rules of classical narrative by eschewing eyeline matches and shot-reverse shot patterns, and continually moving the camera, if only minimally, to keep his framing decentered, just as the introduction of characters totally extraneous to the narrative disavows narrative continuity. These kinds of compositions seem "improvisational," but in fact it is the audience, positioned as subject in a universe of

Film still from *Pull My Daisy* (1959), directed by Robert Frank. Courtesy of the Museum of Fine Arts, Houston.

flux, that must continually improvise, reorient itself, and sort out the wealth of visual cues, thus frustrating any attempts at identification. Likewise, the nonsynchronous sound of Kerouac's monologue of beat verse, stream of consciousness, and narrative doubling of images, while the actors merely mouth their words, distances the audience.

Although very much a collaborative effort, the film does include among its characters a small boy: Pablo Frank in his first screen appearance. The boy is seen in three scenes, which emphasize the family ties of the beats.[22] In the first scene he eats cereal and is packed off to school by his screen mother. In the second he is seen wandering among the grown-ups. In the third he is allowed to play a small tuba with the adult jazz musicians before being carried off to bed. More significant is the last scene in the film, in which the child is absent, yet present, as the father angrily kicks the boy's chair before leaving his scolding wife to go out drinking with the boys. The chair represents his responsibilities as a father, which he chooses to ignore. The interest in showing a beat family, as well as the tensions between husband and wife, may reflect Frank's own dichotomy as beat photographer and filmmaker and father of two children. It's mere speculation to read a lot of biography into the film, since the character of the son is based on Neal and Carolyn Cassady's son, Jamie. But the use of Pablo seems significant, especially in the light of Frank's later attempts to involve his children in his filmmaking.

OK, End Here (1963), Frank's third professional 35mm film, includes at least two overtly autobiographical moments. In the first, the couple pass a suburban father who is attempting to shoot a home movie of his family with the Empire State Building in the background. The family makeup is identical to Frank's: a wife, a male and female child. The son revolts against his father's directorial prerogative: "I don't want my picture took," he repeats. In *Life Dances On* (1979), Frank refers to the earlier scene by holding up a small statue of the Empire State Building, having just filmed his second wife, June Leaf, who asks him why he is always filming. In *OK, End Here* Frank cuts to silent home movie footage, reduced to a square on a white screen. The scene is totally superfluous in terms of the narrative and can only be understood as Frank's self-critical insert about his relationship to his own family.

The second autobiographical moment involves the letter in the restaurant, which actually may or may not have been written by Frank to his first wife. In the letter the woman's ex-husband talks about his inability to write, his attempts not to tell lies, and a long letter written in a drunken stupor and left behind in a Zürich railway station. Responding indirectly, the wife in the film says to herself: "It's so hard not to forget. At least photographs stop everything. They stop the passing of time." This is a phrase Frank will repeat in *Conversations in Vermont* (1969). Together these two scenes address Frank's belief in the power of photographs not only to record a moment in time, but also to communicate that moment to others, unlike words, which apparently disappear in the noise of other people's preoccupations. At the same time, the home-movie sequence hints at his family's resistance to images, a theme that will be picked up more strongly in the autobiographical films.

Shot over a period of three years, and incorporating both documentary and fictional footage, real persons and actors, black and white and color material, dialogue written by Frank and improvised by his actors, *Me and My Brother* (1968) was Robert Frank's most complex film to date. Produced by Helen Silverstein and shot in 35mm, that is, for a commercial, theatrical market, the film was perceived as a typically chaotic product of the hippie movement and ultimately received little commercial distribution, although it was picked up by New Yorker Films for a few years. Frank began the project as a film about Julius Orlovsky, the catatonic brother of poet Peter Orlovsky, but it soon evolved into a much larger project, concerning the nature of mental illness and American society's response to it. Among the problems inhibiting a unified structure, however, were Frank's inability to coerce the real Orlovsky brothers into "acting," forcing him to use professional actors midway through the film; the insistence of a financial backer that Frank switch to shooting in color; the on-again-off-again shooting schedule over three years;[23] Frank's decision in the editing room to multiply the levels of reality by emphasizing the film-within-a-film structure. Thus, *Me and My Brother* is as much about the nature of filmmaking as it is about Julius Orlovsky. Frank's opening statement, printed over an image of the Bible like a solemnly delivered oath, reads: "In this film all events and people are real. Whatever is unreal is purely my imagination."

The film begins with a fictional scene about the making of a homosexual porno movie in which Peter and the director are trying to get Julius to participate. Julius, for his part, is staring at walls. As an opening scene, it reverberates with disturbing meanings that color the rest of the film. First of all, the act of making a sex film becomes a metaphor for the whole film. Peter's characterization of a sex film as a beautiful idea, a gift to mankind, offers a libertarian view of the proceedings but fails to recognize the exploitive voyeurism of much commercial film pornography, just as Frank ultimately fails to deal with his own film's voyeuristic elements. The homosexual lovemaking is reprised later in the film, when Frank inserts a lesbian love scene, again calling attention to the film's voyeurism even though Frank shoots it in a nonexploitive fashion. The first sex scene also allows the question, is Frank possibly exploiting others in the film?

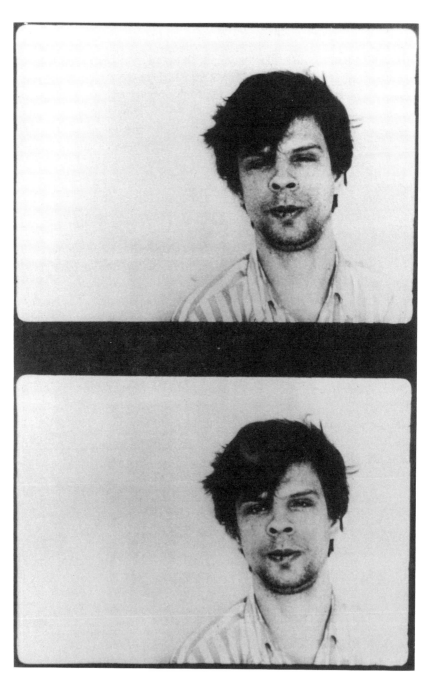

Film still from *Me and My Brother* (1965), directed by Robert Frank.
Courtesy of Museum of Fine Arts, Houston.

The porno director, like the film's real director and everyone else in the film, continuously browbeats Julius (played in this scene by Joseph Chaiken) with supposedly well-meaning questions, attempting to force a response. When the director doesn't get one, he becomes belligerent: "If you want to tell me what you're thinking and feeling, I'd be more than happy to listen. . . . You'd see your brother and friend [in the sex film]. Then you'd see your face. . . . It's perfectly normal. All you have to do is behave as you would in real life."

These attempts to get Julius to act, to speak, to react, to answer questions, to stand up, to look into the camera, to walk away are repeated throughout the film by his brother Peter, by Allen Ginsberg, by a psychiatrist, by a social worker, by a dentist, by the doctors in the psychiatric wards, and most of all by Frank himself. At one point, Frank, played by the actor Christopher Walken with Frank's voice dubbed in, says: "I can't get Julius to do what I want. . . . It's very difficult working with him." Julius just keeps staring into space, silently, whether Frank's camera is near or far. In a most tragic way, these scenes presage Pablo's resistance to his father's inquisitive camera in the later autobiographical films.

The film's last scene, on the other hand, makes clear why Julius (the real one) refuses to cooperate with the camera gazing at him. Again Frank points the camera, forcing Julius to reposition himself within the film frame: Frank asks him to say something "to the camera." Looking away from the camera, Julius says: "The camera seems like a reflection of disapproval or disgust or disappointment or unhelpfulness or unexplainability . . . to disclose any real truth that may possibly exist." The camera is clearly identified with the father, whose controlling gaze has the power to record privileged moments and register its disapproval, thus laying bare the weaknesses of the child. For the object of the camera's voyeuristic gaze there is little room to maneuver, except to deny his or her participation, to look away from the camera, to remain silent. Frank ends the scene by again asking Julius to look into the camera, which Julius does, sticking his face almost into the lens (another form of resistance). Frank then asks Julius to give his name and address. Julius cooperates momentarily (looking away from the camera) but then walks out of the camera's range, mumbling something about it being too chilly. Frank yells "cut" off-frame; the film ends with black leader. Thus, while Julius, after ninety minutes of silence, finally cooperates briefly, it is clear that he is still uncomfortable with the camera's presence, that he sees it as just another device to define his image from the outside, as the father gives definition to the son.

At another level, Frank's film is obsessed with images and the gaze. In the opening scene, the porno director tells Julius that it is perfectly normal to watch sex, to look at oneself on the screen (or in the mirror), calling attention to the Janus head of voyeurism and narcissism. In the film's second scene, Frank cuts to a screening of *Me and My Brother,* where he records the virulently negative and positive responses of the audience. Thus, in his opening scenes, Frank addresses both the issue of voyeurism vis-à-vis the audience, and the positioning of the subject as voyeur and narcissist.

At the second screening, Frank's real voice in the guise of his fictional body is heard giving directions to the real Julius on screen and to the fictional Julius standing in front of the screen. The dichotomy between real and fictional spaces is broken down, both shown to be products of the filmmaker's manipulations. Although the film is ostensibly about the "real" Orlovsky brothers, their fictional counterparts are shown first in the film. The method of juxtaposing the real and the fictional version of Julius within the same scene is repeated a number of times in the film, for example, in the bookstore sequence, where Frank intercuts footage of Ginsberg and Julius with the later filmic reconstruction of the scene.

At other times, Julius and other characters are shown gazing at slides, photographs, paintings; or "audiences" off screen are heard commenting on the film, criticizing actors. These are continual reminders that all persons in the film, whether on camera or off, are engaged in the act of seeing, fascinated by the look. Such insertions not only distance the real audience but also deflect any real critique of the filmmaker's methods by inscribing the voyeuristic gaze into the body of the film. For example, during the first screening we see and hear the audience, or later, an obnoxious woman off-screen screams that an actress on screen doesn't know what she's talking about, while a male voice heaps continuous praise on the same.

A moment earlier the same actress, looking to get a part in the film, complains to the cameraman, another Frank surrogate, played here by Rosco Lee Brown: "You are some kind of blackmailer, because you are always watching privacy." The problem is, of course, more complicated, as Frank realizes when he has her express: "Wouldn't it be fantastic, if you didn't have a piece of celluloid between you and what you saw. If the eye were its own projector, instead of a camera." In other words, what she wants is the perfect kind of voyeurism: it is the desire of the subject to see directly the "reality" of the image, without being present, gazing without being seen.

In point of fact, though, Frank is continually inserting celluloid between "reality" and the audience through his filmmaking practice. Not only is the editing extremely disjointed, not only are many of the scenes out of sync or nonsynchronous (voice-over), but Frank also applies the whole catalogue of visual special effects to layer his images: double exposures, split screens, strobe effects, freeze frames, rapid editing, actors shot in front of projected films or slides, overlapping sound from one scene to the next. All of these devices tend to distance the subject, making the material abstract, a function of ideas.

Me and My Brother is a long and highly complex film, dealing with many issues not discussed here. It also seems a product of its time in the sense that Frank's understanding of mental illness is in keeping with romantic notions common to the counterculture movement of the late 1960s. The actor playing the psychiatrist, for example, says of Julius: "He expresses something we all feel, but keep inside us. He is like a saint, full of poetry." At another point, the cameraman notes that Julius seems to be a meeting place, a common denominator for us all. Such statements, which view psychosis as just another state of consciousness, of being in dream-time or on LSD, privilege the mentally ill as somehow living freer, because they are not restricted by the mores of bourgeois society. Given the socially propagated images of mental illness as an aberration and abnormality, and the desire of the counterculture to create more sympathy for psychotics, for example, in Ken Kesey's *One Flew over the Cuckoo's Nest,* Frank's position is defendable. It seems unlikely, however, given his own experience with Pablo a few years later, that Frank today would direct *Me and My Brother* in quite the same way.

Conversations in Vermont is the first of Frank's overtly autobiographical films, made during the breakup of his marriage to Mary in 1969.[24] It was funded with a small grant from KQED-TV, a public broadcasting station in San Francisco, and conceived as part of a series featuring such artists as Frank Zappa, Ann Halprin, Robert Nelson, Yvonne Rainer, Andy Warhol, and Walter de Maria. The series was planned to "free as much art as could stand it from the closeted environment of the commercial gallery, to put it in the way of life as people were then living it."[25] Frank notes: "I think it was a very successful film—because it was the most honest film I've ever done."[26]

Despite the film's title, *Conversations* begins with a monologue. In a series of flash frames that slowly come into focus, the camera sees Frank cleaning the lens. An ambulance siren is followed by a Bessie Smith blues number and other ambient sound on the track. The film cuts to a long series of photographs of Frank and his family: "This film is about the past," Frank says, before beginning his explication of the photographs, his marriage, their first home, the birth of Pablo. "This film is about the past and the present. The present comes back in actual film footage which I took," Frank continues his narration, while the camera pans over photographs of Mary, the children, friends, shots from *The Americans.*

Only then does Frank cut to live footage from his trip to Vermont, showing Pablo and Andrea cleaning the manure out of a barnyard stall, while

Film still from *Chappaqua* (1967), directed by Conrad Rooks, cinematography by Robert Frank. Courtesy of Museum of Modern Art, Film Stills Library.

Frank photographs them. From the very beginning, Frank establishes his control over the images, and thus the scene has symbolic implications regarding his relationship to his children. As signified in the first shots, he is the filmmaker, the photographer, the narrator/father in whose power lies the articulation of family history. This authority is enhanced by the fact that many of the photographs are too small—some are seen only as contact sheets—or disappear too quickly, or are obscured by overexposure, for the audience to decode their meaning, forcing the viewer to accept Frank's interpretation.

Throughout the rest of the film, Frank returns again and again to the photographs of his family, showing them to Pablo and Andrea, discussing them with his children, while attempting to communicate his memories and feelings about them. While the sound track records conversations, dialogues between Frank and his offspring, the camera and father in these photographic sequences position both his children and the audience as viewers and listeners of his story, of history. It is clear that Frank defines himself through the images his camera produces: at the end of the first sequence, he twice dissolves photographs over filmed images of himself. For him the photographs are a means of communicating with his children, of bridging the communication gap between parents and children, as he tells Andrea and Pablo. He tells Pablo that he learns things about the past from photographs, confessing that the photographs show him how "tight Mary and I were about living our own way," regardless of the children.

Yet Frank's efforts to communicate with his children fail, not because he doesn't try, but because the images themselves hold no meaning for them, other than as a record of their father's experience. Frank repeatedly asks Andrea and Pablo if they remember, if they can read their own meanings into the images, but they can't. Pablo says he doesn't remember the time when the photographs were taken. Andrea doesn't remember ever seeing the "old photographs." The images remain abstractions for them, products of their father's memory, which they perceive with polite distance. Like Frank's mother in *About Me,* they are "blind" to the father's power; like their mother, Mary, shown without eyes for a brief moment in the film's first sequence, the children cannot see what Frank does.

Like Frank's mother and father in Zürich, the children also resist their father's controlling camera gaze. When Frank asks Andrea how she likes being on public television, she is visibly uncomfortable. At other times they scrupulously avoid looking at the camera. The camera for its part is constantly intruding, moving, panning, tracking, rapidly zooming in and out. By emphasizing its subjectivity, it is also a constant reminder of their father's power. While attempting to signify the camera's verisimilitude, its closeness to reality, Frank's nervous camera movement and editing ultimately fragment spatial reality, thus abstracting his children in the visual narrative. Like their mother, seen in a short film clip from Frank's 1958 "home movie" of Mary as a goddess on a beach,[27] they become film fictions. In no single sustained sequence do the children articulate their desires (the longest sequence with Andrea ended as an outtake, used in *Life Dances On*). They, like Mary and Frank's own mother, are denied speech, because this is a narrative of patriarchy.

Ironically, the film ends with an image of the children lost in the crowd of their school choir. Earlier Frank asks them if singing helps them get in contact. While singing is associated with their reality, Frank is unable to visualize them individually in their own chosen medium for definition. The final images show all the students with Pablo and Andrea as silhouettes, unrecognizable as individuals in their father's gaze. *Conversations in Vermont* is, then, a fairly depressing film, because it documents conversations that fail to communicate. Frank seems ultimately unable to visualize anything but his own reality, while his children remain ciphers, images on photographic paper, rather than real persons with their own desires.

About Me: A Musical, ironically, deals ostensibly with music, that is, a form of expression closer to his children than film. Most of the musical groups performing in the film are members of the counterculture, the generation of Pablo and Andrea. Frank presents examples of Indian raga music, jazz, rock music, folk music, communal music, and soul music, but the film, as Frank's title suggests, is not really about music, and therefore not really about the world of his children, but rather about Frank himself. Cofinanced by a grant from the American Film Institute, Frank introduces the film as follows: "My project was to make a film about music in America. . . . Well, fuck the music. I just decided to make a film about myself. This here is the young lady playing me. Her name is Lynn Reyner and she is a very good actress." Frank proceeds to intercut footage of various impromptu musical performances with footage of his female alter ego acting the part of Robert Frank, "real" footage of the making of the film, and sound bites of Frank narrating his true feelings about his purpose. Wearing a chenille bedspread and prancing around Frank's Bowery loft while answering the inquisitive questions of reporters/actors/friends, she says she is trying to get the past, the present, and the future all in one, which is exactly what Frank attempted in *Conversations.*

As in *Conversations,* Frank retells his own past, this time through his female medium, narrating her immigration to America, the birth of her children, and stating that she always tried to be successful, to make money, to be an artist. Having her dress in a bedspread may be just another countercultural joke about the poor, suffering artist in bourgeois society, or it may be related to the persecution she (and Frank?) feels at the hands of her interrogators. She ends by noting that her children have now gone away, that they have problems. Frank, significantly, then cuts to the Zürich sequence discussed above, which transfers the oedipal dilemma one generation.

It is revealing that Frank should choose a woman to play his role and that she should play the role of a musician, rather than a visual artist. She, unlike Frank, is not possessed by the need to make or keep images. At one point, when asked why she produces art at all, she responds by pulling out a drawer of old photographs, throwing it on the table, and declaring, "That is my past. I have to get rid of all this shit... I can make a musical out of it."[28] Frank does make a musical, although the film can hardly be called a musical in the classical sense. On the other hand, he is not so much dealing with his own personal past as replying to the detractors of his work as a public artist. He does this indirectly through his focus on music.

For Frank, music is another form of self-expression, one that communicates in some manner, but which also brings people in closer contact with themselves. This also means bringing people closer to nature, especially in the cultural context of the 1960s counterculture. Not surprisingly, many of the musical sequences are filmed out of doors, in open fields, on mountain tops, in the country, rather than in a concert hall. The one exception proves the rule. Frank films five black convicts marching through an endless prison corridor, then in a basketball gym, while on the sound track they sing a beautifully harmonious a capella soul gospel song. When they finish, the audience learns that most of them are in prison for life. Incarcerated within prison walls until death, surrounded by mean-looking white security guards, they are permanently cut off from nature, from the roots of their culture, yet their singing is an expression of their desires and their freedom as human beings. It is possibly one of the most uplifting moments in any of Frank's films.

Music is also identified with innocence, with a world uncorrupted by adult necessity, rationality. In one scene of a group of communal musicians in New Mexico, Frank holds his camera on the group after they have finished their number, because the children can now be heard plunking out their tunes on a small vibraphone. At another point the artist notes that she likes to listen as a young woman plays a halting improvisation on a piano, because it "brings out the child in me." In fact, much of the music in the film is not professional, nor even competent, for example, the violin playing of Frank's living companion: it is merely heartfelt. The improvisational, unprofessional look of Frank's film, with all its "mistakes" in lighting, editing, false camera movement, is likewise supposed to communicate honesty.

Frank's aesthetic filmmaking strategy, which he had practiced for the first time in *Me and My Brother* and *Conversations in Vermont,* was subject to critical debate. Frank deals with this criticism directly through the question and answer sessions between the artist and her public. But her answers are for the most part evasive, leaving the impression, as one person puts it, that she doesn't seem "too sure about anything." At another point, she refuses to discuss her separation of the personal and the political, certainly a central question of the 1960s.

Life Dances On (1979), constructed of old footage and a new interview with Pablo, is dedicated to the memory of Frank's daughter, Andrea, who had died in a plane crash in Guatemala in December 1974, and of Danny Seymour, a close friend and an artistic collaborator on a number of Frank's films, who disappeared in 1973 with his boat in the Atlantic Ocean. Returning to the overtly autobiographical mode of *Conversations* and *About Me,* it includes scenes with Marty Greenbaum, another collaborator; interviews with a Bowery bum, Billy; and clips from an unfinished fiction film with Frank's second wife, June Leaf. Through Frank's documentation of his son's deepening psychosis, Pablo's insistence on endless non sequiturs, and the parallels Frank draws with the mentally ill Bowery inhabitant, Billy, *Life Dances On* also signifies Pablo's ultimate resistance to his father's image-making.

The film opens with an outtake from *Conversations,* a scene in a Vermont barn in which Andrea says she doesn't want to live in New York City, where she grew up. Ironically, although the scene is there to remind the audience of Andrea alive, it also allows Andrea to articulate her desires in a way that was totally absent from *Conversations.* By including the outtake here in a memorial film, Frank gives her a voice in death that he had denied to her in life. Andrea remains invisible for the rest of the film, until the end, when Frank superimposes iris shots of Andrea's photographic image over film images of a barren Nova Scotia landscape. By overlapping the images of her and Danny Seymour with the landscape shots, Frank articulates his memory of them in the present reality of his living in Mabou. Visually, the shot is also a reminder of the view of Frank as a baby in his father's stereoscope, seen in *About Me,* articulating similar feelings of nostalgia, but also making it painfully evident that Frank's images could not protect his child.

After the dedications to Andrea and Danny Seymour (shown smoking a joint in an outtake from *Cocksucker Blues*), Frank begins the film proper with new footage of Pablo in his own apartment. "I want to hear what you have to say," he asks Pablo, whereupon Pablo responds with a series of non sequiturs: "January 12. . . . June 24. What will West Coast volcanoes do? After that Mars and the moon. It's baseball and Mack trucks. Kentucky strip." Frank tries again, asking Pablo why he can't enjoy life like other people, but again Pablo resists. Adamant in his refusal to cooperate with his father, Pablo finally escapes the camera's gaze, returning with a deck of cards. He shuffles the deck and produces the king of spades with a meaningful "ooohhh." For Pablo the playing card refers to the dominance and power of the father. The interview is extremely painful to watch, because it represents Pablo's most radical denial of his father.

Frank wishes to communicate with his son, but Pablo seems to mistrust both language and the camera. When Frank returns to the interview at the end of the film, he is almost pleading with Pablo: "I'm just trying to get the energy together to make this film." Pablo responds by removing a crucifix from his mouth and referring his father to a chapter from the Bible, Job 38:22, which Frank quotes before the endtitles: "Have you visited the storehouse of snow or seen the arsenal where hail is stored." The verse can be interpreted as another non sequitur or as Pablo's symbolic circumscription of his relationship with his father as something cold.[29] In either case, it is clear that Pablo is retreating to a space where his father cannot follow, a space that in clinical terms denotes psychosis.

Interestingly, the one moment of communication that occurs between father and son is only heard and not seen. It involves a dialogue about a short, apparently unfinished fiction film Frank produced, starring himself and June Leaf, in which they find an old camera and June attempts to teach a blind man to make images. The wind is blowing terribly in the scene, and according to Pablo, who has his own interpretation of the film, June "was trying to teach the blind man to photograph the wind." Pablo is then heard laughing before Frank cuts to an iris shot of June blowing into a clicking windmill. The iconography of blindness, the camera, the iris, as well as the clicking noise, replicates almost exactly the Zürich sequence in *About Me*. Only this time the oedipal narrative of the father is interrupted by the son, who for one brief moment is allowed to reinterpret the images. Yet, for the most part, Pablo resists his father's control over history by refusing to cooperate.

Frank realizes this denial, as the sequence following the first part of the interview demonstrates. In it Frank turns his camera's gaze on Billy, who repeatedly maintains that the filmmaker and everyone else is "reading his mind." Later, Billy berates the filmmaker for reading his mind and invading his privacy by continually turning his camera on him. Like Frank's wife,

June, in another sequence, Billy seems to be asking why Frank needs to make these pictures, why he is obsessed with images.

Frank responds indirectly in a sequence on a New York street in which the filmmaking crew asks passersby to name the five most important American photographers. No one remembers Robert Frank's name until coached by a member of the crew. It is as if Frank is denying not only his official achievement as a photographer, but also his power to control images. *Life Dances On* certainly documents his powerlessness as father.

Home Improvements continues in the tradition of Frank's autobiographical films. Using a ½-inch video recorder, Frank filmed from November 1983 until March 1984, then edited. The present version lasts twenty-nine minutes, apparently cut down from a much longer version.[30] Two catastrophes in his personal life, June's exploratory cancer operation and Pablo's mental illness, structure the main body of the video. As in his earlier films, Frank films Pablo and his wife, June, interrogates the past through his photographs, uses the camera as a personal diary by speaking off-camera.

The video begins with Frank's sixtieth birthday party and other "home movie" footage: June on the telephone, a neighbor's baby. In a close-up of a diary, Frank reveals that he is worried about June's health. Later we see her in the hospital and finally back at work in her shed. Much more interesting, however, are the two scenes where June apparently takes the camera into her own hands. During the birthday party, she films Robert in extreme close-up, while he expresses his hope that his dreams will come true.

In a later sequence, June not only photographs Robert, but also takes over the authorial narrative voice. Talking about a pair of hands she made of sheet metal, June says: "I made them for this guy that I'm so crazy about. Isn't he cute?" Frank, who has remained in the center of the camera's gaze, objects, then says: "I was thinking of Pablo eating glass and rocks," then admits that things could be worse: "Well, on the other hand, you [June] pulled through. You could be dead or sick." Significantly, here it is Frank who is a little embarrassed at being the object of the camera's gaze, of being defined as cute. He allows the moment but immediately deflects the conversation away from himself to his son Pablo, who so often has resisted his father's attempts at definition and resists them again in this film.

As in *Conversations* and *Life Dances On*, Frank again shuffles through photographs of Pablo as a baby; the car photo from *The Americans*; Pablo as a teenager, together with Frank, from *Life Dances On*; in a series of mental hospitals, questioning the photographs and himself about the origins of Pablo's illness. As in *Conversations*, Frank asks whether he and Mary were at fault, but also whether Andrea's death contributed. Unlike the earlier films,

Frank seems much less certain about the power of the images to give him answers. In fact they are nothing if not silent, fragments of the past without messages. At the end of the sequence he promises to not give up.

Later, Frank films Pablo at the Bronx Psychiatric Treatment Center. Pablo is silent, answering his father's questions with barely a nod or a grunt. When Frank asks Pablo to say something, Pablo leaves the frame, resisting his father's camera, as so often in the past. Frank films another inmate instead, who is laconically pushing a broom (reminding us of a similar scene of Julius in *Me and My Brother*). He asks Pablo if he remembers Julius Orlovsky, who likewise denied Frank's power to control his image by refusing to cooperate, refusing to articulate himself in a way that would define him. Walking out of the hospital, his camera dollying forward, Frank says he still has hope. But on the subway home he films a sign and graffiti, which together read:

SYMPTOMS
It was dark

And in fact, *Home Improvements* is a dark film, whether Frank is quoting Kerouac while filming old newspapers blowing in the wind or his own reflection in a Mabou window. Nine years later, in September 1994, Pablo killed himself days before the National Gallery of Art opened *Robert Frank: Moving Out,* an exhibition representing the culmination of Frank's career. It was a final, tragic act of resistance against a father who had all but given up any pretensions to power.

After *Home Improvements,* Frank wrote a letter to John Szarkowski of the Museum of Modern Art, offering to give him all of his photographic negatives from 1947 to 1970, as well as the rights to the material. In *Home Improvements* he has someone drill holes in a stack of his prints, thus destroying their value as objects, but also signifying his own doubts about their value. The scene will be replayed in *Candy Mountain,* when Elmore Silk burns his guitars. Thus, Frank makes good on a threat he had articulated as early as *About Me.* The past, as captured in photographs, has become meaningless, because their power is false; they have not helped him cure Pablo's illness, nor have they anything to do with his present life. His next series of films will continually rework a discourse on the powerlessness of the author.

Candy Mountain started as a small, half-hour film project, which Rudy Wurlitzer tried to put together for Frank but expanded into a full-blown, 35mm commercial film when Wurlitzer's foreign financiers got excited about the script.[31] The film was shot for $1.3 million, using a French, Swiss, and Canadian crew, and starred professional actors and rock musicians, including Kevin O'Conner, Bulle Ogier, Tom Waits, Leon Redbone, and Dr. John, who had previously appeared in *Energy and How to Get It*. It has been distributed commercially in the art house network, where it has done reasonably well. Codirected by Frank and Wurlitzer, the film, with its straightforward narrative and relatively conventional camera style, is Frank's most accessible project in over twenty years.

In the film, a down and out musician named Julius Book searches for the elusive and reclusive Elmore Silk, a master guitar builder, whose craftsmanship, as much as his invisibility, has made him a legend. Julius wants to cop a few guitars from Silk and possibly get him to sign a contract, hoping thereby to turn his own fortunes and generate a career as a rock musician. Traveling on the road from New York to the wilds of Canada, the would-be exploiter is himself exploited, finally finding his grail in the winter snows of Nova Scotia. Silk turns out to be a false god, and Julius no less broke at the end of the film than he was at the beginning—only a lot farther away from his dream.

One of the final images of the film is of a dead-end road, looking out onto the ocean. It is literally the end of the road for both Julius and Silk, who burns his guitars at the site. It is also an apt metaphor for Frank and Wurlitzer's loss of faith in freedom on the road, a concept nurtured by Kerouac's beats and the counterculture of the 1960s. Julius's trajectory on the road from new vehicles to junk heaps, and finally as a careless hitchhiker, marks his progressive loss, his journey to the edge, just as virtually all of the characters Julius meets are transients, living in broken-down trailers, in shacks that don't belong to them, lamenting their missed opportunities and broken-down dreams. Frank's camera, except for the opening panorama of New York City and a few shots at the end in Nova Scotia, are tightly composed, claustrophobic, projecting interior landscapes rather than the open expanses associated with road movies of the past. When asked what happened to his band, Julius replies: "Suicide, incest, ambition, betrayal. Big trouble." Like Julius himself, everyone lies in the film, everyone is looking out for number one. As far as Frank is concerned, these are the motors driving consumer society, a throw-away society, where only the self-promoters and the opportunists get ahead, where only radical denial protects the individual from exploitation.

Clearly, the character of Elmore Silk is patterned after Frank himself. Like Frank, whose road has taken him from Switzerland, to New York, across the back roads of America, and finally to Mabou, Silk escapes his own past. Like Frank (and Wurlitzer), Silk has left the comfortable confines of New York, where he could be earning substantial sums of money for the commodities

Film still from *Candy Mountain* (1989), directed by Robert Frank, with
Kevin J. O'Conner and Tom Waits. Courtesy of George Eastman House.

Film still from *Candy Mountain* (1989), directed by Robert Frank, with Kevin J. O'Conner and Tom Waits. Courtesy of George Eastman House.

he produces. Like Frank, the photographer, Silk is tired of meeting the expectations created by his own legend, tired of producing the myth on demand. Like Elmore Silk, Frank is a recluse, often uncooperative vis-à-vis the media, unable and willing to promote himself.[32] Like Frank, who has holes punched in his photographs in *Home Improvements,* Silk decides to physically destroy his guitars, the very objects that trap him in myth, opting instead to accept a Japanese pension and disappear into the West. Frank, too, has refused to be trapped in his own myth.

Frank's next film, *Hunter* (1989), was also a road movie, a journey through a landscape as foreign to Frank as the moon. Shot on 16mm color in Germany's Ruhr Valley in the autumn of 1989, the thirty-six-minute film was Frank's first European film production. The project came about as a result of an invitation from the Cultural Foundation of the Ruhr, in cooperation with West German Television (WDR) and Paul Hoffmann, director of the Cinematheque in the Ruhr, who now distributes the film.

In his treatment to the film, written before ever setting eyes on the Ruhr, Frank states: "This is about a man who's destiny is—not to find a destination. A man who fears that he will never find what his imagination compels him to look for. . . . A photographer's Fate: look around you carefully the shortest Day will be here soon." The quote clearly refers to Frank's own work, his own search for truth. A stranger in a strange land, Stephan Balint travels by car through the Ruhr, speaking only English with a thick Hungarian accent. He picks up a hitchhiker, a music student, then throws him out again; tries to talk to a Turkish family, a lawyer who is to represent him in a legal claim, a prostitute who tries to explain to him why he can't get a free ride, kids in a classroom. His questions are either not understood or misunderstood, for example, when he asks why happy German children become such tough adults. It is a dark film, filled with fear and loathing, Frank obviously depressed by the idea of being in the country responsible for the Holocaust. The film ends with a German war song on the sound track, the hero being gunned down by an invisible assailant, and a graffiti image: "We are always alone... until death." Less personal than many of his other films, *Hunter* is nevertheless an intensely subjective reaction to a given situation and environment.

As if to further confound his critics and admirers, Frank's 1990 autobiographical video is called *C'est vrai (It's True),* a sixty-minute tape made for French television, supposedly shot in a single take on Beta SP between 3:45 and 4:45 P.M. on 26 July 1990. The film begins with Frank and his "assistant," played by Kevin J. O'Conner (Julius in *Candy Mountain*), setting up the mobile camera and then walking, running, driving (in a panel truck), riding (on the subway), and talking their way through lower Manhattan in real time. Along the way, they happen to meet numerous friends and acquaintances who stop to chat, including Bill Taylor and Peter Orlovsky.

In point of fact, nothing is actually true in the film. The single take has a hidden splice when Frank drives through a tunnel. Every moment has been carefully choreographed to give the appearance of a seamless reality, while the filmmaker remains almost invisible, but nevertheless in control. Like the scene of the two thieves making a deal on a street corner, the tape is supposed to look like life as it happens, but is in fact a total fiction. But happily, not even Frank can take the enterprise completely serious. He has his assistant berate him for his lack of organization, cackling, "Daddy looking for the truth!"[33]

Frank's film *The Last Supper* (1992) goes one step further in Frank's deconstruction of the myth of the "author" by having the artist disappear altogether. In the film a group of friends, relatives, and hangers-on meet one afternoon in an abandoned lot in Harlem to celebrate the birthday of a well-known novelist, obviously Frank's alter ego. While the impoverished black residents of the neighborhood periodically march through the scene, the white guests wait patiently for the guest of honor, who never arrives. When the guests flee at the first sign of darkness for fear of being trapped in Harlem, the black residents are treated to the leftover dinner, the last supper.

As in *Candy Mountain,* Frank is again actively deconstructing the myth of the artist, refusing to confirm to the image society has chosen for him. In keeping with the film's title, it is suffused with religious iconography. But the novelist is not the messiah, even if bread, fish, and wine are served at the party, and many of the guests are there to be healed by him, to pay homage to him, to soak up his aura, to make him a mirror for their own desire. Like the lawyer who wants desperately to be the novelist's friend, or the three Japanese women seeking an autograph, or the female stranger who has brought him her wooden cardinal as a gift, the guests are there for their own selfish reasons. One of the guests quotes Godard: "Society never makes a man, it destroys him." Never has Frank so clearly renounced his audience, nor has his vision been so negative. No wonder the novelist refuses to make an appearance.

Just as the novelist never appears, so does Frank remain invisible in the film, but ironically, he is nevertheless present. As the novelist's wife puts it: "A portrait of people remembering an artist is a self-portrait. It's always a self-portrait." This statement must be understood as Frank's invitation to the viewer to read the statements of various individuals in the film in terms of

Frank's autobiography. Thus, the novelist's son's tirades against his father reprise those of Pablo's against Frank, accusing him of "stealing people," of exploiting him and others for the sake of "fucking art" without ever "revealing himself." The novelist's old friend carries an empty frame with glass, which can be understood either as another metaphor for cinema or for Frank's unwillingness to continue work as a photographer. Talking of the novelist, the friend states: "He's old. He's falling apart. What does a person do when he's finished?" A farewell to his audience? Hardly. Frank has produced two more films in the last three years: *Moving Picture* (1994) and *The Present* (1996).

It seems striking that in all of his films, Robert Frank is both present and absent: present through his control of the image and his directorial questions and comments from off screen, absent because he rarely places himself at the mercy of the camera's gaze. This making himself inaccessible to the viewing subject becomes a signifier of his power over the cinematic apparatus. He is the voice of god, the father, coming from the off. As Kaja Silverman notes: "The voice-over is privileged to the degree that it transcends the body. Conversely, it loses power and authority with every corporal encroachment."[34] The potency and authoritative knowledge of Frank's voice from the off aligns him with the symbolic father.

In *Me and My Brother,* the audience sees Frank only in the guise of surrogates. He is played by actors, although on the sound track his Swiss-German accented voice is unmistakable and heard throughout the film. In *About Me,* he again chooses a surrogate, albeit a female one, to play his part, although again his voice is heard, unidentified as the film's first voice-over. In *Conversations in Vermont,* Frank's voice is omnipresent as the narrator of the photographs, but he is usually only shown with his back to the camera. In the later autobiographical films, Frank is occasionally seen, but only briefly, before the camera swishes back to the persons being questioned by Frank's off-camera voice. In *This Song Is for You, Jack,* Frank is again heard on the voice-over, but not seen. *Home Improvements* marks somewhat of a change, because here Frank for the first time not only turns the camera on himself, but also allows, if only briefly, his wife to actually control the camera's narrative.

Despite their autobiographical or personal nature, though, Frank's films are more often about people around him, his family and friends, than about himself. Certain biographical details make an appearance again and again in his films, but they seem to be a part of the official biography, the public persona that is Robert Frank. There are few moments in any of these films in which Frank consciously reveals anything about his true self.

If anything, the films reveal Frank's unconscious attempts to control the world through images, through the gaze of his camera, to improve family relations, to make his children and his wife happy by somehow willing it through his photographic and filmic expertise. Like his own father, Frank identifies the camera with the power of the father. His voice beyond the image's parameters questions, sometimes bullies, always observes, signifying his omnipotence within the realm of the narrative.

Obsessed with the look, with the camera as a means of patriarchal control, denying the power of narrative to any of the women in his life, Frank at one and the same time rebels against the father through his supreme distrust of language. His films are constructed as visual experiences, where the use of language on the sound track is always of secondary importance. The extremely fragmented style of his films is a function of his distrust of verbal expression, their ambiguity an attempt to escape the literal meanings of words. Frank grew up in a German-language culture, where the use of written language is formalized to a much higher degree than in English, and where Swiss-German dialect is the lingua franca. His use of the camera is, ironically, also a revolt against the father, who, as a German national, ridiculed his son's use of Swiss-German as barbarous, a sign of the uneducated masses. Frank refuses to be controlled, refuses to be defined or pigeonholed by the camera's gaze. In his films nothing is ever final. Their very structure, their fragmented editing, their wildly gyrating camera movement, their off-the-cuff style defy interpretation or leave plenty of room for conflicting and ambiguous meaning. While such a structure can under circumstances expose the cinematic apparatus, thus in some way liberating the spectator, Frank's continuously moving camera remains a synecdoche for the power of the voyeuristic gaze. As Christian Metz notes: "The way the cinema, with its wandering framings (wandering like the look, like the caress), finds the means to reveal space has something to do with a kind of permanent undressing, a generalized strip-tease, a less direct but more perfect strip-tease, since it also makes it possible to dress space again, to remove from view what has been previously shown, to take back as well as retain."[35]

Thus, Frank's films both profess knowledge and deny power to the spectator, their meanings ultimately ambiguous. The same has been argued about his photographs, especially his book *The Americans*.[36] Ultimately, Frank's positioning of the spectator in a patriarchal narrative, in which the power of the father's look is played out against the silent articulations of the mother, is not liberating, even though Frank desperately wants to believe in the power of the camera to change reality, if only as a medium of knowledge. In his autobiographical films, he is continuously reading other images, hoping to learn about the present from their past. Ironically, both his photographs, as rephotographed in his films, and his moving images are treated as a discursive text in which he positions himself as author/narrator while at the same time undercutting their power to enunciate a fixed meaning. His films continually document the camera's failure to communicate. In this sense they also expose the powerlessness of the father, of the camera, because real life keeps slipping out of frame, beyond the camera's gaze. Small wonder that his latest films are all discourses on powerlessness, on the flight of the author, on Frank's revolt against his own myth.

In contrast to Robert Frank, who has struggled to maintain control over his environment via the lens of the camera, Danny Lyon has made films about living without power. Searching out the poorest and most outcast elements of society, those who lack any power at all, Lyon has celebrated their liberation. As a result of his acceptance of his subjects, Lyon has not fallen prey to the cultural pessimism of Robert Frank, but rather has sought to discover a different kind of utopia.

8 Danny Lyon

THAT SPACE OF AN ABSOLUTE FREEDOM

Rather than focusing his camera on the institutions of power, or even their relations with other classes, Danny Lyon, in his photographs and films, has subjectively documented the disenfranchised, the poor, the migrants, the homeless, the insane, Chicanos, prisoners, bikers. Lyon's vision of the institutions of power, when it is articulated at all in his films, is that of a dystopia. By its very invisibility, power becomes a structuring absence in the lives of his documentary protagonists. He sees American society in general as completely compromised by the seduction of power. Steve Baer, in *Little Boy* (1977), states Lyon's only slightly exaggerated version of the American ruling class's hard line: "Why reward people who don't behave themselves? . . . Basically it takes the strain off of everybody in the world to know there is a ready-made punishment for anybody who doesn't do what he's supposed to do every minute of every day." Here is a society in which punishment becomes the ultimate weapon of control, a society in which order is programmed into its very structures. Lyon superimposes the American flag and atomic bombs over a close-up shot of Baer as the latter describes nuclear energy's need for a law-and-order society and the "control" atomic weapons provide. The implication is that fear of punishment, fear of freedom, acts as a coercive force to control the middle class.

More importantly, the ideology of the middle class, of the silent majority, inscribes within it the power of the institutionalized elite. "Doing what you are told," failing to question the institutions of power, means to deny humanity, individuality, and freedom. For Danny Lyon the middle class is

Film still from *Little Boy* (1977), with Steve Baer, directed by Danny Lyon. Courtesy of Danny Lyon.

unfilmable, because they hide their true emotional condition.[1] They are unwilling to expose themselves without lawyers present to protect them.[2]

Lyon's use of a superimposition of atomic bombs to visually demarcate the power of the institution also points to the inability of the image of man alone to function as a metonymy of power relations. This becomes clear when compared to Lyon's image of the sheriff in *Willie*, one of the only other scenes in Lyon's films where a representative of the law articulates a position. Unable to explain Willie's condition beyond the recitation of the statistics of crimes and misdemeanors, the seemingly benign sheriff notes that they should have put him away sooner. Yet, the image itself cannot reproduce the effects that institutional power have had on Willie's psyche. It is the prison system in its totality, not any one individual, that has deformed a human being. The social formations of power are most effective at their institutional base.

According to Michel Foucault, all power is inscribed in social formations: institutions of incarceration, the judiciary, laws, taxes, and the economy. In modern society, social control is accomplished less through the use of overt violence against a general population—as it was in feudal systems—and more through the seemingly benign force of rational government:

> The development of the disciplines marks the appearance of elementary techniques belonging to a quite different economy: mechanisms of power which, instead of proceeding by deduction, are integrated into the productive efficiency of the apparatuses from within, into the growth of this efficiency and into the use of what it produces. For the old principle of "levying-violence," which governed the economy of power, the disciplines substitute the principle of "mildness-production-profit."[3]

Foucault thus defines power as a system of control manifestly structured into the institutions of society. He theorizes that the discourses of the mainstream, the dominant ideology, are in fact not only tools for social control, but its very structuring principle. According to Foucault, the institutions of power order their economies by breaking up the populations into controllable units, thus allowing them to reduce the potentially threatening power of uncontrolled masses. Foucault writes: "That is why discipline fixes; it arrests or regulates movements; it clears up confusion; it dissipates compact groupings of individuals wandering about the country in unpredictable ways; it establishes calculated distributions."[4] Those failing to conform are relegated to the periphery, are institutionalized, are incarcerated. Thus, power, while manifested in the ratio of institutions, is often invisible in its daily regulation, hidden beneath the veneer of social normalcy.

These actual articulations of power are rarely seen in the films of Danny Lyon. Power as manifested in social relations between the empowered and the powerless, managers and workers, the contented middle classes and the *Lumpenproletariat* remain seemingly invisible, even in prison. In *Llanito* (1971), proud but desperately poor Mexican Americans speak, as do retarded Anglos, but not the institution of the asylum, nor the corporate estates that control the land of New Mexico and its people. In *El otro lado* (1978), the life of undocumented Mexican migrant agricultural workers is visualized without the physical presence of the feared U.S. Immigration and Naturalization Service (INS). In *Willie* (1985), prisoners are seen in their cells or working out, guards remain in the background, and prison officials are completely invisible.

The one exception that proves the rule is *El mojado (The Wetback)* (1974), a short film about undocumented Mexican workers in New Mexico in general, and specifically about "Eddie," who builds an adobe for the filmmaker. That film begins with a long interview with an INS border guard, who is quoted as saying: "This is the most interesting part of the job. It's like a hunter, you know. Only you're stalking human beings. And that makes it a lot more fun." The film goes on to illustrate the rounding up of "wetbacks" and INS interviews with their catch. Yet even here, INS representatives are only shown in very brief shots, usually remaining invisible off-camera.

The very fact that Danny Lyon fails to engage in a dialogue with the institutions of power indicates he is less interested in their existence than in the ways they affect social structures at the bottom strata of the pyramid of power. Yet, Lyon does not view his film protagonists as merely victims of social and political repression. He does not take the patronizing view that his film, or any film, will help them out of their misery. As Lyon's literary alter ego notes in his book *The Paper Negative,* "Anyway, they're not the ones who need help. If anyone needs help, it's us."[5]

Daniel Joseph Lyon was born on 16 March 1942 in Brooklyn, New York. His mother, Rebecca Henkin, had been born in a Jewish household in Russia and emigrated at the age of seventeen to the United States in 1924. His father, Ernst Frederick Lyon, originally came from the Saar region of Germany but was forced to flee the Nazis in 1935, having previously completed his medical studies. Danny grew up in Queens, listening to his father and grandparents speak German, but the adults refused to teach the language to the children. While Danny was aware of his Jewish roots, his family was secular and modern, supporting the Spanish Civil War and later the civil rights movement.[6]

After finishing high school in the New York public school system, Danny went to the University of Chicago in 1959 to study ancient and medieval history. There he took a documentary film course with Gerald Mast and began publishing his photographs in the student magazine and yearbook, and winning prizes at local photography competitions. Encouraged by Hugh Edwards, a curator at the Art Institute of Chicago, Lyon decided to become a photographer after receiving his B.A. in 1963. Having traveled to the South for the Student Non-Violent Coordinating Committee in Atlanta in 1962, Lyon became their staff photographer. Lyon's photography gained instant recognition when in 1964 his photographs of the civil rights movement in the South were used in *The Movement: Document of a Struggle for Racial Equality*, with a text by Lorraine Hansberry.[7] The participatory nature of Danny Lyon's photographs in *The Movement* was to become a hallmark of his style, and the photographic book his preferred medium of expression.

In 1966 he had his first one-man exhibition at the Art Institute of Chicago, followed by participation in the exhibition *The Photographer's Eye* at the Museum of Modern Art. Two years later, in 1968, Lyon published *The Bikeriders*,[8] having spent some time from 1963 to 1966 hanging out with the Chicago Outlaws Motorcycle Club. There followed *The Destruction of Lower Manhattan* (1969),[9] which documented the disappearance of historic nineteenth-century buildings south of Canal Street, funded by a grant from the New York State Council on the Arts; *Conversations with the Dead: Photographs of Prison Life, with the Letters and Drawings of Billy McCune, #122054* (1971),[10] about the Texas state penitentiary system; *The Paper Negative* (1980),[11] about children and prostitutes living on the street in Colombia; *Pictures from the New World* (1981),[12] a summary of his twenty-year career as a photographer; *Merci Gonaives* (1988),[13] about living conditions in Haiti in the last years of the "Baby Doc" dictatorship; and *I Like to Eat Right on the Dirt: A Child's Journey Back in Space and Time* (1989).[14] The list of exhibitions of his photographic work is too lengthy to list here.

In more than twenty-five years, Danny Lyon has also created a substantial body of films. Given the richness of his films, it is surprising that his film work has suffered from critical neglect. J. Ronald Green locates this indifference in the fact that Lyon's films have fallen between the critical cracks, because they are neither wholly social documentaries, nor are they purely poetic expressions of subjectivity.[15] Pamela Allara has suggested that photo-historians are much more comfortable with the overt politics of Lyon's photography, while his films after 1969 turn towards a more subjective point of view.[16]

Most critics writing about Lyon's films and photographs have long since recognized the social periphery as his turf. In one of the earliest essays on Lyon's films, Karen Cooper notes his "intense personal concern with marginal men: the poor and the outlawed, the prisoners, victims, and outcasts of

Danny and Nancy Lyon, during the production of *Willie* (1985). Courtesy of Danny Lyon.

society."[17] Allara, likewise, comments on Lyon's identification with "people who operate on the fringes of society," drawing parallels between Lyon's work and that of his famous predecessor, James Agee: "Perhaps more than any documentary artist since Agee, Lyon has been concerned with identifying with rather than simply identifying his subjects."[18] J. Ronald Green has perhaps most sympathetically deepened the discussion by suggesting that Lyon's films are not merely socially concerned documentaries, but rather film poems, which demonstrate a "unique and personal way of associating images, sounds, stories, and facts."[19] Furthermore, Green notes that Lyon is a master in the use of eccentric similes, extended, symbolic metaphors, metonymies, repetition, and mediation.[20]

While these critics are sympathetic to the plight of the socially marginalized in the United States, others are critical of Lyon's "depressing" images and even more critical of the filmmaker's openly subjective point of view.[21] One critic complained of Lyon's constant intrusions, going so far as to accuse him of contributing to Willie Jaramillo's turning into a criminal by making him the subject of several films.[22] Other more mainstream film critics, for example, the *New York Times* critic, have worried that Lyon lacks a "developed cinematic style," meaning his films lack the professional polish of traditional documentary forms.[23] Even Cooper discovers a lack of clarity and focus in the editing of some of Lyon's films, as does Katherine Dieckman, who complains that the ambiguity in *Willie* makes the film "ineffective."[24]

Lyon's films do give up any pretense to objectivity, the theoretical basis of all theories of social documentary. Superficially, his style is comparable to cinema verité with its hand-held camera, long camera takes, and seemingly rambling, non-narrative structure. Unlike cinema verité, though, Lyon is always a active participant, influencing the situation in front of the camera, much like an amateur moviemaker. Michael Renov in his analysis of the various levels of intercession and mediation in documentary film defines documentaries in the style of home movies as films "dependent upon a special relationship between those filmed and the one filming."[25] He specifically mentions Lyon's *Willie* in this context: "Lyon's work displays an utter disregard for the presumed adulteration of filmmaker intervention. The shaping presence can never be forgotten; Lyon frequently carries on full-blown conversations from behind the camera which he wields with a fluency born of 20 years experience as a still photographer."[26] Lyon's amateur film aesthetic consciously removes him from the polished forms of traditional documentaries, which maintain a pretense of objectivity through their narrative construction, even while making their ideological agendas invisible. Lyon purposefully acknowledges his own subjectivity through his film form. In this way he resembles his erstwhile film mentor, Robert Frank.

While Frank's subjectivity in his films activates a struggle with the personal and the familial,[27] Lyon has constituted his social spaces and class relations in *terms* of the familial. Frank's real family and Lyon's social outcasts and misfits who become sons, brothers, fathers are thus similarly defined in direct personal relationship to the filmmaker controlling the image. It is Lyon and Frank's diametrically opposed conceptions of power that divide them: Frank articulates power almost exclusively in terms of the personal, while Lyon sees power as an all-pervasive social force acting on the personal. Lyon's subjects are exposed to the harshest social environments, the result of what he sees as the ruling classes' compulsion to control, yet this power remains for the most part invisible and abstract, like the National Anthem, which at the end of *El mojado* represents the power sending Eddie back across the desert to Mexico.

Rather than focusing on a dystopia of the powerful, Lyon instead finds a vision of utopia in those American societies at the edges and, at times, beyond the social order. Disconnected from the discourses of power, Lyon discovers in these communities an ability to articulate their own humanity in personal relations, in a sense of culture and history, in their own discourses on myth and religion. Against the dystopia of total institutional control and power, Lyon sets a utopia of romantically infused anarchy. His peasants and prostitutes, aliens and agnostics, define through their very existence the failings of the power elites to keep everyone "behaved." His films are thus discourses on un-power, on the resistance of the periphery to institutionalized reason, on what Michel Foucault has called "the danger of unreason, and the space of an absolute freedom."[28]

Danny Lyon's first film, *Social Sciences 127* (1969), begins and ends with its hero, the tattooist/photographer Bill Sanders, lecturing on tattooing in what appears to be a college classroom. This is in fact only a ruse, since Lyon subsequently makes clear that Sanders's knowledge is hardly taught in an institution of higher learning. The latter exists ostensibly for the production of knowledge in a "production-profit" system. Sanders, on the other hand, turns his knowledge against the institutional conception of education when he quizzes a female client on the Latin root of *fellatio*, while ornamenting her naked breasts.

For Danny Lyon, Sanders is a scientist. Working out of a storefront in a poor section of Houston, Sanders philosophizes while making tattoos, then documents his work with a camera. His polaroids mimic the scientific method of inquiry, taxonomy, classification. Like his near namesake, August

Sander, Bill Sanders uses photographic media to capture human bodies. Each image is framed similarly. They are hung with thumbtacks, side by side, row by row, for comparison and classification. Yet, unlike the production of knowledge within the institution of learning, where classification functions as an instrument for social control, Sanders photographs are not rarified. They are in fact throwaway objects, as ephemeral as the serendipity at their root. They are indexes of a freedom beyond institutional control. As Danny Lyon later notes in *Pictures from the New World*: "When the sunlight faded the pictures he would just replace them. 'I've got stacks of them,' he said. Bill Sanders knew more about what a photograph is than most museum curators."[29] For Lyon photography and film are a means of exploring freedom. Lyon is in part fascinated by the Sanders photographs because of their negative value: they lie outside the official canon, as established by the institution (museum).

Interestingly, Lyon comments on Sanders the photographer, not Sanders the tattoo artist, although it is clear that he is equally fascinated by, even obsessed with tattoos.[30] In *The Bikeriders*, Lyon already includes a number of images of tattooed bodies, although the tattoos seem incidental to the focus of the image. In *Conversations with the Dead*, Lyon's camera places tattoos at the center of attention: a Madonna, a head of Christ, a tiger, naked women, scenes of fantasy and seduction. In *Llanito, Little Boy, Born to Film*, and especially the prison scenes in *Willie*, tattoos are very much in evidence.

While acknowledging his fascination with tattoos, Lyon is unable or unwilling to articulate an explanation. Tattoos have functioned as signs of opposition to middle-class norms. Until the 1960s, tattoos were an almost exclusively lower-class phenomenon and socially unacceptable except in bohemian circles. Likewise, the middle-class children of the counterculture embraced tattoos as a signification of difference from their straight parents. But tattoos, as *Social Sciences 127* and Lyon's other work demonstrate, signify more than mere opposition. Their sheer variety qualifies them as personal narratives and myth, indeed as expressions of cultural independence, even when their owners are incarcerated. Especially in the context of Lyon's prison images in *Willie*, tattoos signify a creativity physically inscribed on the body, a freedom that the institution cannot take away.

Lyon himself has two tattoos. *Media Man* (1994), Lyon's latest film, includes a tattoo contest in which various participants are shown on stage and in the crowd, sporting their tattoos, many of them extremely large and complex. At the end of the scene, Lyon asks his wife, Nancy, if she has any tattoos (she says no), then bares his two for the camera, noting that they cost $2 and $7 on Clark Street (Chicago) and in Houston, respectively. However, as I will point out in more detail below, Lyon treats this tattoo-*kultur* differently in *Media Man* than in previous films. Though still a sign of personal freedom, they are no longer identified with social outcasts. Indeed, the tattoo contest is a family party, babies and children very much in evidence within Lyon's field of vision.

Lyon's second film, *The Destiny of the Xerox Kid* (1970), is to date also his only foray into fiction filmmaking. Starring Robert Frank's protégé, Danny Seymour, the twenty-five-minute short was also Danny's first attempt at making a film about film, a subject he would tackle more successfully in *Born to Film*. Lyon, who refuses to show the film although he admits to having a 16mm print, describes it as follows: "The main character is trying to create immortal life, using film and tapes. He wants to create the immortal machine. It was supposed to be a guide to my work. The hero finally overdoses on cocaine."[31]

With *Llanito*, shot in New Mexico, Lyon moved into an environment that would preoccupy him for at least the next fifteen years. The initial attraction seems to have been his desire to get as far away as possible from New York, Chicago, and his middle-class, German-Jewish intellectual upbringing. (Ten years later he would, in *Born to Film*, once again embrace those roots, having in the meantime himself become a father.) He began *Llanito* by filming his neighbors with a 16mm camera and soon discovered a world apart: Spanish-speaking, and therefore cut off from the English-speaking, middle-class mainstream, struggling, poor, but proud. With the exception of the Santa Fe railroad train roaring through the film's frame at the beginning and end, signs of the new, moneyed Southwest are not to be seen.

Instead, Lyon films Chicanos, Native Americans, and a group of retarded white males. The unifying element among these seemingly disparate groups is not the squalor discovered by some critics, but rather the ability of these people at the periphery to articulate their own personal myths. Over the image of the train penetrating the landscape, a voice-over of a Hispanic American relates the history of Spanish conquest in New Mexico. Lyon retells the story at the beginning of *Little Boy* and most completely in his book *The Paper Negative:*

> The first white man to set foot in New Mexico was actually black, a slave of the shipwrecked explorer Cabeza de Baca. . . . [Francisco Vásquez] Coronado and the main expedition followed the next year in 1540. . . . With the exception of one successful Indian uprising, the Spanish ruled continuously until 1821 when the Mexican Revolution made New Mexico part of Mexico instead of Spain. This lasted until the American Army marched in with General Kearney. He reached Santa Fe in 1846 and announced that the United

States would protect the New Mexicans from the Indians, which they didn't, respect their laws, which they didn't, and make them a part of the United States, which they couldn't bring themselves to do until 1912 because, let's face it, the people here didn't speak English; many of them still don't.[32]

Like the Spanish-speaking minority, Native Americans relate their 20,000-year history of the Llanito valley, while an institutionalized retarded youth narrates Christ's passion in a high-pitched voice. Allara calls the latter sequence "unquestionably one of the most bizarre religious testaments ever recorded," a quote Lyon liked so much that he reprinted it as a blurb in his brochure for the video distribution of his films.[33] The importance of these historical and mythical narratives is twofold. On an elementary level, they present a counterhistory to the one articulated in standard textbooks of white, middle-class America. Like most racial and ethnic minorities, Mexican Americans and Native Americans have been written out of the historical discourses of the dominant culture. More importantly, though, is the sense of unity and strength that these narratives provide. Indeed, their history has survived in oral traditions, despite official institutional neglect, because it has functioned and been used by its narrators as an oppositional force.

Song and dance play a similar role in defining a native culture in opposition to that of the commercially controlled mainstream. Thus, in *Llanito* Lyon has Indians practice a native song on a street corner; later they sing in a living room. In *Los niños abandonados* (1975), *Little Boy, El otro lado,* and *Willie,* songs and stories also play a central role in the lives of the protagonists. In *El mojado,* Lyon films his "hero," Eddie, building an adobe as if it were a cultural event, and indeed, it is a particular architectural expression of the Mexican-American culture of the Southwest. Much like tattoos, and other works of art adorning the walls of his protagonists' homes, their songs and crafts are an index of personal creativity and freedom, because they have survived without the official sanction of the dominant culture.

It is this understanding of even naive art as personal expression that possibly allowed Lyon to reevaluate his own father's simple home movies and include them in *Born to Film.* Indeed, the film opens with Danny and his son, Raphael, looking at 16mm footage of the Pendleton Round-Up, shot by his father, Ernst Lyon, a medical doctor who was a refugee from Nazi Germany.[34] The film continues to cut away to shots of Danny taken by his dad as Lyon and his son make their film, thus weaving together a tapestry of family history and personal identity as an artist.

In contrast to this "amateur" art, Lyon often cuts away to images of American TV or sounds of American radio in his films. These images and sounds

Film stills collage from *Los niños abandonados* (1975), directed by
Danny Lyon. Courtesy of Danny Lyon.

from melodramas, westerns, and top-forty radio function in ironic counter-point to Lyon's images of his protagonists. In *Llanito,* Willie talks about the dead he has known, while *Dark Shadow* can be seen on a portable television, juxtaposing the real horror of his life with the media's fake horror. In *Little Boy,* Lyon cuts to a TV version of the reconciliation between the U.S. Cavalry and Indians, while his images of the reservation only demonstrate govern-ment neglect of Indian interests. At other times, these official images are simply background noise, ignored, because they have no reality in the lives of the protagonists. That the official media are mistrusted in these commu-nities is evident when Willie tells the filmmaker in *Llanito:* "They say you are just a spy or something. And tell and report how we are."

Shot in Colombia in 1974, *Los niños abandonados* documents the lives of a group of street urchins in the seaport town of Santa Marta. Sleeping on the steps of the church, picking scraps of food off the plates of restaurant pa-trons, defecating in the street, playing in the sand at the beach, these children survive in spite of official neglect. Lyon has called the children "saints."[35] They are presented as a mixture of innocence—commensurate with their age—and world-weary experience, in keeping with their horrific social con-dition. The squalor in which these children live cannot be ignored, yet, un-like such Latin American fiction films as *Los olvidados* (1953, Luis Buñuel) and *Pixote* (1981, Hector Babenco), which view these kids solely as victims, Lyon sees in their social relations a microcosm of a utopian anarchy.

While a twelve-year-old boy, Joselyn, appears to be the focus of attention, Lyon makes clear that the group is nonhierarchically structured. Living out-side the institutions of society, they have created codes of conduct based on mutual caring and respect. Each boy maintains his individuality within the group. Having nothing, the group of male children shares everything: they eat and cook together, play together, swim together. There are scenes of great tenderness, especially the images of the children sleeping. Ivan, the bard of the group, sings self-composed songs, narrating their common daily strug-gle to survive. Their songs (like their games, which are constructed from bottle caps and cigarette butts found in the street) are expressions of their identity and autonomy. Abandoned by the society around them, they have learned of necessity to cope and survive in a space of absolute freedom. At the same time, they retain moments of childlike innocence, for example, when they are shown building sand castles on the beach. In such moments they are no different in the sight of Lyon's lens than Lyon's own frolicking, nude children in *Born to Film.*

El otro lado is similarly conceived and constructed. The film opens with Mexican music played by a village band before cutting to a scene in the woods, where two families are apparently feuding over a piece of land given by the government. The scene proceeds as each side calmly explains their position. Significantly, no government officials or police are in evidence. Like the abandoned children in the earlier film, the peasants are capable of putting a democratic process into practice in a nonhierarchical fashion, without coercion from the institutions of power.

This spirit of solidarity continues when Lyon follows a group of villagers who illegally cross the border into Texas to work as migrants in the orange groves. Sleeping in the fields despite unseasonably cold temperatures, the "wetbacks" work together, while one of their number watches out for the feared U.S. immigration authorities. A title tells the viewer that the men have successfully waged a strike for higher wages. They likewise cook together, share tortillas and stories. On Sundays they wash in the irrigation ditches, before relaxing in the sun, playing poker, singing songs, trading narratives about outfoxing La Migra, the immigration men, who periodically enter the fields to destroy their belongings.

Again Lyon constructs out of the very squalor of their living conditions an image of a free society completely outside the control of the ruling power elites, yet able to maintain a high degree of harmony and individual humanity. Both *Los niños* and *El otro lado* present their societies as surviving without institutionalized government, their social relations governed by a natural law rather than the "law of the disciplines." This concept of a natural law is central to the philosophical precepts of anarchism. Emma Goldman wrote in 1917: "A natural law is that factor in man which asserts itself freely and spontaneously without any external force, in harmony with the requirements of nature. For instance, the demand for nutrition, for sex gratification, for light, air, and exercise, is a natural law. But its expression needs not the machinery of government, needs not the club, the gun, the handcuff, or the prison."[36]

Like the ideal societies of the anarchists, Lyon's communities at the fringes function without governments, without private property, without any forms of social control other than the free wills of their constituents. For Danny Lyon it is a cause for hope that even the inevitable force of the institutions of power, which will eventually use "the gun, the handcuff, the prison" against them, cannot take that experience of freedom away from them.

In *Little Boy*, Lyon returns to the New Mexican landscape and environment of *Llanito*. Referring to the first atomic bomb, dropped on Hiroshima in August 1945, *Little Boy* juxtaposes the historical narratives of the natives to the institutional narrative of atomic annihilation, and images of industrialization to an archaic landscape of farming and sheep herding. In contrast to the earlier film, though, Lyon here inserts images of an actual political struggle against the corporate monopolies. Native Americans are seen demonstrating against a New Mexico coal gasification program, which is encroaching on Indian lands. It is Lyon's most overtly political film, not only because of its discourse on the atomic bomb and government culpability, but also because it allows the socially marginalized Native Americans to directly articulate their attacks on the ruling elites: "The whole political apparatus is behind the corporate power scene. . . . Corporations could exist without controlling the political system, because of the corruption of the tribal elders and politicians." The argument gains strength when Lyon cuts to nineteenth-century photographs of Indian and Chicano natives, thereby underscoring their rights to lands that are now being expropriated for mining and thus made useless for farming. Inhabitants of the reservation are seen dancing and singing before and during the protest; earlier, a young man plays guitar, yet another sign of their cultural and political autonomy.

Little Boy also marks the return of Willie Jaramillo, the protagonist, from *Llanito*. Willie, now eighteen, has left his childhood behind and has been forced into the vicious circle of crime and punishment in New Mexico's system of institutional incarceration. At the film's opening, Willie has just been released from three years of prison after assaulting Bernalillo policemen. The film closes with Willie again on his way to prison for assault, while dreaming of "a good Christian woman, reading aloud to him from *The Bible*, and a little farm." Earlier he is seen in the abandoned truck he calls home and in jail, awaiting trial. He is still a somewhat cocky kid, a loud-mouthed teenager whose love for his family marks him as still innocent.

Willie, made seven years later, documents the continuation of Willie's trouble with the law. The film opens with Willie preparing for yet another trial, having already spent over five years in jail. Willie is now clearly marked by the prisons and mental hospitals he has seen. He has become addicted to thorazine, a powerful narcotic administered by doctors and prison officials to the presumably insane as a method of keeping them docile and under control. The "treatment" is as much the cause of Willie's situation as its result. Lyon has called Willie "another certified graduate of America's vegetable factories."[37] Willie Jaramillo died in 1996 after ten days in the Sandoval County Jail. "He had a very high temperature and when they finally took him to the hospital he died the same day," writes Danny Lyon, who, with his wife, Nancy, bought a gravestone for him on which are written the words: "When the roll is called up yonder, I'll be there."[38]

In *Willie* the Sheriff tells the camera that Willie has a record as long as his arm: disorderly conduct, assaulting officers, resisting arrest. In the larger

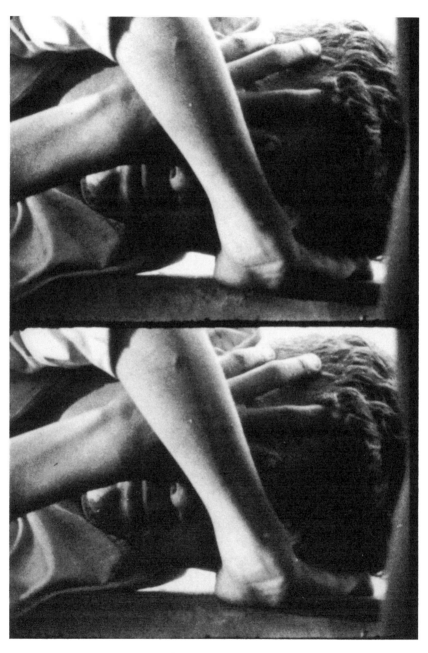

Film still from *Los niños abandonados* (1975), directed by Danny Lyon.
Courtesy of Danny Lyon.

Film still from *Little Boy* (1977), directed by Danny Lyon. Courtesy of Danny Lyon.

scheme of things, they are minor crimes, but they have branded him in the eyes of the authorities as dangerous, possibly insane. Lyon shoots a scene with Willie, sitting in his underwear, drinking beer under a highway bridge, talking about solitary confinement, the Santa Fe prison riot he survived, his homeless state. He sings a song. Lyon intercuts the scene with footage of Willie as a child in *Llanito* and as a teenager in *Little Boy,* reminding the viewer of his innocence and lost potential.

Clearly, Lyon identifies with his protagonist, seeing his struggle as a most radical form of rebellion against the power of the state, rather than viewing him as an insane or incorrigible convict. This power to empathize is also characteristic of Lyon's photography. In writing about *Conversations with the Dead,* Max Kozloff notes: "As for the photographer, the man who permits us to observe certain miseries, he makes no pretense at objectivity. The sense of his offerings as documents informs every image, but they are too emphatically wrought to maintain any of the usual clinical or journalistic distance. He identifies with these cast-offs, however much he felt the strain of shooting them, a strain eventually unbearable after 14 months of close-up work."[39] Indeed, Lyon has confessed that he "empathized completely with the rage and frustration of Willie."[40] In contrast to some characterizations of Willie as "an animal," Lyon presents him singing a song, dancing to a Beatles tune, narrating his own drawing of Christ at Calvary, thus exposing Willie's gentle and human sides. At the same time, he sees Willie as unequipped to deal with the disciplines of power, with the state's regime for the maintenance of order.[41] Thinking himself innocent and a victim, Willie fails to understand that the institutions of power can and will use prisons, mental institutions, physical force, and drugs to isolate any threats to their established order.

While Danny Lyon's films of outlaws and outsiders construct an image of America as a hostile environment in which the spaces of freedom are severely delimited by institutional police powers, where freedom can survive only at the fringes of straight society, his autobiographical films find that freedom in the act of creation itself, in the creation of the artist's own subjectivity and in the cradle of the family. *Born to Film* (1981), as noted above, is Lyon's first film to return to his familial roots after a long period of rebellion. Made in a period where Lyon was fighting a custody battle for his son, Raphe, the film brings together three generations of the Lyon family: Danny's late father, Ernst Lyon, himself an amateur filmmaker; Danny; and Danny's son, Raphe, who is shown learning the craft of filmmaking.

Cutting his father's footage into his own film allows Lyon to relate his family history to his son and teach him some of his own values. Thus, the family is seen as the ultimate protection against a hostile environment, a point that seemingly underlies a number of Lyon's films. For example, in *Los niños abandonados* the boys survive, because they have formed substitute families. In *Born to Film* Lyon cuts away several times to homeless people, even to corpses on the street. In the later films with Willie, it is the very absence of a visible family that is in part responsible for the boy's descent into the treadmill of institutional punishment. This point is expressed directly in *Born to Film* by Billy McCune, a convict who has spent twenty-six years in prison in solitary (and is first seen in Lyon's photo series, *Born to Lose: Fifteen Photographs of the Texas Department of Corrections*), and who has received parole from a life sentence. Sitting in Lyon's garden as he watches some screaming children frolic, Billy admits ruefully that he missed all that: "Screaming children, plates breaking, cats jumping out of bags." Becoming a father might have protected him from society and from himself, the film seems to imply.[42]

Danny Lyon's latest film, *Media Man* (1994), returns to the autobiographical and familial discourse of *Born to Film,* a subject he also worked through in his photography book about his children, *I Like to Eat Right on the Dirt.* But the film also manages to tie together the other strands of Lyon's creative work, indeed much of Lyon's life. Taking a humorous and, at times, romantic look at his own past, Lyon visits many of the sites of his previous encounters with an America at the bottom of the social scale. Throughout the film Lyon is also seen fishing in various rivers, in different parts of the country (summer, fall, winter), talking about various kinds of flies and with a variety of fisherman about their catch. The working title of the film was "The Media Man Goes Fishing," and, indeed, the film's central metaphor is fishing.

In one scene some black men from Mississippi are seen fishing, because they are out of work and unwilling to buckle under the "pencil slavery" of present-day America. Here, then, fishing represents a self-sufficiency and freedom from institutional control, which characterizes other marginal groups in Lyon's films and even Lyon's own life. At the beginning of the film, Lyon proudly presents his victory garden, while simultaneously thumbing his nose at the philistines of the National Endowment for the Arts, noting that pesticides make his tomatoes fit for NEA consumption. Not one to kowtow to the authorities of state censorship (another method of institutional control), Lyon financed this film by himself and for years has been distributing his films out of his own home, thus guaranteeing his own freedom of expression.

However, the film's loose construction, its open-ended editing, its snippets of dialogue and very brief scenes suggest that Lyon is also fishing for images, traveling around the country to see what his camera can catch. In the course of the film, he shows us his children in Clintondale, New York, on

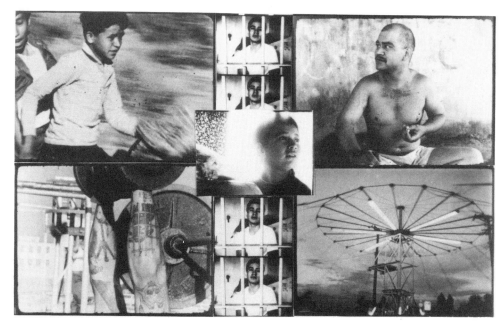

Film stills collage by Danny Lyon (1986), from *Willie* (1985), directed by Danny Lyon. Courtesy of Danny Lyon.

Film still from *Born to Film* (1981), with Danny and Raphe Lyon, directed by Danny Lyon. Photo by Nancy Lyon. Courtesy of Danny Lyon.

Belzoni, Mississippi 1994

For Chris and Martha

with thanks Danny Lyon

Signed film still from *The Media Man* (1994), directed by Danny Lyon.

the Fourth of July and during Halloween; a black Baptist church choir in Mississippi (the site of a photograph in *The Movement*); playground, murder, and traffic scenes from New York City (where he grew up); the tattoo contest mentioned above; a demolition derby in New Jersey; a Mexican-American classic car convention in Bernalillo, New Mexico, where he lived for many years; and, finally, an old westerner attempting to sell junk as rare art. While the focus is still on individuals and groups at the social margins, there is no sense of victimization, nor do the instruments of institutional power ever make an appearance. Instead, Lyon is celebrating their and his independence from mainstream America, from white-bread, born-again, conservative, institutional society. And it is a family affair: both in the sense that Lyon's family (his wife, his son) are a part of the crew, and in the sense that Lyon continually cuts away to children and families at these various folk festivals, suggesting again that families are the last line of defense against the powers of the state.

Lyon's intense partisanship for his protagonists, then, goes beyond the filmmaking experience. He is still friends with Willie's brothers, as he is with Billy McCune and others who have been the subjects of his films and photographs. But Lyon's subjectivity is also an aesthetic strategy, completely in keeping with the philosophical premises of his work. His films eschew the kind of "objective documentary" techniques favored by mainstream media, because such an aesthetic creates a seemingly unbroken narrative of reality, which simultaneously, invisibly deforms reality through ideology. It is the evening news with its claims to balance, all the while presenting a single point of view, and the media's insistence on positivism that Lyon sees as another strategy of the institutions of power to control public discourse. Its invisibility increases its power.

Lyon's films, on the other hand, are montages of discontinuities, rather than continuities, narratives of subjectivity, rather than objectivity, images of folk culture, rather than a disingenuous American commercial culture. While Bill Sanders parodies the methodologies of institutionalized rationalism, Lyon subverts that rationalism by overtly proclaiming the subjectivity of his protagonists, allowing them the freedom to express themselves, regardless of their "appropriateness." Lyon's protagonists are seldom articulate, often awkward, certainly not telegenic. They are, however, genuine in their attempts to narrate their lives at the bottom. It is indeed their very unreason in the face of institutionalized order that Danny Lyon sees as a space of absolute freedom.

The final chapter focuses on a photographer and filmmaker, Ed van der Elsken, whose work is virtually unknown in America. Even in Europe he is better known as a photographer than a filmmaker, since much of his film work was financed by and produced for Dutch television. If we view the aesthetic discourses engaged in by the photographers and filmmakers in this book as a movement towards ever more overt forms of subjectivity, then Ed van der Elsken represents the most radical position on the spectrum. More than any other photographer/filmmaker discussed here, van der Elsken exposed his inner life in his images, giving both his narcissism and his voyeurism free reign.

9 Ed van der Elsken

THE INFATUATED CAMERA

In one of his earliest films, *Reis rond de Wereld* (*Journey around the World*, 1960), there is a shot of Ed van der Elsken, naked except for a skimpy bathing suit, balancing himself in the wind between two ship's masts, taking a photograph. The image is shot from slightly below against a clear sky, so that it is impossible to tell how high the photographer has climbed, but the impression is one of a precarious height, not without danger. Looking out over the horizon, van der Elsken's quick movements with the tool of his trade betray his energy, his self-confidence, and his fanaticism—when it comes to his work. More than once on this trip around the world, documented on film and in his book, *Sweet Life* (1966), he placed himself in mortal danger to get a photograph. In Durban, South Africa, van der Elsken went alone to a working-class beer hall in a black township, despite the fact that race riots had occurred earlier that summer and Europeans were seriously discouraged from entering such environments.[1] In the south Mexican state of Chiapas, van der Elsken was nearly stoned to death, according to his own account, when he photographed a religious ceremony at which no person of European descent had ever been present.[2]

Following the shot of van der Elsken on the ship's mast, there is a slow pan down to the mostly naked body of Gerda van der Veen, his wife. She is sitting on deck in a bathing suit, smiling at the camera as it languidly caresses her legs, hips, and breasts. Another shot, later in the same film, shows Gerda under a waterfall, washing her body. Again the camera moves up and down her loins, the film's overt eroticism accentuated by the cool, rushing water flowing over her body. Again and again in this film, as in his photographic and film work in general, Ed van der Elsken's camera searches out the female form, discovering and taking pleasure in its eroticism.

Thus, we have encapsulated in these two images at sea the two essences of Ed van der Elsken's subjectivity, revealing his narcissism and his voyeurism. For him, the camera had meaning only if it allowed him to look, to see, and to be seen. While other photographers have endeavored to hide or downplay their subjectivity or avoided the self-revelatory elements structurally inherent in their craft, van der Elsken flaunted them.

More than any other photographer/filmmaker discussed in this book, Ed van der Elsken broke down the boundaries between his professional and private sphere, photography and real life. More than most photographers in the latter half of the twentieth century, van der Elsken's images are documents of his identity as a person, an artist, a lover, a family man. He became famous as a street photographer who created overtly subjective portraits of life on the wild side, having invented the genre almost single-handedly, and independently of his colleague, Robert Frank. Yet, while Frank's subjectivity always maintained a distance, holding back the inner core of his personality in order not to betray to a public audience his private secrets, van der Elsken has exposed himself with a vengeance, ruthlessly documenting his obsessions, neuroses, and flaws regardless of the public consequences. In much of his photography and film work, the image maker is at the center of attention, manifesting himself not only through his particular point of view, but also by often appearing in front of the camera. His film *De verliefde camera* (*The Infatuated Camera*, 1971), for example, is a self-portrait in which van der Elsken places his private life and his work on public view. More than once in his photography and films, he has published images of himself naked in bed with various women. In his final film, *Bye* (1991), a horrific, feature-length exploration of the process of dying from cancer, van der Elsken again turned the camera on himself, shooting into a mirror, documenting his physical decay and his emotional struggle. This lack of regard for the sensibilities of the representatives of power who "protect" public morals turned him into a bête noire in some circles and certainly did not always help to further his professional career. But if van der Elsken finds a place in the history of photography and film, it will indeed be for his uncompromising attitude toward himself and his subject matter.

Ed van der Elsken's career as a filmmaker was more underground than most. One searches in vain for articles or reviews about his films in non-Dutch language periodicals and books. Despite a thirty-year career as a filmmaker, his films have almost never been screened at international festivals,

Frame enlargement *Journey around the World* (1960), with Ed
van der Elsken, directed by Ed van der Elsken. Courtesy of Nederlands
Filmmuseum.

and even in Holland they have been shown mostly on Dutch television, for which they were often produced. Unlike his protégés, colleagues, and friends, among them Johan van der Keuken, Fons Rademakers, Jan Vrijman, and Hans Keller, van der Elsken's name does not make an appearance in the standard histories of Dutch cinema.[3] Even in the Netherlands his position in the film world is controversial, despite the fact that he worked for years as a cameraman on the films of other directors. Neither of the two Dutch film periodicals, *Skoop* and *Skrien,* has to date published articles on van der Elsken's career as a filmmaker. When van der Elsken died in 1990, *Skrien* ignored the event altogether, and *Skoop* published an eight-line obituary, giving three times as much space in the same issue for their farewells to Leonid Trauberg and Joan Bennett.[4] Why this neglect? When he won the Dutch National Film Award in 1971 for his film *The Infatuated Camera,* there were protests from within the industry.[5] If the truth be known, van der Elsken was not well liked by his colleagues. As Evelyn de Regt notes: "At the television studios in Hilversum, however, Van der Elsken was not a popular cameraman. Most directors found his images too little in focus, too sooty, and felt his camera moved around too much. They were also wary of his tendency to meddle with the shots and pass comment from behind the camera. He was generally at loggerheads with the cutters, because he did not agree with the editing."[6]

In 1991 van der Elsken's *Bye,* completed six months before his death, received an award for the best Dutch documentary broadcast on television. Since then, interest in his films has slowly begun to increase, with a major retrospective in 1996–97 at the Nederlands Filmmuseum in Amsterdam, the Centre Européen de la Photographie in Paris, and the Filmmuseum in Munich. However, lack of preservation and availability still hampers research into his film work.[7] A number of his films exist only in fragmentary or incomplete form.

The perceived lack of technical perfection in Ed van der Elsken's film work was a function of his film aesthetics. Although his films have little in common with the aesthetics of cinema verité, he appropriated their technology to his own aesthetic ends. Due in part to his training as a photographer, in part to character traits that often made it difficult to work with him, van der Elsken functioned best alone or with his wife (who handled sound). In an industry that thrives on group dynamics and effort, such a "lone wolf" status made him a pariah. At best, he managed to work with a sympathetic director when hired as cameraman. He liked to shoot fast and with a high degree of flexibility for camera movement, filming in real locations under available light conditions. His early films were shot with a 16mm silent

Bolex, which he later had modified with a home-made blimp, a synchronous motor, an aluminum breast harness to give him a steady image, and special, light-sensitive lenses.[8] In 1964 he bought a 16mm Eclair Cine camera, which, when used in conjunction with an Uher tape recorder, could shoot synchronous sound under the most difficult of production conditions. In the early 1970s, he switched to a Super 8mm film camera to shoot more cheaply and, more importantly, more inconspicuously. After completing several more films in 16mm in the 1980s, he used Betacam, U-matic, and Super VHS cameras to record his last film. The utilization of these semiprofessional and amateur film formats indicates that van der Elsken was more interested in the spontaneity and freedom of movement that low-tech equipment could give him than in the technical perfection of professional equipment, demanding larger film crews and increased setup time. Van der Elsken was certainly not alone in developing such a fast and loose aesthetic, given the international film avant-garde's predilection for light, portable equipment, but he was an anomaly within the Dutch television industry in the 1960s.

The two television companies for whom van der Elsken free-lanced most often, AVRO and VPRO, depend on maintaining a subscription base of at least 100,000 viewers to gain access to the two national Dutch TV channels. Given their economic base, and the fact that these companies were traditionally connected to the Catholic and Protestant churches, respectively, they could ill afford radical programming. Yet Ed van der Elsken's films hardly fit into the category of standard TV documentaries. The aesthetically conservative programming policies of Dutch TV began to change in the late 1960s, when VPRO, in particular, embarked on a strategy of inviting more adventuresome filmmakers to direct films for them. Among the film directors to profit from this trend, in which van der Elsken had been a pioneer, were Johan van der Keuken, Hans Keller, and Wim Schippers.[9] Thus, Dutch television offered van der Elsken an occasional forum (as well as financing) for his films but also possibly hindered their reception in avant-garde film circles.

Eduard van der Elsken was born on 10 March 1925 in Amsterdam. His parents, Eduard and Huberta van der Elsken, owned a modest furniture shop. After completing commercial high school, van der Elsken decided in 1943 to go to art school, having previously realized that he was not cut out to become a salesman in his father's store. However, the fear of being drafted by the German *Arbeitsdienst* in what was then still Nazi-occupied Holland forced him to go into hiding in the countryside around Noord-Branbant. When the Allies liberated the south of Holland after the Battle of Arnhem in September 1944, van der Elsken joined a mine-clearing brigade, having become a pacifist.

After the war, van der Elsken apprenticed with a series of studio photographers and began taking pictures in Amsterdam's red-light district in 1947. In 1950 he hitchhiked to Paris, where he spent the next five years. In autobiographical texts, van der Elsken made much of the fact that he slept under the bridges of Paris like a clochard, but, if indeed he ever did sleep under a bridge, it was only for his first night in Paris. In point of fact, he almost immediately took a job, working for Pierre Gasmann, the head of Magnum's photo lab, making prints for such photographers as Ernst Haas. But van der Elsken lasted only six months, eventually giving up "darkroom slavery" for the life of a free-lancer. In the mean time, he had become acquainted with the bohemian circles on the Left Bank. However, neither the intellectuals who read Sartre or Camus, nor the international colony of artists drew him to the area around the Avenue Saint Germain de Prés, but rather the homeless youth who survived by sleeping in cafés and the Metro, and by committing petty larceny and prostitution. Living on the street, often without identification papers, many of them alcoholics or drug addicted, these kids were a lost generation, orphaned and victimized by the war. Van der Elsken was particularly taken with Vali Myers, a sometime dancer and artist who lived on the street and became an important inspiration for his photographic studies. Through her, he gained access to the grudging, camera-shy youth.

When Edward Steichen met van der Elsken in Paris in 1953, he bought eighteen of the photographer's portraits and included them in his exhibition, *Post-War European Photography,* held at the Museum of Modern Art in New York the same year. Peter Pollack, curator at the Art Institute of Chicago, saw the exhibition and subsequently organized a one-man show of the same prints in Chicago and at the Walker Arts Center in Minneapolis. But it was not until the publication of van der Elsken's book *Love on the Left Bank* that he experienced an international breakthrough, the photographs having been previously published in the *Picture Post* and in Dutch magazines.[10]

Interestingly, while van der Elsken had taken the photographs without a specific concept in mind, he was able to create for the book a fictitious, first person, "cinematic" narrative consisting of images and text, much like a *photo-roman. Love on the Left Bank* relates the story of Miguel, a young, homeless Mexican youth who falls hopelessly in love with Ann (Vali Myers), also homeless, a "red-haired girl who danced like a Negro" and preferred to sleep with blacks. Obsessed with Ann, Miguel follows her around, watching her make love to men and women alike. Eventually, after spending a few months in jail, the boy finally sleeps with Ann but realizes it meant nothing to her. He returns to Mexico, where he gets a letter from Ann telling him he had probably contracted a venereal disease from her. Both the stark pho-

tographs and the sexually frank narrative shocked some contemporary reviewers, still trapped in the repressed 1950s, but the book also garnered critical praise, especially in Germany.

The book's layout was also something new for the time and underscored
the cinematic aspects of the *roman*. It begins with a long shot of Paris by
night, the Eiffel Tower in the background, much like any good Hollywood
film. It moves to an establishing shot of the neighborhood by night, with the
Café Mabillon in the foreground, where much of the action takes place. On
the following two pages are six images, three of them laid out on top of each
other, simulating film stills and showing the atmosphere of the café: jazz
musicians, singers, dancers. On the next two pages, van der Elsken presents
a close-up of "the girl with red hair who dances like a Negro." Thus begins *A
Love in Saint Germain de Prés*, as the book was called in Dutch and German.

In 1957 van der Elsken traveled to French Equatorial Africa at the invitation of his brother-in-law, having previously married Gerda, his second wife.
The three-month journey resulted in a second book, *Bagara*, published in
1958. The year 1959 saw the publication of *Jazz*, a book about the blooming
jazz scene in Amsterdam, which included photographs of Chet Baker, Dizzy
Gillespie, Lester Young, Miles Davis, Oscar Peterson, Ray Charles, and Ella
Fitzgerald on stage.[11] Taken under available light conditions, the photographs are extremely grainy due to the pushed film stock, giving them a
sense of immediacy in keeping with the subject matter. He developed this
grainy, high-contrast black and white, at times slightly out-of-focus style
even further in *Sweet Life*. Over the next three decades, van der Elsken published fourteen more photography books. In almost every case he was responsible for the layout, as well as the texts, which cultivated an overtly autobiographical, chatty tone. Highly idiosyncratic in choice of subject matter,
the photographs reflect his lifelong obsession with observing street life and
his need to expose his own position as a maker of images. It was an aesthetic
he would also apply to his films.

Ed van der Elsken's first contact with the cinema had come in the late
1940s, when he spent some time in an art house in Amsterdam. In 1955 the
Dutch television station, AVRO, produced a program based on his Saint
Germain des Prés photographs. Although he was unsatisfied with the program, his interest in filmmaking was sparked. In the same year, he and a
friend, Jan Vrijman, were commissioned by VPRO to make a documentary
about the European Center for Nuclear Research in Geneva, but the two
film novices' footage and sound were completely unusable because of technical inadequacies. Two more films by the pair, though completed, were not
much better.

In 1959, van der Elsken received a contract from the Royal Dutch Ship Owners Association to make a film for Princess Margriet of the Netherlands (the godchild of the Merchant Marine) in honor of her coming of age in 1961. Van der Elsken and Gerda were to be given free first-class passage on any freighter in the Dutch fleet for an around-the-world sea voyage. To further finance the voyage, van der Elsken contracted for a series of short travelogues for Dutch TV (AVRO), and he and Gerda wrote journals for Dutch illustrated magazines. They set sail in August 1959 for Africa, sailed around the Cape of Good Hope to China, the Philippines, and Japan, traveled on to the United States and Mexico, and returned to Amsterdam in September 1960. A 35mm reflex camera in one hand, a 16mm Bolex film camera in the other, van der Elsken documented everything. The results were a ten-part series on AVRO; a documentary, *Van Varen* (*About Sailing,* 1961); a seventeen-part photo-reportage in the Dutch Catholic illustrated magazine, *Katholieke Illustratie;* and a book, *Sweet Life.*

The footage for the series, *Journey around the World,* broadcast in roughly ten-minute segments between 1959 and 1960, was sent en route to Hilversum with instructions for editing and a script for the narration. Only a thirty-eight-minute montage apparently survives, edited without sound. Since the footage has no head titles, but the editing is very sophisticated, it is likely that the footage was reedited by van der Elsken himself.[12] Indeed, the surviving film is edited without much regard for temporal or spacial continuities in a stream of consciousness, free-form style.

As stated above, the film begins with Ed and Gerda on board a freighter. The next sequence has them traveling through the United States, sleeping in their car, camping out, and horseback riding. Cut to Japan, after a brief scene in the van der Elsken's stateroom, where Ed is developing 35mm film and Gerda is banging out a journal on a portable typewriter. A montage of numerous Japanese men and women bowing, even when telephoning, is followed by shots in Africa and Mexico before the film cuts back to a wild west show in the United States. Later, a sumo wrestling sequence is followed by wrestlers on American television, cut together with two black Americans on the street in Harlem, fighting, and a fist fight between black children. Still later, van der Elsken creates an elaborate sequence of Philippine strippers, Africans dancing, Native Americans dancing, a Zulu dance spectacle, North African dancers, and a Noh performance. At another point, he cuts together a sequence of stone lions from various parts of the world, an obvious homage to Sergei Eisenstein's *Potemkin* (1925).

Without a narration, the footage is identifiable only with the help of *Sweet Life.* In fact, many of the still images in the book are found in a slightly

Frame enlargement *Journey around the World* (1960), with Ed
van der Elsken, directed by Ed van der Elsken. Courtesy of Nederlands
Filmmuseum.

different form in the film; for example, a scene of African fisherman pulling in their nets, sandwiched between Coney Island beach shots and footage taken at a Sea World–type aquarium in California, is only identifiable through van der Elsken's photographs of the same scene taken in Freetown, Sierra Leone.[13]

A comparison of the photos and film scene reveals the similarities and differences in van der Elsken's vision in the two media. First, it needs to be noted that van der Elsken's photographs, as was his style, cover the page completely, without borders, so that the two photographs on facing pages literally bleed into each other.[14] The photograph on the left is taken from very close to the shore and shows a group of African men (covering the bottom two-thirds of the image) pulling fish from a net, the horizon and sky marking the upper third of the image. In the upper left-hand corner, we see a fish suspended in the air, as if completely independent from the group. The photo is backlighted, so that many details are eliminated, leaving a high-contrast image in which the men and fish appear almost as silhouettes. Interestingly, another seemingly larger fish, suspended in the air, is at the focal point of the second image, in which the sky covers the top two-thirds of the image, and the upper bodies of the men are seen at the very bottom of the image. These two photographs are cinematic in the sense that their open compositions invite us to imagine the space beyond the frame.

Second, the montage of the two images essentially duplicates a long-shot–medium-shot construction, a standard convention in film editing. On the other hand, the simultaneity of the two images, allowing the viewer to compare and contrast the images, is only possible in photography. None of the ten shots in the film sequence duplicate the two photographic images in the book. We see the net being hauled in, the fish being pulled from the net and thrown up on the beach, where they are tossed up the beach even farther to women who carry away the fish in baskets. In Sweet Life, van der Elsken explains this process in his "captions" at the front of the book. Moving his camera frequently to follow the movement of objects and persons, he presents an activity in time, thus focusing much more attention on the process. The mysteriously flying fish of the photographs, suspended above the heads of the men and pregnant with symbolic meaning, loose their metaphoric quality in the film, becoming no more than a detail in a scene from everyday life in Africa.

Clearly, van der Elsken's point of view is that of a tourist with an eye for the picturesque. Noticeable is his concentration on individuals and groups interacting in public spaces. Architecture, except for a few rare shots of Hong Kong and New York, seems to be of little interest to him. Public events—bull

fights, baseball, wild west shows, sumo wrestling, public dance displays—
allow him to capture exotic occurrences, while his street images of pedestrians likewise focus on those views most appealing to a European audience
before the age of mass tourism. While a certain percentage of the shots were
evidently made with the acquiescence of the subjects, who pose for the camera, many shots have an improvised, fleeting look to them. Van der Elsken's
biographer, Evelyn de Regt, notes that it was on this trip, specifically in
Japan, that van der Elsken discovered his own style of photography: "With
his Japanese work, he revealed the kind of reality and moments he was looking for—moments in which a series of minor dramatic incidents converged,
partly in reaction to his dynamic presence."[15] Even when the subjects are
posing, then, they hardly have time to become conscious of their position, so
their image is more a reflection of the photographer's subjectivity than a collaboration with the person depicted.

In contrast to the many photographs of poverty published in *Sweet Life*
without pathos or a sense of social injustice, only a few such sequences are
seen in the film. Given that van der Elsken's main goal was to produce a
"travelogue" and "propaganda" film, he undoubtedly felt the need to censor
himself when holding his Bolex.

About Sailing was completed after van der Elsken's return to Holland. The
narration and style of *About Sailing* was necessarily impersonal, because the
goal of the twenty-minute film was to present the Dutch merchant marine
in a positive light. The short opens with seamen taking leave of their loved
ones on the pier before setting sail. On board, the work of officers and crew,
as well as their private living quarters, are visualized. The next segment de-
picts various harbors of the world, then follows the sailors on shore leave:
Disneyland, strip joints in the Philippines, Coney Island. Here the film
strikes a melancholy note, when the narrator points out the essential loneliness of the sailors, who are always "observing life from the outside." The film
ends, however, with a patriotic image: a waving Dutch flag, backlighted by
the sun.

An atmosphere of romantic adventure is immediately created with the
film's first image, a silhouetted sailboat, gliding across a shimmering sea. The
well-composed, balanced images, with a number of prominent low-angle
shots of seamen and officers, contribute to the "heroic," larger-than-life
mood of the film. The sense of romanticism is also underscored by the film's
narration, which is consciously literary, unlike the conversational tone of
van der Elsken's later films. Utilizing repetition in a manner that clearly re-
produces the poetic cadences of Pare Lorentz's *The River* (1937), the narrator chants the names of ports of call, goods loaded and unloaded. Given the

Frame enlargement from *Bewogen Beweging* (1961), directed by Ed van der Elsken. Courtesy of Nederlands Filmmuseum.

film's wholly different intentions, it is not surprising that only a few shots from the film ("sea world," Disneyland) remind us of *Sweet Life* or *Journey around the World*.

In the same year as *About Sailing*, van der Elsken completed the first of a series of films about artists and art exhibitions. *Bewogen Bewegung* (*Moving Motion*, 1961), a project initiated by the director of the Stedelijk Museum in Amsterdam, Willem Sandberg, documented in slightly less than five minutes an exhibition by the same name. The Stedelijk exhibition, which included work by Jean Tinguely, Moholy-Nagy (*Light Prop*, 1930), and mobiles by Alexander Calder, presented moving sculptures. Accordingly, van der Elsken decided to move his camera in a fashion that would accentuate the dynamism of the art on display, the camera taking on the wholly subjective view of a museum visitor. Beginning with a pan up a sculpture outside the museum's main entrance, van der Elsken tracks through the museum's exhibition hall. After cutting to shots of various sculptures in motion, intercut with reaction shots of visitors, especially children, he creates a fast-paced montage of moving sculpture parts, as if the sheer dynamism of the exhibition has led to a mental breakdown of the filmmaker/visitor. The film closes breathlessly with a fast-action track through the exhibition from back to front, stopping periodically and briefly at a number of sculptures, before ending in front of the museum, where the film began. Van der Elsken thus tries to reproduce the literal path of the visitor through the exhibition hall, as well as the subjective emotions, conjured up by the art on display. In particular, the final minute of the film, where the moving camera races past, around, and in between visitors and sculptures, is an impressive piece of camera work, given the need to work under available light conditions and continually pulling focus to keep the image sharp. The overt subjectivity of the film, emphasizing the spectator's position as a consumer of art, placed it in sharp contrast to the normally staid conventions of art historical documentaries.

The year 1961 also witnessed the production of another film by van der Elsken, *Karel Appel: Componist*. The Dutch action painter, Karel Appel, had been a friend of van der Elsken since their time together as bohemians in Paris in the early 1950s.[16] Earlier in 1961, van der Elsken had made a very short film, *Appel-iep* (*The Appel Elm*), which showed Appel painting the trunk of an elm tree in his studio, then taking it to a public park, where the reactions of passersby were filmed.[17] Van der Elsken was hired by the Philips Radio Company to photograph Appel while he composed the "Musique barbare" for Jan Vrijman's film, *De werkelikjheid van Karel Appel* (*The Reality of Karel Appel*, 1961).[18] Recording Appel's composition in the studio, and bits

Frame enlargement from *Karel Appel: Componist* (1961), with Karel Appel, directed by Ed van der Elsken. Courtesy of Nederlands Filmmuseum.

of dialogue between Appel and his sound engineer on a small tape recorder while photographing the two men, van der Elsken decided afterwards to make a film of his recorded sound, still images, film footage, and some footage he had shot in New York in Appel's studio a year earlier while on his world tour. The result was an experimental film, rather than a documentary, a free-form collage of images and music, black leader with sound and still photographs, moving-camera shots and snippets of mostly unintelligible dialogue. An artist at work, playing drums, endlessly mixing recorded sounds, listening, splicing audio tape, dancing in euphoria, sitting in a corner in exhaustion: van der Elsken's film covers all the bases of the creative process in repetitive detail. The result, however, is not a chronological explication of the creation of a work of art, but rather a chaotic, at times emotional outburst, much like Appel's scream on the sound track, which opens the film as the camera lingers on a portrait of the artist. "The creative man stands in disarray with his self-expression. And he stands alone," says Appel in one of the few intelligible verbal statements in the film. *Karel Appel: Componist* ends with the artist signing his name to a painting, while van der Elsken can be heard on the sound track saying: "So that was it." The film was shown at the Stedelijk Museum.

Sandberg hired van der Elsken a year later to document in photographs the construction of a much talked about exhibition at the Stedelijk, *Dylaby.* The photographs were published in the exhibit's catalogue. He also made a film, *Dylaby* (1962), visualizing the completed "dynamic labyrinth." The artists participating in the conception of the labyrinth included Robert Rauschenberg, Tinguely, Niki de St. Phalle, and Daniel Spoerri. Again, van der Elsken applied the point of view technique of a visitor to the exhibition, panning and tracking in his opening shot from the exhibition's entrance through a hall to the exhibition proper. Again, he inserts throughout the film reaction shots of the audience viewing the installation. This exhibition was interactive, allowing visitors to participate in dancing the twist, a shooting gallery, and a balloon room for kids. Ten minutes in length, the film moves at a much slower pace than *Moving Motion,* attempting through its roving camera and composition to duplicate the actual experience of reception, down to the fact that some scenes are extremely dark, almost invisible, because the museum visitor was asked to feel his/her way through a dark, tactile environment. In Daniel Spoerri's "Upside-Down Room," on the other hand, van der Elsken's camera moves 180 degrees around its own axis, approximating the perceptual chaos encountered by the visitor entering the room.[19]

In 1965 van der Elsken produced an eight-minute documentary about the international short film festival in Oberhausen, Germany, *Oberhausen, XI: Westdeutsche Kurzfilmtage* (1965). As in the two previous films, van der Elsken begins with a shot outside the festival hall, then cuts to the cleaning ladies in the empty projection space. A fast-action sequence shows the audience taking their seats until the theater is filled. After panning over the crowd and a few close-ups of individuals, van der Elsken presents a montage of shots filmed off the screen. The clips of films from the festival are not in chronological order, but edited according to their subject matter: shots of Martin Luther King Jr. (*The March*, 1964), Fidel Castro, flood victims in Asia, and a Nazi Party rally (*The Daily Life of Gestapoman Schmidt*, Poland) are followed by erotic shots from various films and by films documenting sensational events: boxing (*Cassius le Grand*, William Klein), bullfights, auto racing *(Autorennen),* horse racing (*A Sunday at the Races*, Yugoslavia), and the production of a Hollywood film epic (*Hollywood in Deblatschka Pescara*, Germany). The awards ceremony was depicted as a montage of eighteen different handshakes. In fact, van der Elsken tries throughout to inject humor into the film. The erotic sequence thematizes male audience voyeurism, for example, by intercutting a shot of a leering man with screen images of beautiful women, followed by scenes from the films of various men looking at women. As in earlier films, van der Elsken also includes his own photographs, for example, of a legendary all-night panel discussion. A group portrait of the festival's filmmakers, on the other hand, is occasion for a perceptual joke: it appears to be a photograph, because everyone in the image is absolutely motionless, except that one person in the group is consciously moving ever so slightly. The film ends with a humorous little animation of the 111th Oberhausen Film Festival in the year 2065. The film was broadcast on VPRO.[20]

While beginning work as a film-stills photographer and cameraman for hire, for example, on Fons Rademaker's *The Spitting Image* (1962) and Jan Vrijman's *On the Bottom Rung of Heaven* (1963), van der Elsken initiated his first personal project, a thirty-minute film, *Welkom in het leven, lieve kleine* (*Welcome to Life, Little Darling*, 1963).[21] The occasion was the birth of his second child with Gerda, Daan Dorus.

The film opens with Ed, Gerda, and their two-year-old daughter, Tinelou, driving through Amsterdam, then cuts to shots of Gerda and Tinelou at home in their flat: a home movie. A slow pan from the window overlooking the Nieuwmarkt Square introduces the next segment, which presents a portrait of the neighborhood. After another "home" sequence, which includes numerous portraits of mother and child, van der Elsken cuts to a sequence

Frame enlargement from *Karel Appel: Componist* (1961), with Karel Appel and Jan Vrijman, directed by Ed van der Elsken. Courtesy of Nederlands Filmmuseum.

of a carnival on the Nieuwmarkt. The film ends with a scene of the birth of the new baby.

Welcome to Life is the first of van der Elsken's overtly autobiographical films, demonstrating many stylistic elements that would be typical of his later films. The portrait of his neighborhood, for example, consists of numerous pan shots of pedestrians on the street, often aware that they are being filmed, sometimes not. Similar in style to his street photographs, these images replicate the gaze of a person sitting in a sidewalk cafe, people-watching. Second, the camera work is extremely mobile, in particular in a scene where van der Elsken stumbles upon a street fight—the camera literally darts through the crowd, around the men involved, without actually showing the fight—and in the later carnival sequence, in which the editing further emphasizes the dynamism of the movement. Third, van der Elsken cuts together whole sequences of still photographs, which create a completely different rhythm in contrast to the moving image sequences. These shots are intimate, rather than public: Gerda resting on a sofa, close-up portraits of his wife and daughter. Lastly, van der Elsken's narration is consciously chatty, as if talking to a friend or showing home movies to an assembly of relatives who live elsewhere.

The film is literally framed by two shots in the mirror, creating, respectively, a self-portrait of the artist and cameraman with child, and a portrait of the now expanded family. More than ten years earlier, van der Elsken had taken a number of auto-portraits in mirrors: alone with his Leica (1951), with the two children of his first first wife, Juliette and Madeleine (1951), with Vali Myers (1952), with his wife, Ata Kando (1952).[22]

Images in the mirror turn up again and again in van der Elsken's films. Why? The mirror allows the photographer to gaze through his lens at the objects of his desire and to look at himself looking, bringing both narcissistic and voyeuristic urges into play. Such mirror images are, thus, pregnant with psychoanalytic meaning. They remind us of what Jacques Lacan has called the pre-Oedipal, narcissistic phase of development of the ego, "the mirror phase," when primary identification occurs: a child looks in the mirror and recognizes his body as a coherent whole.[23] For the first time, he sees himself as an identity within the world. With the realization of lack in the Oedipal phase, the security of primary identification is forever lost. The gaze into the mirror, then, represents a futile attempt to recuperate the plentitude and security of identity in primary narcissism. The mirror into which van der Elsken points his camera reflects in a Lacanian sense, therefore, not the real, but rather the idealized, symbolic self, thus satisfying his narcissism. Indeed, the image of van der Elsken looking with his child in the mirror exactly replicates Lacan's description of the parent holding the child up to the mirror: "By clinging to the reference point of him who looks at him in a mirror, the subject sees appearing, not his ego ideal, but his ideal ego, that point at which he desires to gratify himself in himself."[24] But narcissism is also invariably linked through the symbolic order to voyeurism. According to Lacan's interpretation of Freud, the scopic drive (scopophilia) is rooted in the subject, in the fact that in the act of gazing the subject sees himself.[25] The mirror allows the filmmaker to see himself looking, thus increasing the overt voyeuristic pleasure of the subject.

Few photographers or filmmakers have so overtly defined themselves not just as authors outside the text, but also the subject within the text. But in the context of *Welcome to Life,* the two mirror images of van der Elsken with his camera also point to the film's extreme self-reflexivity, it's exposure of the cinematic apparatus. From the film's very beginning, van der Elsken intercuts numerous photographs and live-action shots of the process of filmmaking. Early on we see Tineloe interviewing her doll with a microphone; later we see the filmmaker in a photograph, holding his portable tape recorder; still later we see him interviewing a mechanic who is testing his car's engine. Thus, *Welcome to Life* is a portrait of his family, his neighborhood, and his self-image as a photographer and filmmaker. It is the first of many.

Van der Elsken had found the topic that fascinated him the most: his own life. This turning inward may be the reason he never completed the only overtly political film he ever attempted, *Grenzen van het leven* (shot in 1963, shortly after *Welcome to Life*).[26] According to his biographer, van der Elsken was to receive, but apparently did not, a commission from the Dutch Ministry of Education, Art and Culture to shoot a film in the Waterlooplein district of Amsterdam, which was to be torn down to make way for the new Amsterdam city hall. On the surface the project sounded good: a film about the street life van der Elsken loved. The unedited footage begins with a building being torn down in winter, then moves on to capture street life in the working-class neighborhood: children going to school through dark, dirty streets, houses falling apart, a seaman returning home, an old couple with a retarded child. But the film also goes indoors to document the abject living conditions of a poor family. The scenes of four children going to sleep in the same bed, while a television flickers in the background, remind one of the leftist films of the pre–World War II period. These scenes were apparently supposed to be juxtaposed to scenes in an automobile show (we see Porsches, Rolls Royces), where the wealthy seem to frolic. Van der Elsken must have realized, however, that this "dialectic montage" was too thin to base a whole film on it. Or perhaps he lost interest in the project when the funding failed to materialize.

Significantly, *The Infatuated Camera,*[27] a thirty-five-minute film that van der Elsken made eight years later, begins with the birth of a child, just as the earlier film ended with one. The crucial difference in the two birth sequences is that it is not his wife or child, nor the event, that is of interest to the camera in the new film; rather, it is van der Elsken, the photographer, documenting a birth, who is placed at absolute center stage of the narrative. The sequence ends, predictably, with van der Elsken looking directly into the camera, smiling, self-satisfied.

As if to confirm that van der Elsken is both the author outside the text and the subject within the text, the greater part of the film that follows has van der Elsken talking directly to the camera in his trademark conversational tone about his photography, his world travels, his meetings with famous people, and his erotic adventures. In a scene in the middle of the film we see van der Elsken, bare chest exposed, conducting a photo shoot with naked female models. The models are clearly visible, but discreetly in the background, so as not to detract the audience's attention from the body of the photographer, which seems charged with phallic energy. In the two very long closing shots, van der Elsken is seen driving his convertible through an open field, declaiming a political and social manifesto to the camera, while in the second shot, thanks to a fish-eye lens, the wife, children, and landscape rushing by frame his image.

The rest of the film records van der Elsken's comments as he pulls photographs from his files and film scenes from the shelf, narrates their content, and explicates their meaning. The images fall roughly into two categories: erotic and photo-journalistic. After the birth sequence, van der Elsken pans over a series of black and white photographs of nudes, cuts to a preteenage couple kissing, then to color photographs of a couple intensely making love and a film sequence of the same couple. Later, he shows us images of himself in bed with a black prostitute (Africa), then erotic photos from his "playboy" phase in the late 1960s. On the sound track, the photographer matter-of-factly confesses his pleasure in seeing well-formed human bodies, his reveling in the sensuality of naked flash, and his unapologetic voyeurism, but the images also document his unadulterated exhibitionism.

The narcissistic tone of the erotic image sequences also marks the photo-journalistic sequences. Repeatedly, we are shown van der Elsken with famous persons (Prince Sihanouk, Sukarno, Castro) and hear of his adventures while traveling around the world as a photo-reporter and filmmaker. Due to the running commentary, even the photo-journalistic images are

Frame enlargement from *Grenzen van het leven* (1963), directed by Ed van der Elsken. Courtesy of Nederlands Filmmuseum.

marked by the author's overt subjectivity and his narcissism, identifying him as "the point of absolute textual origin."[28] Whether consciously or unconsciously, van der Elsken exposes himself completely, leaving viewers no other choice but to admire him, that is, identify themselves with him, or to reject completely his narrative of self-absorption. Given such uninhibited exhibitionism, it is not surprising that the film was so controversial when it won a Dutch film prize. One critic called it an "outrageously self-indulgent portrait of a photographer."[29]

Van der Elsken's next film, *Death in the Port Jackson Hotel* (1972), returned him symbolically to the hallucinatory days of his Parisian youth. In Edam (Holland) and southern Italy, van der Elsken filmed a portrait of Vali Myers, who had metamorphosed herself into a hippie, living in a country commune with thirty dogs and a lover twenty years her junior. The film opens with a sequence in which van der Elsken talks about *Love on the Left Bank* and Vali Myers, then cuts to an audio recording of Vali talking about the young people depicted in the book, while we see images from the book. The sequence begins and ends with van der Elsken's famous photograph of Myers kissing herself in a mirror—an image of narcissism par excellence— then cuts to van der Elsken filming himself and Myers in a mirror set up outside on the photographer's farm. He asks her to talk about "a long time ago," but she doesn't have much to say about the subject, seemingly embarrassed that the question reveals her age. In the next two sequences, Vali is shown riding a horse and talking about her drawings, one of which gives the film its title, while van der Elsken's camera scans the artwork. (She had, in fact, become a relatively well-known artist.) The second half of the film is shot in an isolated valley in Italy, where Myers lived with her animals.

Interestingly, van der Elsken gives Myers her own voice in the film, carrying on a dialogue with her, allowing her plenty of space to tell her own story. She relates her opium addiction and her "death trip," manifested in her lifestyle and art, and talks of her love of the animals, who returned her to life. As if to prove the point that communion with nature is life embracing, van der Elsken films her fully clothed, making love with her boyfriend while leaning against a tree, just as later we see dogs copulating while Vali talks about being in heat. Van der Elsken returns obsessively to an extreme close-up of Vali's tattooed mouth, which gives her an animal-like appearance. Yet, his goal is not to present her as a freak, as one might suspect, but rather to tell a story of redemption, the meaning of which would not escape van der Elsken. After the breakup of his marriage, he too would withdraw to his farm, which would provide him with the subject matter for his next personal film.

In 1980 van der Elsken produced *Avonturen op het land (Adventures in the Country)*, a feature-length, personal documentary shot with a super 8mm camera, as well as a book of color photographs.[30] The film is a microcosmic look at the natural and social environment to be seen and experienced within a few miles of van der Elsken's farm in Edam. Ironically, the film opens with an almost two-minute shot of van der Elsken setting up his camera and a telephoto lens the size of a cannon to film the surface of the moon. The obvious symbolism of the phallic lens, used to visually penetrate the moon (a female sign), is accentuated by the sensuality of the shot's lighting. From the very beginning, van der Elsken keeps up a running commentary on the images, often describing exactly what the viewer is seeing. In a sense, then, this film, too, is a home movie in which the photographer is the center of attention. The opening shots of the moon and setting sun—the telephoto abstracts the images' articulation of space—announce the romantic undercurrents clearly visible in the film and in van der Elsken's relationship to the material.

The film proper begins with an aerial view of the farm, surrounded by fields and water, then cuts to a long sequence at a local "rodeo," where farmers drive their livestock through the streets. This sequence is extremely fast-paced due to van der Elsken's panning shots, which follow the action, similar to the way he shoots pedestrians in other films. Later sequences present the birth of various animals, the family horse, birds in nests, bunnies and more birds, frogs and tadpoles in the creek, winter landscapes, underwater scenes of microscopic organisms, a tug-of-war at a local festival. Everything is fair game for van der Elsken's inquisitive camera, and many shots are extremely beautiful, marked, as it were, by the photographer's lyrical attitude toward nature. As in his earlier films, van der Elsken also seems absolutely fascinated by bodily functions, especially birth and sexuality (we see various forms of animal life copulating), which also structures the film's overall narrative, moving as it does from spring through the seasons to winter and back to spring, birth and rebirth.

Just as *Welcome to Life* and *The Infatuated Camera* featured extremely graphic scenes of human birth, *Adventures in the Country* almost obsessively gazes at animal births. Van der Elsken films in close-up the birth of a black lamb, a white lamb, a calf born by Caesarian section, freshly hatched birds. A short film, *Paardeleven (A Horse's Life)*, obviously shot around the same period, features both copulation and the birth of a horse, as well as the erotically charged image of a naked woman riding bareback. This continual return to the site of expulsion from the womb, to the moment when life first infuses a tiny body, seems to have endlessly fascinated van der Elsken. Birth is life-affirming, but also a frightening realization of sexual difference. The image of the gaping orifice of the vagina signifies the terrible lack of female sexuality (the veterinarian literally has to reach into a ewe's uterus and pull out the fetus, at one point) and the fear of castration. Indeed, in another scene, van der Elsken presents the spectator with close-ups of a castration, as if to indicate that, as Freud noted, birth and the fear of castration are inevitably linked in the symbolic order. The castration scene, in retrospect, takes on its own eery, symbolic significance, given van der Elsken's own very real castration, as discussed in *Bye*.

Een Fotograaf filmt Amsterdam (*A Photographer Films Amsterdam*, 1982) returns to familiar van der Elsken territory. The film consists basically of two parts, which alternate throughout film. In the first shot and in numerous subsequent scenes, van der Elsken drives through Amsterdam at breakneck speeds shortly after dawn to avoid traffic (replicating the opening shot of *Welcome to Life*), naming streets and buildings as he goes. From one sequence to the next, van der Elsken covers, in ever wider concentric circles, the whole city and some of its suburbs, until, in the final scene, he flies around the city in a small plane to visualize its geography and topography.

The second set of images returns us to the photographer as *flâneur,* strolling through various neighborhoods, gazing at life on the street. In keeping with van der Elsken's by now firmly established mode of operation, his camera focuses most often on well-endowed young women, while he sometimes comments on their appearance. Van der Elsken also has an eye for the exotic, the abnormal, the weird, the fanciful, and the carnivalesque. As in previous films, the pedestrians usually become aware of the camera and that they are being filmed while van der Elsken is shooting. But the artist has fallen on hard times with his method; van der Elsken has no other choice but to document that resistance. Some people make faces, others shout at him or cover their faces, at least five individuals make an obscene gesture with their middle finger. Unlike the voyeur who wishes to remain hidden, seeing without being seen, van der Elsken is very honest about his predilection, so that he takes such resistance in stride, often cracking a joke from behind the camera. Would any one else in the postfeminist era have dared to make a film in which male voyeurism is its *raison d'être*?

Ed van der Elsken began work on his last film, *Bye*, in December 1989, fourteen months after learning that he had terminal prostate cancer, and finished it in June 1990, six months before he died.[31] Much of the film was shot by van der Elsken in a mirror, so that he could record his own thoughts and document the progress of the disease, which would inevitably end his life. In terms of its subjectivity, it is one of the most brutally honest films about dying ever made, filled with anger, resentment, sadness, pain, but also joy, hope, even humor. Shot with a video camera, the VPRO-financed film alternates between black and white and color scenes, the former shot with an experimental video camera that the Philips Company had given van der Elsken in 1982.[32]

The film opens with an eight-minute black and white take of van der Elsken reading a long statement, in which he admits that this will be his last film because he has incurable prostate cancer, that he had always tried to make photographs and films about the things that grabbed him emotionally, fascinated him, including this last adventure. He then goes on to describe in almost clinical detail the activities of the doctors who "castrated him," and bungled the job, so that he nearly bled to death. He then talks about the course of the infection, the period of remission, and the renewed growth of tumors six months after the operation. Close to tears at several points, angry at the doctors and at fate, van der Elsken nevertheless manages a smile when he takes leave of "the little guys in the metal kidney-shaped dish" (his testicles). Having read his statement, he begins his narrative in the present tense by switching to color film, noting that he can now begin improvising and reacting (typical of his film style). Holding the camera himself for the first time, he tries to get out of his wheelchair and take a few steps while shooting into the mirror, a task he is able to complete with utmost difficulty. He complains bitterly that every photo-journalist in the world is now in Berlin (filming the Wall going down) or Rumania (it is December 1990), but that he is tied to his wheelchair. There are seemingly no retakes, just lengthy video shots with van der Elsken progressively showing the signs of his fatal illness.

Over the course of the next eighty minutes, van der Elsken addresses the camera repeatedly, describing various treatments, drugs, and therapies he is being subjected to, as well as his feelings, especially toward his wife and child, and toward death. It is a narrative of intense, continuous pain—he considers euthanasia at one point—physical and emotional setbacks, moments of relief when a new drug manages to remove the pain, at least temporarily, and a kind of pride that he is still able to work and produce images through all of it. He talks about various photo projects, books, and exhibitions, and interviews Ata Kando, his Hungarian-born first wife, and a Hungarian photographer who have come to visit him.

Halfway through the film, van der Elsken inserts an "intermission": a five-minute film, *Fietsers* (*Bicyclists,* 1965), he originally shot for VPRO featuring lyrical scenes (shot with an extreme telephoto lens) of Amsterdam's bicycle culture, with Vivaldi on the sound track. At another point, he shoots footage of nature outside his bedroom window, reminding the viewer of his earlier film, *Adventures in the Country.* In the final shot, van der Elsken says goodbye: "Do your best. Show the world who you are. Bye." The film closes with another musical interlude: a montage of photos from his last photo book, *Once upon a Time,* and a Jacques Brel chanson.

If narcissism and voyeurism were the driving forces behind much of van der Elsken's earlier film and photographic work, creating an illusory image of wholeness through primary narcissistic identification, then in *Bye* we witness the documentation of a radical separation from the self, whereby the subject can only face death by objectifying himself, describing his castrated body, as if it belonged to another. At one point he takes off his shirt and shows us his pelvic area, where a graph has been drawn directly on his skin to guide the doctors administering the radiation treatment. Holding his penis, he notes that the doctors have warned him to keep it out of the way of the radiation. At another point he lays out all his X-ray and bone scans on a light table, so that his tumors can be viewed in frightening detail. In order to come to terms with his lack, he puts on a cap inscribed "the boss" and from which is protruding a giant phallic cigar. Van der Elsken knowingly plays with such fetishistic signifiers, thereby creating another moment of humor, which also distances the subject.

Indeed, the film's radical formal structure, consisting almost exclusively of single long takes in which the filmmaker directly addresses the audience, works to keep the viewer from identifying with the subject. As a result, van der Elsken blocks any emotions of pity that might have been conjured up, given the emotional power of the narrative, had another filmmaker been at work. On the other hand, he makes a bid for immortality in this final exhibitionistic extravaganza. He states that he has to finish the film, because there is another book project that awaits completion. He even jokes about making another feature-length film from beyond the grave, because so many people are interested in knowing what it is like. He adds that he will again play the central role. Van der Elsken knows these images will outlive his physical existence, will in fact give him a form of immortality. Metaphorically, the camera has power over death.

To the very end, then, Ed van der Elsken remained true to his libidinal drives. Certainly, his almost exclusive focus on his own subjectivity make him an object of interest, especially for those viewers interested in the more personal cinema of the avant-garde. Indeed, van der Elsken's film work must be seen in the tradition of such overtly autobiographical filmmakers as Jonas Mekas, Carolee Schneemann, Andrew Norton, Tom Chomont, and Robert Huot. Ed van der Elsken's films may be the most flagrantly self-revelatory of the group, exhibiting at both a conscious and subconscious level positive and negative aspects of his personality and personal life. Whether his films will find a new audience, posthumously, remains to be seen.

10 Conclusion

In the past, photography has lent itself much more readily than film to authorial analysis, because still photography has traditionally been a medium for individual artistic expression. As a result, the standard histories of photography are based on an analysis of the work of individual photographers and photographic schools, much as traditional art history has been similarly constructed as a narrative of great artists and art movements. Film history, on the other hand, has oscillated between narratives of "auteurs," that is, of outstanding film directors who managed to establish a personal style, and studies of national and transnational cinemas, which focus more heavily on the historical, political, and social dimensions of cinema. Such aesthetic and historical debates, whether the cinema is a product of individual aesthetic vision or a collective endeavor, have in fact been the direct result of the complicated and multilayered process of film production. In the past fifteen years, both photographic history and film history have witnessed a sea change in the sense that materialist, linguistic, and psychoanalytic methodologies have increasingly been brought to bare on these disciplines, the result of which has been a deemphasis on studies of authorship.

By focusing on individual photographers as filmmakers, this book has in a sense swum against contemporary currents. It has assumed that while film production is generally a collective activity, making questions of authorship problematic, photographers have preferred to work in those cinemas and film genres that allowed for a greater, rather than lesser, degree of control over the film production process. Given their previous training as photographers, who work essentially alone, such a choice seems natural for the filmmakers involved. It has been further argued that avant-garde and independent documentary are two film genres that allow for a greater amount of artistic freedom and therefore have drawn to them photographers looking to expand their horizons in the other photographic medium. By looking at the careers of a number of photographer/filmmakers from Europe and the United States, and from the beginnings of the century to the present day, it has been demonstrated that many photographers have managed to remain surprisingly consistent when moving from one medium to the other. In some instances, this consistency has been most visible in their usage of the formal possibilities of the two media of film and photography, that is, they have manipulated in strikingly similar fashion those technological elements common to both media: lighting, optics, framing. In other instances, this consistency has been the result of developing a personal vision toward a complex of thematic concerns. What has also become clear, however, is that while the photographer's choice of one medium over another might initially be a matter of opportunity, rather than concept, the ultimate usage of film, rather than photography, is a deciding factor in the conceptual framework of the final product.

Due to their dissimilar formal characteristics and differences in the manner of reception, films communicate differently from photographs, and vice versa. Photography allows for a perception in time, the cinema for perceptions through time. Photographs are usually constructed as a closed system of meaning, making them more readily available for metaphoric and symbolic coding. Films communicate more readily on an iconic level, because the film frame is not a closed system, but rather a rectangle that at least theoretically allows for a glimpse beyond the frame. On the other hand, photographs hide much more than they show; a mystery always remains, giving the viewer a great deal of freedom in terms of the reception of the image. And films are so structurally complex in terms of their layering of coded messages through image, sound, and text that they, too, cannot be reduced a single level of meaning. The reception of a photograph usually occurs on an individual basis and is governed by the materiality of the object itself, while film reception is invariably a collective experience, based on the immateriality of the image on the screen. Photographer/filmmakers are, as this book demonstrates, intensely aware of the differences between the two media and have consciously exploited such differences.

Viewed chronologically, the films of the photographers discussed here demonstrate that there has been an ever-increasing tendency away fom discourses of objectivity toward overtly subjective modes of address. While photographer/filmmmakers in the first half of the twentieth century still held the belief tht the real world could be documented in film and photography in an objective fashion, that visual artists and audience shared a set of precepts about the nature of reality and its mass-mediated representations, a generation of post–World War II artists has increasingly turned their sights inward, convinced that an objective view is impossible, that the conscious construction of their own subjectivity is their only honest alternative. In this sense, these photographer/filmmakers are following a trend very much in evidence in all modern and postmodern art.

But what are we to make of the future? In the new electronic age of digital media, both film (moving images) and photography (still images) have moved ever closer together, both in terms of their formal characteristics and in terms of their use value. In cyberspace, on CD-Roms, on the internet, moving images and still images are constructed of the same electronic particles, plus and minus. It is probably a given that for all practical purposes, the photographic, that is, chemical technology at the base of film and photography will whither away, replaced by digital forms. The spaces of reception of the two media will, then, be the same: the video monitor. Both film and photography will have lost varying degrees of materiality, inherent in each medium. Given this new discursive space, one may ask, what new formal methodologies will photographers and filmmakers devise for this new space? Will the individual photograph cease to exist as a unit of meaning, replaced at best with series of still images? In what way will both electronically constituted media define new ways of seeing? Such questions cannot, of course, be answered here. They will, however, become increasingly important as we move into the next century and the age of instantaneous electronic information.

Notes

1. Paul Gsell in Auguste Rodin, *L'Art: Entretiens réunis par Paul Gsell,* as quoted in Paul Virilio, *The Vision Machine* (London: British Film Institute, 1994), 1 (trans. Julie Rose).

1. PHOTOGRAPHERS AND FILM

1. See Martin Sopocy, "A Narrated Cinema: The Pioneer Story of Films of James A. Williamson," *Cinema Journal* 18, no. 3 (fall 1978): 1–28.

2. See Charles Musser, *The Emergence of Cinema: The American Screen to 1907* (New York: Charles Scribner's Sons, 1990), 29ff.

3. A Swiss group in Zürich has put together an interesting series of such films. See the program brochure *Film und Fotografie* (Zürich: Filmstelle VSETH/VSU, 1991).

4. At the back of this volume, a filmography lists the most important photographers and their work in film.

5. Charles Wolfe, "Introduction," *Wide Angle* 9, no. 1 (1987): 4 (special issue on film and photography).

6. Pamela Allara, "Danny Lyon: From Photographs to Films: The Subject Imaged," in *Danny Lyon: Pictures from Films—Films from Pictures* (Medford, Mass.: Tufts University, 1983), n.p.

7. See Gene Moskowitz, *"Si j'avais quatre dromadaires,"* *Variety,* 14 December 1966.

8. See "G. G. Passion," *Monthly Film Bulletin*, May 1967, 80.

9. Swedish photographer Rune Hassner to the author, 19 December 1995.

10. The work of Allan Sekula, Sally Stein, Abigail Solomon-Godeau, Jan Zita Grover, and Douglas Crimp is particularly important in this respect.

11. My own work on avant-garde cinema has consistently included the studies of the links between photography and film. In particular see Ute Eskildsen and Jan-Christopher Horak, *Film und Foto der 20er Jahre* (Stuttgart: Gerd Hatje Verlag, 1979); and Jan-Christopher Horak, ed., *Lovers of Cinema: The First American Avant-Garde,1919–1945* (Madison: University of Wisconsin Press, 1995).

12. Curated by Katherine Schlesinger, the exhibition and film program was shown at the Photo Center Gallery of New York University in November and December 1987.

13. Tom Smith, *Moving Pictures: Films by Photographers* (New York: American Federation of the Arts, 1990, program brochure). The program included Man Ray's *L'etoile de mer* (1923), Ralph Steiner's *Mechanical Principles* (1931), Harry Callahan's *Motions* (1947), Willard Van Dyke's *Valley Town* (1940), Weegee's *Weegee's New York* (1948), Elliot Erwitt's *Beauty Knows No Pain* (1971), Ruth Orkin's *Little Fugitive* (1953), Cartier-Bresson's *Le retour* (1946), William Klein's *Broadway by Light* (1958), Paul and Menno de Nooijer's *At One View* (1989), Bruce Weber's *Broken Noses* (1987), and Danny Lyon's *Born to Film* (1981).

14. Many of the films were made available to the series through the artists themselves, since few of these films were in nontheatrical distribution.

15. The Strand exhibition catalogue does treat Strand's film work in much more detail. See Sarah Greenough, *Paul Strand: An American Vision* (Washington, D.C.: National Gallery of Art, 1990).

16. See exhibition catalogue by Sandra S. Phillips and Maria Morris Hambourg, *Helen Levitt* (San Francisco and New York: San Francisco Museum of Modern Art and Metropolitan Museum of Art, 1991).

17. Rudolf Arnheim, "On the Nature of Photography," *Critical Inquiry* 1, no. 1 (September 1974): 151, reprinted in *New Essays on the Psychology of Art,* by Rudolf Arnheim (Berkeley: University of California Press, 1986), 102–14. Clearly, Arnheim is influenced here by post–World War II developments in both film and photography. As in his earlier work, Arnheim emphasizes form as a controlling principle but also maintains his view that point of view constructs form.

18. André Bazin, *What Is Cinema?* trans. and ed. Hugh Grey (Berkeley: University of California Press, 1967), 15.

19. Siegfried Kracauer, *Theory of Film: The Redemption of Physical Reality* (London: Oxford University Press, 1960), ix.

20. Bazin, *What Is Cinema?* 21.

21. Vivian Sobchack, *The Address of the Eye: The Phenomenology of Film Experience* (Princeton: Princeton University Press, 1992), 58.

22. Stanley Cavell, *The World Viewed: Reflections on the Ontology of Film* (New York: Viking Press, 1971), 23–24.

23. Ibid.

24. Roland Barthes, *Die helle Kammer* (Frankfurt am Main: Surkamp Verlag, 1985), 115–16.

25. Gilles Deleuze, *Cinema 1: The Movement-Image* (Minneapolis: University of Minnesota Press, 1989), 2.

26. Ibid., 11.

27. Sobchack, *Address,* 60.

28. The literature here is voluminous. A good starting point is Philip Rosen, ed., *Narrative, Apparatus, Ideology: A Film Theory Reader* (New York: Columbia University Press, 1986).

29. See Hans Robert Jauss, *Toward an Aesthetics of Reception* (Minneapolis: University of Minnesota Press, 1982). See also Janet Staiger, *Interpreting Films: Studies in the Historical Reception of American Film* (Princeton: Princeton University Press, 1992).

30. Ferdinand de Saussure, *Course in General Linguistics,* trans. Wade Baskin (New York: McGraw-Hill, 1966).

31. Roland Barthes, *Image-Music-Text,* trans. Stephen Heath (New York: Hill and Wang, 1977), 44.

32. See Jean-Louis Baudry, "Ideological Effects of the Basic Apparatus," in Rosen, *Narrative,* 286–97.

33. Ibid., 291.

34. See David Bordwell, Janet Staiger, and Kristin Thompson, *The Classical Hollywood Cinema: Film Style and Mode of Production to 1960* (New York: Columbia University Press, 1985).

35. Stephan Heath, *Questions of Cinema* (Bloomington: Indiana University Press, 1981), 31.

36. Roland Barthes, *L'obvie et l'obtus* (Paris: Editions du Seuil, 1982), 59–60.

37. Roland Barthes, *Camera Lucida: Reflections on Photography,* trans. Richard Howard (New York: Hill & Wang, 1981), 19.

38. Barthes, *L'obvie et l'obtus,* 92.

39. Christian Metz, *The Imaginary Signifier: Psychoanalysis and the Cinema* (Bloomington: Indiana University Press, 1982), 43.

40. Ibid., 50.

41. Ibid., 57.

42. Christian Metz, "Photography and Fetish," *October* 34 (fall 1985): 81–90.

43. Ben Singer, "Film, Photography, and Fetish: The Analyses of Christian Metz," *Cinema Journal* 27, no. 4 (summer 1988): 13–14.

44. Ibid., 15–16.

45. Raymond Bellour, "The Pensive Spectator," *Wide Angle* 9, no. 1 (1987): 6–10.

46. Ibid., 6.

47. Ibid., 9.

48. Arnheim, "On the Nature of Photography," 151, 154.

49. Telephone interview with Helen Levitt, 2 September 1996.

2. CHRIS. MARKER

1. *La Chine* (1956) could not be found, although it certainly would have been germane to this study.

2. Chris. Marker, *Le dépays* (Paris: Éditions Herscher, 1982), translated into German by Roland Platte and Andreas Eisenhart as *Das Fremdland* (Berlin: Galrev Verlag, 1985).

3. Marker's other photo-book is *La renfermée: La Corse* (Paris: Editions du Seuil, 1981), with a text by Marie Susini. See also Marker and Jean-Claude Carrière (text), "Effets et gestes," *Vogue* (Paris) 752 (December 1994–January 1995): 208–11, 263.

4. One of the best early articles on Marker is Gilles Jacob, "Chris. Marker and the Mutants," *Sight and Sound* 35, no. 4 (autumn 1966): 165–68.

5. Quoted in Ian Cameron, "I Am Writing to You from a Far Country. . . ," *Movie* 3 (October 1962): 14.

6. Text taken from the 35mm print, distributed by New Yorker Films. The complete narration has been published in English as "Sunless" in *Semiotexte* 4, no. 3 (1984): 33–40. German translation, *Sans Soleil: Unsichtbare Sonne,* by Elmar Tophoven (Hamburg: AG-Kino, 1983). There are discrepancies between the German and English texts.

7. Chris. Marker, *Silent Movie* (Columbus, Ohio: Wexner Center for the Arts, 1995), 16.

8. Like many biographical details that Marker has refused to clarify, his exact date of birth is not known. Some sources say 22 July, others 29 July.

9. For example, organized in Germany and shown at the Munich Filmmuseum, a traveling retrospective was torpedoed by Marker when he refused to let any of his films made before 1963 be shown in the program.

10. The film won the prestigious Prix Jean Vigo in 1954.

11. Quoted in Sherri Geldin's foreword to the exhibition catalogue for *Silent Movie*, 6.

12. Chris. Marker has also produced a video in his *Zapping Zone* series (1985–90), which consists solely of photographs: *Photo. Browse* (301 photos). This video was unfortunately not available to the author.

13. Richard Roud, "Chris. Marker," in *Cinema: A Critical Dictionary: The Major Film-makers*, ed. Richard Roud, vol. 2, *Kinugasa to Zanussi* (New York: Viking Press, 1980), 668.

14. Text taken from the 35mm print, distributed by New Yorker Films. See also Marker, *Sans soleil*, 2.

15. See Jeanne Allen, "Self-Reflexivity in Documentary," *Cine-Tracts* 1, no. 2 (summer 1977): 41–42. *Letter from Siberia* was apparently yanked from the Karlový Vary Film Festival when the Russian government protested that the film had been shot in Siberia without permission. In point of fact, they were unhappy with the results after having authorized Marker's shoot. See Gene Moskowitz, "Foreign Films," *Variety*, 26 November 1958, 22.

16. Film script published in Chris. Marker, *Commentaires 1* (Paris: Editions du Seuil, 1967), 58.

17. Marker's fascination with space travel is abundantly apparent in film after film. While he maintains that he contributed nothing to *Les astronautes* (1959)

(James Quandt to author, 26 October 1993), *La joli mai* includes a sequence in which Marker questions a child about space travel at an exhibition of John Glenn's space capsule. In *Si j'avais quatre dromadaires,* Marker inserts a sequence with rocket ships, which, like photography, allow for travel at the speed of light. In *Sans soleil,* we see a Polaris missile launched.

18. Chris. Marker, "Terminal Vertigo," *Monthly Film Bulletin* 51, no. 606 (July 1984): 197.

19. See also Orkun Ertener: "Filmen, als ob sich filmen ließe: Über das Bilder-sammeln und Filmemachen in Chris. Markers *Sans soleil,*" *Augenblick* 10 (June 1991): 44–45.

20. Marker, *Sans soleil,* 2.

21. Translated by the author: "La photo, c'est la chasse, c'est l'instinct de chasse sans l'envie de tuer. C'est la chasse des anges.... On traque, on vise, on tire et—cla! au lieu d'un mort, on fait un eternal." Film script in Chris. Marker, *Commentaires 2* (Paris: Editions du Seuil, 1967), 87.

22. Marker, *Das Fremdland,* n.p. Translated from the German by the author.

23. Marie Susini, *La renfermée: La Corse,* with photographs by Chris. Marker (Paris: Editions du Seuil, 1981).

24. See Musser, *Emergence of Cinema,* 40–41.

25. Marker, *Das Fremdland,* n.p. Translated from the German by the author.

26. Terrence Rafferty, "Marker Changes Trains," *Sight and Sound* 53, no. 5 (autumn 1984): 286.

27. James Quandt, "Grin without a Cat," *Cinematheque Ontario Programme Guide* (fall 1993): 4.

3. HELMAR LERSKI

1. Helmar Lerski, *Köpfe des Alltags* (Berlin: Hermann Reckendorf Verlag, 1931).

2. Ute Eskildsen and Jan-Christopher Horak, eds., *Helmar Lerski, Lichtbildner* (Essen: Museum Folkwang, 1982), 25. This catalogue was published in German and English in conjunction with a retrospective exhibition shown at Folkwang Museum (Essen) in 1982 and the Tel Aviv Museum, March 1983.

3. Curt Glaser, in Lerski, *Köpfe des Alltags,* 10. See also Glaser, "Der Photograph Lerski," *Berliner Börsenkurier* 271 (3 December 1930).

4. *Das Tagebuch* 12, no. 15 (11 April 1931); Herbert Starke, "Köpfe des Alltags," *Der Arbeiter-Fotograf* 6 (1931).

5. See Helmar Lerski, *Metamorphosis through Light/Verwandlung durch Licht* (Freren: Luca Verlag, 1982).

6. For a complete biography of Lerski see Eskildsen and Horak, *Helmar Lerski,* 6–29.

7. Sidney Allan (pseudonym), "A New Departure in Light and Shade Arrange-ments," *Photo-Era* 29, no. 5 (November 1912): 226–28.

8. Anneliese Lerski, ed., *Der Mensch: Mein Bruder* (Dresden: VEB Verlag, 1958), 17.

9. *Der Film*, 25 March 1916, n.p. William Wauer (1886–1962) was an artist, a member of the Berlin Sturm group, a novelist, and a theater and film director.

10. *Der Kinematograph*, 19 July 1916, n.p.

11. Robert Reinert (1873–1928) became artistic director of the Deutsche-Bioscop Film Company in 1917, having previously worked as a scriptwriter for the Projektions-Union, where Lerski and Wauer also worked.

12. *Der Film*, 21 April 1917, n.p.

13. *Die Licht-Bild-Bühne*, 4 August 1917, n.p.

14. The original nitrate negative was discovered in Munich in 1994, and a new 35mm print was generated by the Munich Filmmuseum, allowing for the film's breathtaking cinematography to be fully appreciated.

15. In Munich, Reinert founded the Monumental Film GmbH, which was later subsumed under the Emelka (Münchner Lichtspielkunst) after Reinert became the latter's director of production. *Nerves* was recently acquired by the Munich Filmmuseum from Gosfilmofond (Moscow), which holds the only surviving material.

16. *Der Kinematograph*, 31 December 1919.

17. See reviews in *Der Kinematograph*, 4 December 1922, 10; *Die Licht-Bild-Bühne*, 16 December 1922, 16.

18. Quoted in *Der Film*, 25 January 1925, n.p.; *Die Filmtechnik* 2, no. 23 (13 November 1926): 463.

19. *Die Filmwoche*, 4 February 1925, 135. The tinted print of the film was recently restored through the joint efforts of the Nederlands Filmmuseum (Amsterdam) and the Munich Filmmuseum.

20. Siegfried Kracauer, *From Caligari to Hitler* (Princeton: Princeton University Press, 1947), 112.

21. *Der Filmkurier*, 18 December 1926, n.p.

22. See Bèla Balàsz, *Der sichtbare Mensch oder die Kultur des Films* (Vienna/Leipzig: Deutsch-Österreichischer Verlag, 1924), 73ff.; and Bèla Balàsz, *Der Geist des Films* (Halle a. d. Saale: Verlag Wilhelm Knapp, 1930), 86.

23. *Close-Up* 2 (November 1928): 60.

24. After being forced to emigrate to France and then to the United States in 1933 due to the Nazis, Schüfftan was unable to work legally for years, because he could not join the American Society of Cinematographers. He was eventually vindicated when he won an Academy Award for *Hud* (1960).

25. See *Kinematograph Weekly*, 13 January 1927, 105.

26. Helmar Lerski to Bertold Viertel, 18 January 1930.

27. Helmar Lerski to Charles Peignot, editor of *Arts et Métiers Graphiques*, 1931, Lerski Estate Collection, Museum Folkwang, Essen, Germany.

28. According to Anneliese Lerski, the Nazis had threatened Lerski because of his proposed book, "Jewish Heads." See Eskildsen and Horak, *Helmar Lerski*, 15 n. 55.

29. Postcard, Anneliese Lerski to Helmar Lerski, 6 September 1932.

30. See Jan-Christopher Horak, "Zionist Film Propaganda in Nazi Germany," *Historical Journal for Film, Radio & Television* 4, no. 1 (1984). For a history of Zionist film efforts in the silent period, see also Hillel Tryster, *Israel before Israel* (Jerusalem: Steven Spielberg Archive, 1995).

31. Gal Esser to Leo Herrmann, 22 March 1934, Central Zionist Archives, Keren Hayesod (hereafter KH), 4B/1202.

32. See Curt Kramarski, "The Palestine Film for Palestine: An Interview with Helmar Lerski," *Palestine Post,* 12 July 1935.

33. M. Y. Ben-gavriel, "Lerskys Palästina-Film," *Jüdische Rundschau* 40, nos. 33–34 (26 April 1935): n.p.

34. Karl Schwarz, "Lerskis Film *Avodah,*" in *Jüdische Rundschau* 40, no. 65 (13 August 1935): 7.

35. Curt Kramarski, "*Avodah* at the Rimon Cinema, Tel Aviv," *Palestine Post,* 19 July 1935.

36. Quoted in "The Film of Palestine," *Palestine Post,* 21 May 1935.

37. See *Neue Züricher Zeitung* 1634 (22 September 1935): 2.

38. Arthur Engländer, "Gedanken über den Palästinafilm *Avodah,*" *Selbstwehr* 32, no. 13 (1 April 1938): 6.

39. Arthur Hantke to Leo Herrmann, 27 March 1935, KH, 4B/1202.

40. Leo Herrmann to Palästina Filmstelle, Berlin, 11 March 1936, KH, 4B/1290. An excellent article on *The Land of Promise* appeared recently: Hillel Tryster, "*The Land of Promise* (1935): A Case Study in Zionist Film Propaganda," *Historical Journal for Film, Radio & Television* 15, no. 2 (June 1995): 187ff.

41. Manfred Epstein to Leo Herrmann, 30 April 1937; and Leo Herrmann to Paul Boroschek, 8 July 1937; L. Herrmann to Epstein, 26 April 1938, KH, 4B/1202, 378.

42. Hans Feld to Helmar Lerski, 28 June 1935, Folkwang Museum, Essen. Lost for over fifty years, a nitrate print of *Avodah* was discovered in the Academy Cinema, where Lerski also exhibited his *Metamorphosis through Light* in 1938. It was preserved by the British Film Institute, and a print is now available at George Eastman House and at the Jerusalem Cinematheque.

43. Leo Herrmann to Arthur Bergmann, Prague, 15 March 1936. See also Leo Herrmann to Kol Noa Institute, 26 April 1938, KH, 4B/1202, 378.

44. See Horak, "Zionist Film Propaganda," 49ff.

45. Arthur Hantke to Leo Herrmann, 27 March 1935, KH 4B/1202.

46. The author found this footage in Hungary when he organized a Lerski exhibition in 1982. It has been preserved by the Bundesarchiv, Koblenz, Germany.

47. Quoted in Eskildsen and Horak, *Helmar Lerski,* 25.

48. Interview with Petruschka, Jerusalem, 9 March 1983. See also *Jüdische Rundschau* 17, 26 February 1935. Weissgerber also performed "Hebrew Melody" publicly on 11 April 1935 in Berlin at a benefit concert for the Keren Kayemeth.

49. Max Prager (Vienna) to Leo Herrmann, 3 March 1936, KH, 4B/1202.

50. "Lerski at Seventy," *Palestine Post,* 21 February 1941.

51. According to officials at Histadrut, these films must be considered lost, although I hope they will still be found in the archives of the Labor Council.

52. Manfred Geis, "Helmar Lerski at 75," *Palestine Post,* 28 February 1946; "Vortrag Helmar Lerski," *Mitteilungsblatt Alija Chadascha* 10, no. 12 (22 March 1946).

53. Compare Norman Bertwich, *Ben-Shemen: Children's Village in Israel* (Paris, 1956). Films with similar narrative lines are *My Father's House* (1946), *The Great Betrayal* (1947), and *Out of Evil* (1951).

54. Anneliese Lerski to Ernst Loewy, 15 July 1961; Anneliese Lerski to Stettner, 2 April 1962. No print of *Adamah* in its original form is known to have survived.

55. Quoted in a press brochure for *Adamah.* No date.

56. Ibid.

57. *New York Times,* 11 April 1949, reprinted in *New York Times Film Reviews* (New York: Arno Press, 1970), n.p. See also *New York Herald Tribune,* 11 April 1949.

4. PAUL STRAND

1. P. Adams Sidney, ed., *The Essential Cinema: Essays on the Films in the Collection of Anthology Film Archives* (New York: New York University Press, 1975), xiii–xviii.

2. Janet Bergstrom, "The Avant-Garde," *Screen* 20, nos. 3–4, reprinted in *Movies and Methods,* vol. 2, ed. Bill Nichols (Berkeley: University of California Press, 1985).

3. See Horak, *Lovers of Cinema.*

4. Ironically, P. Adams Sitney makes a similar case for the romantic attitudes of the second avant-garde. See P. Adams Sitney, *Visionary Film: The American Avant-Garde* (New York: Oxford University Press, 1979), 46, 129–30.

5. The first part of this chapter is a revised version of an article that first appeared as "Modernist Perspectives and Romantic Desire: *Manhatta,*" *Afterimage* 15, no. 4 (November 1987): 8–15.

6. Stephen Dwoskin, *Film Is . . . The International Free Cinema* (Woodstock, N.Y.: Overlook Press, 1975), 34; Sheldon Renan, *The American Underground Film* (New York: E. P. Dutton, 1967), 75.

7. Lewis Jacobs, "Avant-Garde Production in America," in *Experiment in the Film,* ed. Roger Manvell (London: Grey Walls Press, 1949; New York: Arno Press, 1970).

8. Scott Hammen, "Sheeler and Strand's 'Manhatta': A Neglected Masterpiece," *Afterimage* 6, no. 6 (January 1979): 6–7.

9. Nancy Newhall, *Paul Strand: Photographs, 1915–1945* (New York: Museum of Modern Art, 1945); Constance Rourke, *Artist in the American Tradition* (New York: Harcourt, Brace, 1938).

10. Dickran Tashjian, *Skyscraper Primitives: Dada and the American Avant-Garde* (Middletown, Conn.: Wesleyan University Press, 1975), 221–23.

11. Naomi Rosenblum, "Paul Strand: The Early Years, 1910–1932" (Ph.D. diss., City University of New York, 1978), 96–105.

12. Theodore E. Stebbins Jr. and Norman Keyes Jr., *Charles Sheeler: The Photographs* (Boston: Museum of Fine Arts, 1987), 17–21.

13. See "Narrative Chronology," in *Paul Strand: Essays on His Life and Work,* ed. Maren Stange (New York: Aperture, 1990), 259ff.

14. Paul Strand, interview with Milton Brown and Walter Rosenblum, November 1971, transcript in the Paul Strand papers, Archives of American Art, 8–9.

15. According to Ted Stebbins, Sheeler made at least two other films in this period. The photographer Morton Shamberg appeared with a parakeet in the first, which may have been shot as early as 1914–15. The second, produced ca. 1918–19, featured Katherine Baird Shaffer, Sheeler's future wife, in a series of close-up nude shots. Neither film survives, so that all that remains are one still from the former, and a series of stills from the latter film. See Stebbins and Keyes, *Charles Sheeler,* 15–17.

16. Another nebulous area concerns the film's original title. Shortly before his death, Strand suggested in a letter to Richard Shales that Sheeler had "proposed that we might make a kind of experimental film about New York together—a silent film carried along by the titles which we took from Walt Whitman's poem." None of the surviving correspondence mentions the title of the film, however, and Strand in later years alternately called it *Manhatta* and *Mannahatta,* so its original title remains unknown. Strand and Sheeler's press release makes no mention of Whitman at all but indicates instead that the intertitles to the film were "by the Rialto," the New York cinema where *Manhatta* premiered commercially. Although some critics have suggested that the intertitles were added later—just as the title may have been changed later to reflect the film's Whitmanesque content—there seems to be ample internal evidence to suggest that the intertitles were in keeping with Strand and Sheeler's intentions and not just a means of legitimizing the film to an intellectual audience.

The film was released under the title of *New York the Magnificent,* a title possibly chosen by the Rialto, possibly to emphasize its position in the program as a "scenic." When the film was screened in Paris in 1922, the title had been changed to *Fumée de New York (Smoke of New York).* Finally, the film appeared at the London Film Society in 1927 displaying the title *Manhatta.* That particular print was preserved by the British Film Institute and is the master material for all surviving prints circulating in the United States.

17. Stieglitz to Strand, 27 October 1920, Stieglitz Archive, Center for Creative Photography, Tucson.

18. Harriet Underhill, *New York Tribune,* 26 July 1921, 6.

19. Robert Allerton Parker, "The Art of the Camera: An Experimental Film," *Arts & Decoration* 15, no. 6 (October 1921): 369.

20. Ibid.

21. Naomi Rosenblum gave a copy of the press release to the Museum of Modern Art Film Department in 1978.

22. *Camera Work* 35 (October 1911); see also Hammen, "Sheeler and Strand's 'Manhatta,'" 6.

23. *Vanity Fair* 15, no. 5 (January 1921): 72.

24. *Vanity Fair* 18, no. 2 (April 1922): 51.

25. Charles Sheeler, *The Rouge: The Image of Industry in the Art of Charles Sheeler and Diego Rivera* (Detroit: Detroit Institute of Arts, 1978).

26. Hammen, "Sheeler and Strand's 'Manhatta,'" 7.

27. Sergei Eisenstein, "A Dialectic Approach to Film Form" (1929), in *Film Form* (New York: Harcourt, Brace, 1949), 45–63.

28. Alfred Stieglitz, "How I Came to Photograph Clouds," *Amateur Photographer & Photography* 56, no. 1819 (1923): 255, reprinted in *Photographers on Photography*, ed. Nathan Lyons (Englewood Cliffs, N.J.: Prentice Hall, 1966), 111–12.

29. Walt Whitman, *Leaves of Grass: Comprehensive Readers Edition,* ed. Harold W. Blodgett and Scully Bradley (New York: W. W. Norton, 1965). All quotes are from this edition.

30. See, for example, Hammen, "Sheeler and Strand's 'Manhatta,'" 7.

31. Alfred Stieglitz, "How the Steerage Happened," *Twice-a-Year* 8/9 (1942): 105–36, reprinted in Lyon, *Photographers,* 130.

32. Abigail Solomon-Godeau: "The Return of Alfred Stieglitz," *Afterimage* 12, nos. 1–2 (summer 1984): 22.

33. Paul Strand, "Photography and the New God," *Broom* 3, no. 4 (1922): 252–58; reprinted in Lyon, *Photographers,* 143.

34. Lyon, *Photographers,* 141.

35. Ibid., 143.

36. Greenough, *Paul Strand,* 41.

37. Ulrich Keller, "An Art Historical View of Strand," *Image* 17, no. 4 (December 1974): 11.

38. Paul Strand, "Realism: A Personal View," *Sight and Sound* 18 (January 1950): 23–27.

39. See Rosenblum, *Paul Strand.* See also Greenough, *Paul Strand,* 166 n. 62.

40. Quoted in Calvin Tomkins, "Profile," in *Paul Strand: Sixty Years of Photographs* (Millerton, N.Y.: Aperture, 1976).

41. See Jan-Christopher Horak, "G. W. Pabst in Hollywood or Every Modern Hero Deserves a Mother," *Film History* 1, no. 1 (June 1987): 57, reprinted in *The Films of G. W. Pabst: An Extraterritorial Cinema,* ed. Eric Rentschler (New Brunswick, N.J.: Rutgers University Press, 1990).

42. See William Alexander, *Film on the Left: American Documentary Film from 1931 to 1942* (Princeton: Princeton University Press, 1981), 70.

43. Greenough, *Paul Strand,* 44.

44. For an excellent summary of the film's production history see Alexander, *Film on the Left,* 70–74. See also William Alexander, "Paul Strand as Filmmaker, 1933–1942," in *Paul Strand: Essays on His Life and Work,* ed. Maren Stange (New York: Aperture, 1990), 148–60.

45. Henwar Rodakiewicz, "Documentary: A Personal View," *Film Library Quarterly* 2, no. 3 (summer): 35.

46. Sidney Meyers, "Paul Strand's Photography Reaches Heights in *The Wave,*" *Daily Worker,* 4 May 1937, quoted in Russell Campbell, *Cinema Strikes Back: Radi-*

cal Filmmaking in the United States, 1930–1942 (Ann Arbor: UMI Research Press, 1982), 131.

47. Alexander, *Film on the Left,* 77.

48. Paul Strand, *Photographs of Mexico,* with a foreword by Leo Hurwitz (New York: Virginia Stevens, 1940), reprinted as *The Mexican Portfolio* (New York: Aperture/Da Capo Press, 1967).

49. Katherine C. Ware, "Photographs of Mexico, 1940," in *Paul Strand: Essays on His Life and Work,* ed. Maren Stange (New York: Aperture, 1990), 113.

50. See John Rohrbach, "*Time in New England:* Creating a Usable Past," and Estelle Jussim, "*Bombed Church,* Host en Moselle, 1950," in *Paul Strand: Essays on His Life and Work,* ed. Maren Stange (New York: Aperture, 1990), 163, 183.

51. See Alexander, *Film on the Left,* 97–101.

52. Campbell, *Cinema Strikes Back,* 166–69.

53. Rohrbach, "*Time in New England,*" 163.

54. For a complete history of the film's production, see Alexander, *Film on the Left,* 206–14.

55. Ibid., 237.

56. Paul Strand, *La France de profil,* text by Claude Roy (Lausanne: La Guilde du Livre, 1952).

57. Paul Strand, *Un paese,* text by Cesare Zavattini (Turin: Giulio Einaudi, 1955).

58. Paul Strand, *Tir a'Mhurain,* text by Basil Davidson (Dresden: VEB Verlag der Kunst, 1962; also London: MacGibbon and Kee, 1969; reprint, New York: Aperture, 1969).

59. Paul Strand, *Living Egypt,* text by James Aldridge (VEB Verlag der Kunst, 1969); and Paul Strand, *Ghana: An African Portrait,* text by Basil Davidson (Millerton, N.Y.: Aperture, 1976).

5. LÁSZLÓ MOHOLY-NAGY

1. Barbara Rose, "Kinetic Solutions to Pictorial Problems: The Films of Man Ray and Moholy-Nagy," *Artforum* 10, no. 1 (September 1971): 73.

2. László Moholy-Nagy, *Vision in Motion* (Chicago: Paul Theobald, 1947), 273.

3. Sibyl Moholy-Nagy, *Moholy-Nagy: Experiment in Totality* (New York: Harper Brothers, 1950), 74.

4. Jeanpaul Goergen, *m-n 100. Zum 100. Geburtstag von László Moholy-Nagy,* program brochure, Bauhaus-Archiv, Berlin, 20 July 1995, 2.

5. Ibid.

6. Jan-Christopher Horak, "Film and Foto: Towards a Language of Silent Film," *Afterimage* 7, no. 5 (December 1979): 11.

7. S. Moholy-Nagy, *Moholy-Nagy,* 79.

8. Compare Rose, "Kinetic Solutions," 72; Terence A. Senter, *L. Moholy-Nagy*

(London: Arts Council of Britain, 1980), 52; and Andrea Kaliski Miller, "Films," in *Moholy-Nagy: Photography and Film in Weimar Germany,* ed. Eleanor M. Hight (Wellesley, Mass.: Wellesley College Museum, 1985), 129.

9. Nancy Nugent, "László Moholy-Nagy: A Chronology," in *Moholy-Nagy: Photography and Film in Weimar Germany,* ed. Eleanor M. Hight (Wellesley, Mass.: Wellesley College Museum, 1985), 138.

10. László Moholy-Nagy, "Constructivism and the Proletariat," *MA* (May 1922), quoted in *László Moholy-Nagy* (Stuttgart: Verlag Gert Hatje, 1974), 16.

11. László Moholy-Nagy, *Painting, Photography, Film* (London: Lund Humphries, 1969), 9; originally published in German as *Malerei, Fotografie, Film* (Berlin, 1925).

12. L. Moholy-Nagy, *Painting,* 24.

13. László Moholy-Nagy, "Produktion-Reproduktion," *De Stijl* 5 (July 1922): 98–100; English translation in Andreas Haus, *Moholy-Nagy: Photographs and Photograms* (New York, 1980): 46–47.

14. Hight, *Moholy-Nagy,* 15.

15. Ibid., 18.

16. L. Moholy-Nagy, *Painting,* 124–37.

17. Ibid., 38.

18. Hight, *Moholy-Nagy,* 45.

19. L. Moholy-Nagy, *Painting,* 122.

20. The script is reprinted in Richard Kostelanetz, ed., *Moholy-Nagy* (New York Praeger Publishers, 1970), 124–30. The photo-montage is published in L. Moholy-Nagy, *Vision,* 285.

21. First published as "Probleme des neuen Films," *Die Form* 5 (May 1932).

22. "Der sprechende Film," reprinted in *i10 Internationale Revue* l, nos. 17–18.

23. "Problems of the Modern Film," reprinted in English in Kostelanetz, *Moholy-Nagy,* 131.

24. L. Moholy-Nagy, *Vision,* 288–89.

25. Quoted in the excellent monograph by Joseph Harris Canton, *The Utopian Vision of Moholy-Nagy* (Ann Arbor: UMI Research Press, 1984), 36.

26. See Goergen, *m-n 100,* 2.

27. See L. Moholy-Nagy, "Neue Filmexperimente," *Korunk* 3 (1933), quoted in Krisztina Passuth, *Moholy-Nagy* (Weingarten, 1968), 381. The film was bought by John Grierson, at that time director of the Empire Marketing Board, who had the film cut up and portions edited into a series of experimental thirty-second advertising films, called Poster films. Paul Rotha, *Documentary Diary* (London: Secker & Warburg, 1973), 136. At least two other Bauhaus alumni were working on similar kinetic light sculptures in film—Kurt Schwerdtfeder designed *Farbenlichtspiel* (1921–23), and Ludwig Hirschfeld-Mack, *Reflektorische Farbenspiele* (1921–23)—both of which, as their titles indicate, involved color film. However, neither artist was able to realize his conceptions on film until the mid-1960s.

28. L. Moholy-Nagy, "Neue Filmexperimente," 34.

29. L. Moholy-Nagy, *Painting,* 28.

30. S. Moholy-Nagy, *Moholy-Nagy,* 75.

31. L. Moholy-Nagy, *Vision,* 273.

32. See *Der Kinematograph* 47 (8 March 1932), quoted in Goergen, *m-n 100,* 2. *A Light Play in Black-White-Gray* was also exhibited at the London Film Society on 20 November 1932 and twice in December 1932 in Frankfurt aum Main and Nuremberg, respectively.

33. Dr. H., "Konstruktives Lichtspiel in der Kamera," *Die Licht-Bild-Bühne* 58 (9 March 1932), quoted in Georgen, *m-n 100,* 3.

34. See Goergen, *m-n 100,* for a listing of all the reviews to the film.

35. Jan-Christopher Horak, "Prometheus Film Collective, 1925–1932: German Communist Kinokultur, Part I," *Jump Cut* 26 (1981): 39–41.

36. S. Moholy-Nagy, *Moholy-Nagy,* 74.

37. Ibid., 78.

38. Ibid., 83.

39. Jan-Christopher Horak, "Parallel Editing Structures in Dziga Vertov's *The Man with a Movie Camera,"* in *Untersuchungen zur Syntax des Films,* ed. Karl Dietmar Moeller (Münster, Germany: MAKS-Verlag, 1985).

40. Sigmund Freud, *Neue Folge der Vorlesungen zur Einfuhrung in die Psycho-analyse. Gesammelte Werke,* Bd. 15 (London, 1938). English translation, *New Intro-ductory Lectures on Psychoanalysis,* standard edition, vol. 22, chap. 4 (London: S. Fischer, 1940), 108.

41. See Senter, *L. Moholy-Nagy,* 28.

42. S. Moholy-Nagy, *Moholy-Nagy,* 83.

43. This film survives at the Galerie Alvensleven, Munich. Barbara Rose mentions *Architects' Congress* but gives the wrong title. She also mentions a second film, *Street Scene: Finland* (1933), but no evidence for the existence of this film has surfaced. See Rose, "Kinetic Solutions," 65. Hattula Moholy-Nagy says about *Street Scene,* "I do not remember hearing about it when my father was alive, and it was not among the films inherited from my mother."

44. The thirty-eight-minute film was apparently first shown at the London Film Society on 10 December 1933: the print names the Film Society as presenter. See also "Film Society Programme (67th Performance)," reprinted in *The Film Society Programmes 1925–1939* (New York: Arno Press, 1972), 272–73.

45. Founded in 1928 at the Swiss château of its patroness, Hélène de Mandrot, CIAM was a liberal, reformist organization of modern architects. Moholy-Nagy belonged to the revolutionary "functionalist" wing of the organization (mostly Germans), which also included a French "formalist" wing. See Charles Jencks, *Modern Movements in Architecture* (Garden City, N.J.: Anchor Books, 1973), 36ff.

46. The Film Society notes state: "The Fourth International Congress for Modern Architecture took place on the miniature Greek liner *Patris II,* starting from Marseilles on July 29th and arriving at Athens on August 1st. The party then spent five days exploring the Greek Archipelago, reassembled on board on August 10th, and

finished up at Marseilles on August 13th. Twenty-five countries were represented. . . . The main topic for discussion was 'the functional town.'" See Jencks, *Modern Movements.*

47. Jencks, *Modern Movements.*

48. See Karol Kulik, *Alexander Korda* (London: W. H. Allen, 1975; and London: Virgin Books, 1990), 149.

6. HELEN LEVITT

1. Sandra S. Phillips and Maria Morris Hambourg, *Helen Levitt* (San Francisco and New York: San Francisco Museum of Modern Art and Metropolitan Museum of Art, 1991).

2. See Maria Morris Hambourg, "Helen Levitt: A Life in Part," in Phillips and Hambourg, *Helen Levitt,* 58.

3. See Lauren Rabinovitz's essay, "Mary Ellen Bute," in *Lovers of Cinema: The First American Film Avant-Garde, 1919–1945,* ed. Jan-Christopher Horak (Madison: University of Wisconsin Press, 1995).

4. Lauren Rabinovitz, *Points of Resistance: Women, Power and Politics in the New York Avant-Garde Cinema, 1943–71* (Urbana and Chicago: University of Illinois Press, 1991).

5. Peter Lehman, "For Whom Does the Light Shine? Thoughts on the Avant-Garde," *Wide Angle* 7, nos. 1–2 (1985): 70. See also Sitney, *Essential Cinema.*

6. Phillips and Hambourg, *Helen Levitt,* 59.

7. Telephone interview with Helen Levitt, 13 October 1993.

8. For complete biographical information, see Phillips and Hambourg, *Helen Levitt,* 45–56.

9. Ibid., 49.

10. Ibid., 53–55.

11. *PM's Weekly,* 11 August 1940, quoted in Phillips and Hambourg, *Helen Levitt,* 25.

12. The earliest documentary evidence of Helen's involvement at CIAA is a letter from Joan McPeak to Leonard Rapport dated 19 April 1942. Thanks to Mr. Rapport for quoting it to me. Also, telephone interview with Helen Levitt, 13 October 1993. See also Bruce Kararoff, "Joris Ivens Records History in the Making," *Knickerbocker Holiday,* 19 July 1943, 19–25.

13. "U.S. and Rockefeller Aim Films at Latin Leaders," *Motion Picture Herald,* 11 April 1942, 23. For a general discussion of the Office of the Coordinator of Inter-American Affairs, see Richard Dyer McCann, *The People's Films* (New York: Hastings House, 1973), 148ff.

14. See "First Latin 'Godwill' Films Arrive in the U.S.," *Motion Picture Herald,* 14 March 1942, 27.

15. Interview with Helen Levitt, 22 January 1994.

16. See Luis Buñuel to Iris Barry, 30 June 1943, Museum of Modern Art Special Collections. See also *Motion Picture Herald,* June 1943; and Luis Buñuel, *My Last Sigh* (New York: Vintage Books, 1984), 182–83, which gives the impression that he resigned in November 1942.

17. Helen Levitt to Leonard Rapport, 22 April 1943, quoted in Rapport to author, 9 February 1994. Interview with Helen Levitt, 13 October 1993.

18. Helen Levitt to Leonard Rapport, 14 September 1943, quoted in Rapport to author, 9 February 1994.

19. There is a photo of Levitt holding a Signal Corps 35mm camera in Phillips and Hambourg, *Helen Levitt,* 56, fig. 45, but according to Hambourg, the footage shot was in 16mm.

20. Ibid., 57.

21. Levitt and Loeb had never intended to release the film and therefore shot it at silent speed. The Museum of Modern Art Film Circulating Library presently distributes prints with an audio cassette of music recorded by MOMA's pianist, Arthur Kleiner, who played for the film at its initial MOMA screening.

22. Helen Levitt, *A Way of Seeing,* with an essay by James Agee (New York: Horizon Press, 1981). According to Maria Morris Hambourg, Agee's involvement in *In the Street* was minimal, confined to one or two forays with the camera. Most of the footage was shot at silent speed (18 fps) by Levitt and Loeb who worked in tandem with two cameras. See Phillips and Hambourg, *Helen Levitt,* 58. There is some debate as to the role played by Agee in the film production. Bergreen gives Agee much more credit, stating that he participated in the shooting (with Levitt) at least three times. See Laurence Bergreen, *James Agee: A Life* (New York: Dutton, 1984), 293.

23. See James Agee and Walker Evans, *Let Us Now Praise Famous Men* (New York: Houghton Mifflin, 1941). See also Phillips and Hambourg, *Helen Levitt,* 63 n. 8; and Bergreen, *James Agee,* 292.

24. Levitt, *Way of Seeing,* v.

25. For a discussion of cinema verité, see Stephen Mamber, *Cinema Verité in America: Studies in Uncontrolled Documentary* (Cambridge: MIT Press, 1974).

26. See Levitt, *Way of Seeing,* plates 15, 20, 51, 53, and 66.

27. Phillips and Hambourg, *Helen Levitt,* 27.

28. See, for example, Julia Kristeva, "Word, Dialogue, and Novel," in *Desire in Language: A Semiotic Approach to Literature and Art* (New York: Columbia University Press, 1980); and Robert Stam, *Subversive Pleasures: Bakhtin, Cultural Criticism, and Film* (Baltimore: Johns Hopkins University Press, 1989).

29. See Mikhail Bakhtin, *Rabelais and His World,* trans. Helene Iswolsky (Bloomington: Indiana University Press, 1984), 235 and all of chapter 3.

30. Ibid., 255.

31. Stam, *Subversive Pleasures,* 96.

32. Ibid., 110. *In the Street* won an award in the experimental film category at the 1955 Cleveland Film Festival.

33. Directed by Julien Duvivier, *Poil de carotte (Carrot Head)* is a sensitive portrayal of a young boy brutalized by his environment.

34. *Los Angeles Times,* 8 April 1949. The film played at the Beverly-Canon Theatre in Los Angeles.

35. Ibid. See also Phillips and Hambourg, *Helen Levitt,* 58; and Bergreen, *James Agee,* 293.

36. "Production Notes," *The Quiet One,* Academy of Motion Picture Arts and Sciences, Clippings files.

37. See *Hollywood Reporter,* 12 November 1948; and *Vogue,* 1 March 1949.

38. Levitt, Loeb, and Meyers edited the film in a cold-water flat on 114th Street, and Meyers handled the final cut. Levitt's brother was brought in for the sound mix. Interview with Helen Levitt, 22 January 1994. See also "Production Notes."

39. See Bosley Crowther, "The Quiet One," *New York Times,* 14 February 1949 and 20 February 1949. See also *Variety,* 15 February 1949; *Fortnight,* 15 March 1949; and *Hollywood Reporter,* 17 February 1949.

40. Walter Rosenblum, *"The Quiet One," Photo Notes,* spring 1949, 24.

41. As scripted by James Agee, who wrote the film's commentary after the film was edited, the film's narrative construction is indeed too tight, and one gets the impression that its psychoanalytic bent was incorporated to please the Wiltwyck people. According to Levitt, psychoanalysis was "all the rage" when they made the film.

42. See *New York Times,* 6 March 1949, Academy of Motion Picture Arts and Science, Clippings files.

43. Interview with Helen Levitt, 22 January 1994.

44. The film was originally titled *The Stairs.* See *Los Angeles Times,* 20 May 1951. See also *Saturday Review,* 12 May 1951.

45. Interview with Helen Levitt, 22 January 1994.

46. The film was almost universally praised, although some of the more moralistic American critics objected to its content. See, for example, A. H. Weiler, "The Savage Eye," *New York Times,* 7 June 1960, 27; *Variety,* 16 September 1959; Paul Rotha, "Eyes on the World," *Films and Filming* 6, no. 4 (January 1960); and *Time,* 23 May 1960. Interestingly, that champion of New American Cinema, Jonas Mekas, was one of the film's most severe critics, attacking its cynicism and disgust with the world, calling it "an imaginary movie made by imaginary film-makers," and a "tutti-frutti." See Jonas Mekas, *Village Voice,* 23 June 1960, reprinted in Jonas Mekas, *Movie Journal: The Rise of a New American Cinema* (New York: Collier Books, 1972), 16–17.

47. According to an unpublished press-release biography of Joseph Strick, *The Savage Eye* cost only $42,000.

48. See *Filmfacts* 3, no. 28 (12 August 1960): 167.

49. Jonathan Rosenbaum, "The Savage Eye/Shadows," in *The American New Wave,* 1958–1967 (Minneapolis: Walker Art Center, 1982), 30.

50. Several of these sequences might be fruitfully analyzed in terms of the carni-valesque, but it is unclear whether Levitt was involved in them.

51. Approximately two-thirds of the budget was put up by Continental, the production arm of Walter Reade Theatres, while independent producer Dana Holdgdon contributed one-third.

52. See *New Republic,* 23 March 1963; *Hollywood Reporter,* 23 April 1963; and *Variety,* 21 March 1963.

53. Eugene Archer, "An Affair of the Skin," *New York Times,* 21 November 1963, 43.

54. Arthur Knight, *Saturday Review,* 30 November 1963, quoted in *Filmfacts* 6, no. 47 (January 1964). See also Judith Christ, *New York Herald Tribune,* 21 November 1963; *Time,* 6 December 1963; and Helen Weldon Kuhn, *Films in Review* 14, no. 9 (November 1963).

55. Played by Diana Sands, the character was only incidently a black women, and the film hardly touches upon race relations. According to *Film Comment:* "A Negro actress . . . plays in AFFAIR the 'straight' role of a human being, a photographer at that, and not a Problem." See unsigned review, *Film Comment* 1, no. 4 (1963): 29.

56. See Phillips and Hambourg, *Helen Levitt,* 58.

57. The photographs published in *A Way of Seeing* and seen in *An Affair of the Skin* are photos 17, 27, 45, 49, 52, and 58. The end credits to the film confirm that all the photographs were taken by Levitt.

7. ROBERT FRANK

This chapter is a shortened and updated version of a much longer essay, first published as "Daddy Looking for the Truth: The Films of Robert Frank," *Afterimage* 16, no. 9 (April 1989).

1. Philip Brookman, "In the Margins of Fiction: From Photographs to Films," in *Robert Frank: New York to Nova Scotia,* ed. Anne Wilkes Tucker (Boston: Little, Brown, 1986), 82.

2. Marita Sturken, "Frank Films On," *Afterimage* 8, no. 5 (December 1980): 18.

3. Anne W. Tucker, "It's the Misinformation That's Important," in *Robert Frank: New York to Nova Scotia,* ed. Anne Wilkes Tucker (Boston: Little, Brown, 1986), 90.

4. Christian Metz, *The Imaginary Signifier: Psychoanalysis and the Cinema* (Bloomington: Indiana University Press, 1982), 60.

5. Mekas, *Movie Journal,* 338.

6. Ibid., 40.

7. See John Brumfield, "The Americans and the Americans," *Afterimage* 8, nos. 1–2 (summer 1980); Jno Cook, "Robert Frank's America," *Afterimage* 9, no. 8 (March 1982); and Stuart Alexander, *Robert Frank: A Bibliography, Filmography and Exhibition Chronology 1946–1985* (Tucson: Center for Creative Photography, 1986).

8. Blaine Allan, "The Making (and Unmaking) of 'Pull My Daisy,'" *Film History* 2, no. 3 (1988): 203.

9. Most of Robert Frank's films are now in distribution through the Museum of Fine Arts, Houston. This availability has increased his visibility.

10. Alexander, *Robert Frank,* 57; Alfred Leslie, "*Daisy:* 10 Years Later," *Village Voice,* 28 November 1968, 54.

11. Allan, "Making,"185–203.

12. William Johnson, "History—His Story," in *Horses, Sea Lions, and Other Creatures: Robert Frank, Dave Heath, Robert Heinecken, and John Wood,* by William Johnson (Belmont, Mass.: Joshua Press, 1986), 22.

13. Ibid., 24.

14. "Chronology," in *Robert Frank,* ed. Sarah Greenough and Philip Brookman (Washington, D.C.: National Gallery of Art, 1994).

15. Johnson, "History," 24.

16. Greenough and Brookman, "Chronology."

17. Alexander, *Robert Frank,* 57.

18. Allan, "Making,"187.

19. Ibid., 197–99.

20. Robert Frank seminar at Visual Studies Workshop, 6 November 1988. The seminar resulted in a monograph with a transcript of the proceedings: William Johnson, ed., *The Pictures Are a Necessity: Robert Frank in Rochester, NY, November 1988* (Rochester: University Education Services, George Eastman House, 1988).

21. Allan, "Making,"187.

22. Ibid., 194.

23. Johnson, "History," 44.

24. Ibid., 50.

25. Quoted in Alexander, *Robert Frank,* 61.

26. Johnson, "History," 50.

27. Alexander, *Robert Frank,* 61.

28. One person looks at them and says they are great images, which seems to be Frank's joke on how his family photographs could become works of art.

29. It is unclear whether Pablo's crucifix is a sign of any religious conviction or just a piece of jewelry. Given Frank's Jewish roots, a "conversion" would be one more piece of evidence of Pablo's flight from his father.

30. Alexander, *Robert Frank,* 146.

31. Steve Dollar, "The End of the Road: A Filmmaker's Journey to 'Candy Mountain,'" *Weekend (Atlanta Journal & Constitution),* 9 July 1988, 16.

32. Ibid.

33. Frank has always claimed that he never read any reviews of his work, but he apparently read the first published version of this essay.

34. Kaja Silverman, *The Acoustic Mirror: The Female Voice in Psychoanalysis and Cinema* (Bloomington: Indiana University Press, 1988), 49.

35. Metz, *Imaginary Signifier,* 77.

36. Cook, "Robert Frank's America," 9.

8. DANNY LYON

1. Telephone interview with Danny Lyon, 30 July 1990.

2. Telephone interview with Danny Lyon, 15 August 1990.

3. Michel Foucault, *Discipline and Punishment: The Birth of the Prison* (New York: Pantheon Books, 1977), excerpted in *Foucault Reader,* ed. Paul Rabinow (New York: Pantheon Books, 1984), 208.

4. Foucault, *Discipline,* 206.

5. Danny Lyon, *The Paper Negative* (Bernalillo, N.M.: Black Beauty Books, 1980), 62.

6. For the most complete biographical information on Lyon, see Ute Eskildsen, "Social Commitment as Personal Adventure," in *Danny Lyon: Photo Film,* ed. Ute Eskildsen and Terence Pitts (Heidelberg: Edition Braus, 1991), 36ff.

7. *The Movement: Document of a Struggle for Racial Equality,* with a text by Lorraine Hansberry (New York: Simon & Schuster, 1964).

8. Danny Lyon, *The Bikeriders* (New York: Macmillan, 1968).

9. Danny Lyon, *The Destruction of Lower Manhattan* (New York: Macmillan, 1969).

10. Danny Lyon, *Conversations with the Dead: Photographs of Prison Life, with the Letters and Drawings of Billy McCune, #122054* (New York: Holt, Rinehart & Winston, 1971).

11. Danny Lyon, *Paper Negative.*

12. Danny Lyon, *Pictures from the New World* (Millerton, N.Y.: Aperture, 1981).

13. Danny Lyon, *Merci Gonaives* (Clintondale, N.Y.: Bleak Beauty Books, 1988).

14. Danny Lyon, *I Like to Eat Right on the Dirt: A Child's Journey Back in Space and Time* (Clintondale, N.Y.: Bleak Beauty Books, 1989).

15. J. Ronald Green, "Bleak Beauty: The Critical Reception of Danny Lyon's Films," *Afterimage* 15, no. 8 (March 1988): 14.

16. Pamela Allara, "Danny Lyon: From Photographs to Films: The Subject Imagined," in *Danny Lyon: Pictures from Films—Films from Pictures* (Medford, Mass.: Tufts University, 1983), 2.

17. Karen Cooper, "The Films of Danny Lyon: Visual Purist with Revolutionary Concerns," *Film Library Quarterly* 9, no. 1 (1976): 7.

18. Allara, "Danny Lyon," 1.

19. Green, "Bleak Beauty," 15.

20. Ibid.

21. See, for example, Andy Grunberg, "Two Masters Return to the Limelight," *New York Times,* 20 September 1981.

22. See Dan R. Goddard, "Indie Night to Include Three American-Made Films," *San Antonio News Express,* 19 August 1985, quoted in Green, "Bleak Beauty," 15.

23. See Vincent Canby, "Films of Danny Lyon," *New York Times,* 3 November 1973.

24. Cooper, "Films," 8; Katherine Dieckmann, "Songs of Innocence and Experience," *Village Voice,* 19 May 1987, 64.

25. Michael Renov, "Re-thinking Documentary: Toward a Taxonomy of Mediation," *Wide- Angle* 8, no. 3/4 (1986): 74.

26. Ibid.

27. See the previous chapter in this volume.

28. Michel Foucault, *Madness and Civilization: A History of Insanity in the Age of Reason* (New York: Vintage Books, 1973), 84.

29. Danny Lyon, *Pictures,* 84.

30. Telephone interview with the author, 30 July 1990.

31. Danny Lyon to the author, 15 August 1990.

32. Danny Lyon, *Paper Negative,* 9.

33. See Allara, "Danny Lyon," 7. See also the brochure, *The Films of Danny Lyon on VHS Video Cassette* (Clintondale, N.Y.: Bleak Beauty, 1988).

34. Interview with Danny Lyon, 30 July 1990.

35. Ibid.

36. Emma Goldman, *Anarchism and Other Essays* (1917; reprint, New York: Dover Publications, 1969), 58.

37. Lyon, *Pictures,* 93.

38. Danny Lyon to the author, 22 August 1996.

39. Max Kozloff, "Conversations with the Dead," *Art News* 69, no. 8 (December 1970): 26.

40. Interview with Danny Lyon, 15 August 1990.

41. See Foucault, *Madness,* 66.

42. J. Ronald Green gives this scene a completely different interpretation, seeing Billy McCune as a sexual deviant who must control his urge to sexually molest prepubescent girls, the crime for which he was sent to prison. While Green's thesis has a certain logic within his own interpretation of the film (which uses McCune's autobiography as evidence) as an exercise in phobiatropic behavior, it does not necessarily contradict my interpretation if one thinks of family morals as also "protecting" against deviant behavior. However, this might be stretching the point. See J. Ronald Green, "Slouching toward Bethlehem: Danny Lyon's Films," in the brochure, *The Films of Danny Lyon* (Cincinnati: Cincinnati Film Society, 1985), 7.

9. ED VAN DER ELSKEN

1. See "Ed en Gerda van der Elsken op hun reis door de wereld," *Katholieke Illustratie* 10 (October 1960): 4–6, quoted in Evelyn de Regt, "Once upon a time: Een biografie," in *Once upon a Time,* by Ed van der Elsken (Amsterdam: Fragment Uitgeverij, 1991), 23. Thanks to Mrs. Anneke van der Elsken for making an English translation of this text, by Karen Gamester, available to me.

2. Ed van der Elsken, *Sweet Life* (New York: Harry Abrams, 1966), caption for photos on 162, 163.

3. See, for example, Peter Cowie, *Dutch Cinema: An Illustrated History* (London: Tantivy Press, 1979). *Directory of Contemporary Dutch Films and Film-Makers,* comp. Matthew Stevens (London: Flick Books, 1990), 87, lists one film by van der Elsken, but without any description.

4. "The End," *Skoop* 27, no. 2 (February 1991): 5.

5. See Peter van Bueren, "Holand spreekt een woordje mee," *Skoop* 7, no. 8 (August 1971): 25–26. The author of the article would like to have seen Johan van der Keuken win the prize and is incensed over the jury selection procedure. Van Bueren calls van der Elsken the "laughing third party," who won only because the "heterogeneous jury" supposedly couldn't decide between Jan Vrijman and Frans Zwartjes. He also quotes a jury member, Charles Boost, who characterized the choice of *The Infatuated Camera* as a scandal.

6. de Regt, "Once upon a time," 45.

7. This chapter would not have been possible without the generous assistance of the Nederlands Filmmuseum and the Rijksvoorlichtingdienst, Amsterdam, which made video copies of van der Elsken's films available to me. At least two important films in the van der Elsken canon were not available for the purposes of this chapter: *Mr. Ed en de sprekende film* (*Mr. Ed and the Talking Film,* 1980) and *Welkom in het leven, lieve kleine (bis)* (*Welcome to Life, Little Darling, Part 2,* 1982), the latter a portrait of his two children, now young adults.

8. I am deeply indebted for most of the biographical information in this and the following paragraphs to Evelyn de Regt's biography in *Once upon a Time,* 9–45.

9. See Cowie, *Dutch Cinema,* 136–37.

10. See Ed van der Elsken, *Love on the Left Bank* (London: Ernst Deutsch, 1956). The book was published simultaneously in Dutch and German editions. See also *Picture Post,* 6, 13, 20, 27 February.

11. A number of these photographs are included in Ed van der Elsken, *Once upon a Time* (Amsterdam, Fragment Uitgeverij, 1991), 72–79.

12. The footage is part of a larger collection of films held by the Nederlands Filmmuseum, Amsterdam. No other completed films of individual segments of *Journey around the World* seem to have survived. Anneke van der Elsken confirmed that van der Elsken most probably edited the abridged version that survives.

13. de Regt, "Once upon a time," 23.

14. van der Elsken, *Sweet Life,* 18–19.

15. de Regt, "Once upon a time," 24.

16. Ibid., 14.

17. Ibid., 27. Johan van der Keuken, among others, assisted on the film.

18. Vrijman's film went on to win a Golden Bear at the Berlin Film Festival in 1962. See Cowie, *Dutch Cinema,* 149. Van der Elsken was credited as stills photographer on the film.

19. Van der Elsken's photographs of Spoerri's room and Niki de St. Phalle's dinosaur sculpture are reprinted in *Once upon a Time,* 68–69.

20. The film is archived in the Nederlands Filmmuseum.

21. Financed by VPRO, the film was broadcast on 15 January 1964.

22. See van der Elsken, *Once upon a Time,* 13–15, 21.

23. See Jacques Lacan, *Ecrits: A Selection,* trans. Alan Sheridan (New York: W. W. Norton, 1978), 1–7.

24. Jacques Lacan, *The Four Fundamental Concepts of Psycho-Analysis,* ed. Jacques-Alain Miller, trans. Alan Sheridan (New York: W. W. Norton, 1981), 257.

25. Ibid., 194.

26. The unedited footage was deposited in the Nederlands Filmmuseum and has been transferred to video. It consists of roughly half an hour of footage.

27. Initially, VPRO had asked a journalist to make a television portrait of the photographer, but van der Elsken was uncooperative, insisting that he make the film himself. See de Regt, "Once upon a time," 29.

28. Silverman, *Acoustic Mirror,* 213.

29. See van Bueren, "Holand spreekt een woordje mee," 25.

30. Ed van der Elsken, *Avonturen op het land* (Busum: Van Holkema & Warendorf, 1980).

31. de Regt, "Once upon a time," 41.

32. Ibid., 38.

Filmography

PHOTOGRAPHERS MAKING FILMS

In compiling this selected filmography, I have attempted to include as many well-known photographers as possible. Clearly, not all those who have made films or worked in television are included. In particular, photographers from Eastern Europe, the Third World, and Japan have been neglected, simply because of a lack of sources to consult. Filmographies include the work of photographers in all capacities, whether as director, writer, camera operator, or art director.

TEVFIK RIZA ERSIN ALOK (18 August 1937, Ankara, Turkey–)
Mountains (1972), *The Palace of Ishak Pasa* (1972), *Time Spent in the Church of Akdamar* (1973), *Prehistoric Rock Paintings in Eastern Anatolia* (1973), *Church Paintings that Influenced the Renaissance* (1975), *A Turkish House in Safranbolu* (1975), *Zoma I* (1979), *Zoma II* (1979), *The Birds of Turkey* (1980), *A Desert Storm* (1981).

MANUEL ALVAREZ-BRAVO (4 February 1902, Mexico City–)
Tehuantepec (1937).

EVE ARNOLD (1913, Philadelphia–)
Behind the Veil (1973).

DAVID (ROYSTON) BAILY (2 January 1938, London–)
TV Commercials (1966–68), *G.G. Passion* (1966), *Beaton by Baily* (1968), *Andy Warhol* (1970), *Visconti* (1971).

JOHN BALDESSARI (17 June 1931, National City, Calif.–)
New York Postcard Painting (1971), *Waterline* (1971), *Title* (1973), *Easel Painting* (1973), *Time-Temperature* (1973), *Water to Wine to Water* (1973), *Ice Cube Sliding* (1974), *Script* (1977), *Six Colorful Inside Jobs* (1977).

MARTINE BARRAT (Oran, Algeria–)
Woman Is Sweeter (1970), *Collection 71* (1970), *Parfum* (1971), *You Do the Crime, You Do the Time* (1973), *Vickie: Queen of the Roman Queens* (1973).

PETER BEARD (22 January 1938, New York–)
Hallelujah, the Hills! (1963, actor), *Longing for Darkness* (1975), *Bicentennial Diary* (1976), *Africa: The End of the Game* (1979, TV).

CECIL BEATON (14 January 1904, London–18 January 1980, Broadchalke, U.K.)
Kipps (1941), *Major Barbara* (1941), *Dangerous Moonlight* (1941), *Young Mr. Pitt* (1942), *Beware of Pity* (1946), *Anna Karenina* (1947), *An Ideal Husband* (1948), *The Truth about Women* (1957), *Gigi* (1958), *The Doctor's Dilemma* (1959), *My Fair Lady* (1964), *On a Clear Day You Can See Forever* (1970).

FERENC BERKO (28 January 1916, Nagyvárad, Hungary–)
Wall's Ice Cream Factory (1936); three publicity shorts for Epidarus Trust, London (1936); two documentaries for Bhavnani Film Prods., Bombay (1939–47); three untitled, abstract, experimental shorts (1948–55); *Design: Language of the Modern Market* (1950); *Ferandina* (1950); *The Sea* (1950); *Night Lights* (1951); *Times Square* (1951); *Aspen, Colo.—Fall* (1953); *Pool Reflections* (1954); Samsonite Luggage shorts (1962); *Crazy Otto* (1964); *For the Record: New York World's Fair* (1965); *Aspen* (1968); *Torn Cristo Curtain* (1972).

WILLI BEUTLER (23 September 1903, Langenöls, Germany–23 September 1978, Hamburg)
Twenty educational films (1939–43).

GUNARS BINDE (27 December 1933, Aluknes, Lithuania–)
Hello, Moscow (1966), *A Moment of the Century* (1967), *By His Own Hands* (1967), *The Salute* (1975).

JEAN CHARLES BLANC (12 February 1942, Royat, France–)
The Painted Truck (1973), *Cinema* (1973).

KURT BLUM (25 August 1922, Berne, Switzerland–)
L'uomo, il ferro e il fuoco (1964), *Auf weissem Grund* (1964), *Expo '64* (1964), *Hellas* (1965), *Rabio* (1965), *Kandinsky* (1966), *Mit Palette und Stichel* (1966), *Terra Sancta* (1970), *Türkei* (1971), *Chile* (1971), *Kunstauktion Kornfeld* (1973).

WALTER BOSSHARD (8 November 1892, Richterswil, Switzerland–18 November 1975, Ronda, Switzerland)
Mao Tse-Tung und Chou-en-Lai (1948).

MARGARET BOURKE-WHITE (14 June 1904, New York–27 August 1971, Stamford, Conn.)
Eyes on Russia (1934), *From the Caucasus to Moscow* (1934).

BRIAN BRAKE (27 June 1927, Wellington, New Zealand–)
Ancient Egypt (1969), *Borobudur: The Cosmic Mountain* (1970), *Batik: The Magic Cloth* (1970), *Ramayana* (1971), *The Eternal Cycle: Festivals of Life and Death* (1973), *Indonesian Safari* (1975).

JULES BRASSAI (Gyula Halász) (9 September 1899, Brasso, Hungary–11 July 1984, Paris)
Tant qu'il y aura des bêtes (1956).

IRVING BROWNING (15 May 1895, New York–1961, New York)
House of Secrets (1929), *Unmasked* (1929), *City of Contrasts* (1931), *The New Legion*

(1934, with Manon Miller), *Edward Steichen: Master of the Camera* (1936), *Getting Your Money's Worth* (1937, camera), *United States Military Academy at West Point* (1940, camera), *Women in Photography* (1941), *Babies by Banister* (194?).

ANTON BRUEHL (11 March 1900, Hawker, Australia–10 August 1982, San Francisco)
The Quarry (1932, with Ralph Steiner).

FRANCIS JOSEPH BRUGUIÈRE (16 October 1879, San Francisco–8 May 1945, London)
Danse macabre (1922, with Dudley Murphy, Arthur Blom), *The Way* (1923, unfinished), *Theory* (1925), *Light Rhythms* (1931, with Oswell Blakeston).

RUDY BURCKHARDT (1914 Basel, Switzerland–)
*145 West 21*st (1936), *Seeing the World: A Visit to New York* (1937), *Haiti* (1938), *The Pursuit of Happiness* (1940), *The Uncle's Return* (1940), *Montgomery, Alabama* (1941), *Trinidad* (1943), *How Wide Is Sixth Avenue?* (1945), *Up and Down the Waterfront* (1946), *The Climate of New York* (1948), *Mounting Tension* (1950), *See Naples . . . and the Island of Ishia* (1951), *Under the Brooklyn Bridge* (1953), *The Automotive Story* (1954), *The Aviary* (1954, with Cornell), *Nymphlight* (1955–57), *A Fable of Fountains* (1955–57), *Verona* (1955), *What Mozart Saw on Mulberry Street* (1956), *Eastside Summer* (1959), *Millions in Business as Usual* (1961), *Shoot the Moon* (1962), *How Wide Is Sixth Avenue?* (1963), *Lurk* (1965), *Square Times* (1967), *Money* (1968), *Tarzam* (1969), *Summer* (1970), *Made in Maine* (1970), *Inside Dope* (1971), *Doldrums* (1972), *Caterpillar* (1973), *Slipperella* (1973), *City Pasture* (1974), *Default Averted* (1975), *Saroche* (1975), *The Bottle of the Bulge* (1975), *Dwellings* (1975), *Sodom and Gomorrah, New York 10036* (1976), *Good Evening Everybody* (1977), *Alex Katz Painting* (1978), *Mobile Homes* (1979), *Neil Welliver Painting in Maine* (1980), *Sonatina and Fugue* (1980), *Rads on Wheels* (1980), *Cerveza Bud* (1981), *Yvonne Jaquette Painting "Autumn Expansion"* (1981), *Bach's Last Keyboard Fugue* (1981), *All Major Credit Cards* (1982), *Indelible, Indelible* (1983), *Untitled* (1984), *The Nude Pond* (1985), *Central Park in the Dark* (1985), *Dancers, Buildings and People in the Street* (1986), *In Bed* (1986), *Zipper* (1987).

RENÉ BURRI (9 April 1933 Zürich–)
After the Six Day War (1967), *The Two Faces of China* (1968), *Braccia si, uomini no!* (1968).

HARRY CALLAHAN (22 October 1912, Detroit–)
Motions (1947).

HENRI CARTIER-BRESSON (22 August 1908, Chanteloup, France–)
La vie est à nous (1936), *Une partie de Campagne* (1936), *Retour à la vie* (1937), *La règle du jeu* (1939), *Le retour* (1946), *Midlands at Play and at Work* (1963), five Süddeutscher Rundfunk films (1964), *Flagrants délits* (1967), *California Impressions* (1969), *Southern Exposures* (1970).

HANS G. CASPARIUS (15 July 1900, Berlin–16 May 1985, London)
Sigi, der eilige Bräutigam (1929), *Ginsterrausch im Hiddensee* (1932, unfinished),

Nomaden der Wüste (1933), *Apocalypse of St. John the Divine* (1949), *The Young Traveller of London* (1954), *You Take the Highroad* (1955), *Simon* (1956), *Fingal's Cave* (1956), *A River Speaks* (1957), *Return from the Sun* (1957), *Ten Bridges* (1957), *Drums* (1960), *Something to Think About* (1962), *The Harvest Is Tomorrow* (1963), *Gayaza* (1963), *A Letter to Japan* (1964), *Children of Our Conscience* (1965), *Sea City* (1965).

LUCIEN CLERGUE (14 August 1934, Arles, France–)
Drame du taureau (1965), *Delta del sel* (1966), *Sables* (1968), *Picasso: Guerre, amour et paix* (1971).

HORACIO COPPOLA (31 July 1906, Buenos Aires–)
Les quais de la Seine (1934), *A Sunday on Hampstead Heath* (1935), *Ainsi naît l'obélisque* (1936).

PIERRE CORDIER (28 January 1933, Brussels–)
Start (1976).

EDWARD S. CURTIS (1868, Whitewater, Wis., 1868–21 October 1954, Los Angeles)
In the Land of the Headhunters (1914), *In the Land of the War Canoes* (1931, sound version of *Headhunters*).

YVAN DALAIN (17 February 1927, Avenches, Switzerland–)
Qui êtes-vous, Monsieur X? (1959), *A l'heure de son clocher* (1960), *Alias Monique* (1972), *Relax, Relax* (1974), *Die Fotografen* (1975), *Die Hände* (1975), *La dernière inspection* (1975), *Menschen im Hintergrund* (1976), *Auf der Suche nach dem Nächsten* (1976), *Analyse d'un crime* (1976), *Madame Bettina* (1980), *Le petit oiseau* (1981), *Sacré Ulysse* (1982), *L'espoir et le souvenir* (1983), *Le rêve* (1984), *Au coeur du racisme* (1984), *Le depart de Dunia* (1985), *Le beau* (1987), *Le pouvoir* (1990), *Monsieur Molière aux champs* (1990).

BRUCE DAVIDSON (5 September 1933, Oak Park, Ill.–)
On Your Way Up (1966), *Living off the Land* (1970), *Zoo Doctor* (1971), *Isaac Singer's Nightmare and Mrs. Pupko's Beard* (1973), *Enemies: A Love Story* (1989).

JACK DELANO (also known as Jack Ovcharov) (1 August 1914, Kiev, Russia–)
Una gota de agua (1947), *Desde las nubes* (1948), *La voz del pueblo* (1949), *Jesus T. Piñero* (1949), *Los peloteros* (1951), *Pablo Casals en Puerto Rico* (1956), *La gaceta* (1966), *Sabios arboles, Mágicos arboles* (1974).

PEDRO DE MORAES (23 October 1942, Rio de Janeiro–)
Homem e profissão (1965), *Em busca de ouro* (1966), *Tempo de mar* (196?), *Cordiais Saudaçoes* (1970), *A linguagem da persuasão* (1970), *A memoria viva* (197?), *Carlos Leão* (197?), *Os inconfidentes* (1972), *Don Orione* (197?), *A memória viva* (1974), *Guerra conjugal* (1975), *Gordos e magros* (1976), *Uma pequena obra* (1977), *O aleijadinho* (1978), *O tempo e a forma* (1979), *A idade da terra* (1980).

PAUL DE NOOIJER (15 June 1943, Eindhoven, Holland–)

Moving Stills (1972), Alone Eight (1973), The Pie (1975), Say Good-Bye (1975),
Transformation (1976), Review (1976), Extra Ball (1976), Tarzan and Jane (1977),
How to Make (1978), Tarting Over (1981), The Third T(h)est (1981), Touring Hol-
land by Bicycle (1981), Tilburg Teachers Trilogy (1981), The Shadow and the Sub-
stance (1982), Three Months Later (1982), Black and White Bathroom (1982), Win-
dow Painting (1982), Nobody Had Informed Me (1989), At One View (1989), I
Should See (1990), A Fortified City (1990), Middelburgfilm (1990), Think (1992),
Rrringg (1992), Greenhouse Effect (1992), Stop Action Faces (1993), The Laughing
Cow (1994), 1945/1995 (1995), Skrien (1995), Exit (1996).

RAYMOND DEPARDON (6 July 1942, Villefrance-sur-Saone, France–)
Venezuela (1963), Israël (1967), Biafra (1968), Jan Pallach (1969), Tchad: L'embus-
cade (1970), Yemen (1973), 50,81% (1974), Tchad 2 (1975), Tchad 3 (1976), Tibesti
too (1976), Numéro zéro (1977), Reporters (1981), Dix minutes de silence pour John
Lennon (1981), Isola San Clemente (1982), Piparsod (1982), Faits divers (1983), Les
années déclic (1985), Une femme en Afrique (1985), New York, N.Y. (1986), Le petit
navire (1987), Urgences (1987), Une histoire très simple (1989), La captive du désert
(1989), Contacts (1990), Carthagena: Contre l'oubli (1991), Face à la mer (1993),
Montage (1994), Délits flagrants (1994), Afriques: Comment ça va avec la douleur?
(1996), Malraux (1996).

JAN DIBBETS (Geradus Johannes Maria Dibbets) (9 May 1941, Weert,
Netherlands–)
Land Art (1968), Fire/Feuer/Feu/Vuur (1968), 12 Hours Ride Objects with Correction
of Perspective (1969), Painting I (1970), Painting II (1970), Vertical-Horizontal-
Diagonal- Square (1970), Horizon I: Sea (1970), Horizon II: Sea (1971), Horizon III:
Sea (1971), Vibrating Horizon (1971), Venetian Blinds (1971), 2 Diagonals (1971,
video), 3 Diagonals (1971, video).

MICHEL DIEUZAIDE (11 December 1951, Tarbes, France–)
Quatre à quatre (1970), Grand Amphi Toulouse (1970), three shorts on Moroccan
agriculture (1974), L'image d'un demain . . . (1976), Post-Scriptum (1976), Michel
Carayon, guerrisseur philippin (1977), Inde du nord (1977), Ets Pignat à Paris
(1978), Tarde Jonda (1980), Portugal 1954 (1981), Les cracks (1981), Un quartier
pietonnier à Bordeaux (1981), L'espace traversé (1982), L'atelier ouvert (1983), A la
mesure du temps qui vient (1985), Rien n'est plus calme qu'un coeur blasé (1986),
Pierre Soulages (1986), Le rideau du Français (1987), Apel—les Fenosa—La terre et
les poètes (1989), Le chemin du Rocio (1990), Vlado Perlemuter: Portrait d'un pianiste
(1990), Madeleine Epouse Milhaud (1992), Humair, solitaire, solidaire! (1994), Pein-
tre et musicien de jazz: Daniel Humair (1994).

TOM DRAHOS (17 November 1947, Jablonec, Czechoslavakia–)
Place de la concorde (1972), Planète Vendôme (1974), Metroshima (1980), Mangeur
de bonbons (1980); India (1991), Prague (1991), Reims (1991), Frankfurt (1991),
Barcelona (1992), Antony (1992), Singen (1992), Sallaumines (1992), Arras (1992),

Copenhagen (1992), *Paris* (1992), *Paysages* (1992), *Mystères* (1992), *Fragments d'après Franz Kafka* (1992, video): *Odradek, Une sentinelle, Chevauchee, Le pont, Une grosse motte, Une petite femme, Carrefour, Le terrier, L'esprit Malin, Le prestidigitateur, K'oua fou ou Wou.*

ELLIOT ELISOFON (17 April 1911, New York–7 April 1973, New York)
Khartoum (1966), *African Heritage* (1967), *Black African Heritage* (1972).

ELLIOT ERWITT (26 July 1928, Paris–)
Czechoslovakia's Last Day of Freedom (1968), *Dustin Hoffman* (1969), *Arthur Penn Films "Little Big Man"* (1969), *Beauty Knows No Pain* (1971), *Red, White, and Bluegrass* (1973), *Beautiful, Baby, Beautiful* (1973), *The Great Treasure Hunt: Japan* (1986).

KÀROLY ESCHER (21 October 1890, Szekszàrd, Hungary–
16 February 1966, Budapest)
Hungarian film industry (1916–27), *Voros Reports* (1918–19).

ROBERT FLAHERTY (16 February 1884, Iron Mountain, Mich.–23 July 1951, Brattleboro, Vt.)
Nanook of the North (1922), *The Pottery Maker* (1925), *Moana* (1926), *Twenty-Four Dollar Island* (1927), *White Shadows of the South Seas* (1928), *Tabu* (1931), *Industrial Britain* (1933), *Man of Aran* (1934), *Elephant Boy* (1937), *The Land* (1942), *Louisiana Story* (1948).

ALAIN FLEISCHER (10 January 1944, Paris–)
Reportages (1965), *Montage IV* (1969), *Règles, Rites* (1969), *Bout à Bout* (1972), *Le rendez-vous en forêt* (1972), *Découpage* (1973), *Un an et un jour* (1973), *Vestiges* (1974), *Dehors dedans* (1975), *Zoo Zéro* (1978), *L'histoire et geographie* (1982), *Pierre Klossowski* (1982), *Rome Roméo* (1991).

HOLLIS FRAMPTON (11 March 1936–30 March 1984, Buffalo, N.Y.)
Clouds Like White Sheep (1962), *A Running Man* (1963), *Ten Mile Poem* (1964), *Obelisk Ampersand Encounter* (1965), *Manual of Arms* (1966), *Process Red* (1966), *Information* (1966), *States* (1967), *Heterodyne* (1967), *Snowblind* (1968), *Maxwell's Demon* (1968), *Surface Tension* (1968), *Palindrome* (1969), *Carrots & Peas* (1969), *Prince Rupert's Drops* (1969), *Works & Days* (1969), *Artificial Light* (1969), *Zorns Lemma* (1970), *Hapax Legomena* (seven films, 1971–72), *Magellan* (362 films, 1972–80), *A & B Ontario* (1984, completed by Joyce Wieland).

MARTINE FRANCK (2 April 1938, Anvers, France–)
Music at Aspen (1970), *What Has Happened to the American Indians?* (1970).

ROBERT FRANK (9 November 1924, Zürich–)
Pull My Daisy (1959), *The Sin of Jesus* (1961), *O.K., End Here* (1963), *Chappaqua* (1967, camera), *Me and My Brother* (1968), *Conversations in Vermont* (1969), *Life-Raft Earth* (1969), *About Me: A Musical* (1971), *Home Is Where the Heart Is* (1971, camera), *Cocksucker Blues* (1972), *About Us* (1972), *Keep Busy* (1975), *Life Dances On* (1979), *Energy and How to Get It* (1981), *This Song Is for You, Jack* (1983), *Home*

Improvements (1985, video), *Fire in the East: A Portrait of Robert Frank* (1986, actor), *Date d'échéance* (1986, actor), *Candy Mountain* (1987), *Run* (1989, video), *Hunter* (1989), *C'est vrai* (1991, video), *Romeo Gigli* (1991), *The Last Supper* (1992, video), *Moving Pictures* (1994), *The Present* (1996).

LEONARD FREED (23 October 1929, Brooklyn, N.Y.–)
Dansende Vromen (1963), *The Negro in America* (1966).

BERNARD LAWRENCE FREEMESSER (15 November 1926, Rochester, N.Y.–18 December 1977, Springfield, Mass.)
John Burton, His Art and Philosophy (1962), *A University and Its People* (1963), *Hey, Follow Me* (1964), *Eugene: 66* (1966).

ROMAN FREULICH (1 March 1898, Czestochowa, Poland–
2 March 1974, Hollywood)
The Prisoner (1934), *Roam Sallion* (1934, unfinished project), *Broken Earth* (1936).

OLIVER GAGLIANI (11 February 1917, Placerville, Calif.–)
One Final Expression (1974).

MARIO GARCÍA JOYA (1938, Santa María del Rosario, Cuba–)
La Ultima Cena (1975), *El recurso del método* (1977), *Los sobrevivientes* (1978).

JEAN GAUMY (–)
Jean-Jacques (1987), *Musicouronne de thiere novel* (1989), *Derrière le mur de Raoul Ruiz* (1989), *Museém de Denis Couchaux* (1989), *Artmafante de Patrick Viret* (1989), *Final d' Irène Jouannet* (1990), *Brisants de François Renaud Labarthe* (1990), *La jeune fille et la mort Michel Spinoza* (1990), *La lampe de l' Esquisse* (1990), *Dockers après la tourmente de Martin Jouando* (1990), *Le baiser de la sirène de Nathalie Masdurand* (1990), *Le rendez-vous banals de Branick de P. Viret* (1991), *Chevaux sauvages d' Australie de Ch. Vandenberg* (1991), *L' autre Célia d' Irène Jouannet* (1991), *La noce de l' esquisse* (1991), *Eaux fortes de J. Christophe Leforstier* (1992), *Terre neuvas* (1992), *La petite amie d' antonio de Manuel Poirier* (1992), *La Sevillane de J. Phillippe Toussaint* (1992), *Le romantiques de Christian Zarifian* (1992), *Fée de J. L. Gonnet* (1993), *Une écaille du dragon de Charlotte Tourres* (1993), *Pas de perdant de Franck Saint Cast* (1993), *En compagnie d' Antonin Artaud de Mordillat* (1994), *Le chant de Mars de J. P. Cayeaux* (1994), *Quelque chose de différent de Bruno Rolland* (1994), *A la campagne de Manuel Poirier* (1994), *Chargée de familie d' Ingrid Gogny* (1995), *Eau douce de Marie Vermillard* (1995), *Les passeurs de Valérie Desnele* (1995), *Le oeil traîne de Stéphane Brizé* (1995), *Omaha Beach de Fabrice Custanier* (1995).

PAOLO GIOLI (12 October 1942, Sarzano di Rovigo, Italy–)
Passando da una situazione ad un'altra (1968), *Tracce di Trace* (1969), *Commutazione con mutazione* (1969), *Immagini disturbate da un intenso parassita* (1970), *Secondo il mio Occhio di vetro* (1971), *Immagini reali/immagini virtuali* (1972), *Del tuffarsie e dell'Annegarsi* (1972), *Cineform* (1972), *Anominatografo* (1972), *Traumatografo* (1973), *Film per flauto da presa* (1973), *Figure instabili nella vegetazione*

(1974), *Quando la pellicola e calda* (1974), *Schermo inciso* (1978), *Schermo—Schermo* (1978), *L'operatore perforato* (1979), *L'assassino nudo* (1984), *Il volto inciso* (1984), *Piccolo Film decomposto* (1985).

PHILIP GITELMAN (–)
Company for Lunch (1964).

ALBERTO GRIFI (1938, Italy–)
La verifica incerta (1965), *Kappa* (1967), *Transfer per Kamera verso virulentia* (1968).

SILKE GROSSMAN (1951, Hamburg–)
Der Pirat ist die Liebe (1984).

JOHN GUTMANN (28 May 1905, Breslau, Germany–)
The Chinese Peasant Goes to Market (1949), *Journey to Kunming* (1949), *Le palais ideal* (1983).

DAVID HAMILTON (15 April 1933, London–)
Bilitis (1976), *Laura: Les ombres de l'ête* (1979), *Tendres cousines* (1980), *Premiers desirs* (1983), *Bilitis II: My Love* (1991).

RUNE HASSNER (13 August 1928, Östersund, Sweden–)
Ensamhet och gemenskap (1959); *Mykonos* (1960); *Athos* (1960); *Min lilla revolution* (1960); *Nimba* (1963); *Arbete pågår* (1964); *Mjölkäggvita i kosten* (1964); *Mjölkbud i Lagos* (1964); *Australien* (1964); *Pengar som vatten* (1964); *Jump Up* (1965); *Myglaren* (1966); *En vacker dag: En smäll* (1967); *Interfences I* (1967); *Ushirika* (1967); *Hjälparen* (1968); *Bilder för miljoner* (eleven parts, 1967–71; English-language version, *Images for Millions* [1973]): *Från hålkamer till bildrör, Niepce, Daguerre och ett kadaver, Nadar, duvor och ballonger, Laterna Magica och rörlig fotografi, Hine och Cole och bild som vapen, Halvvägs mellan Niepce och månen, En djävulsk uppfinning, Photo by Boubat, Ansikten och fragment av blommer, Brassai, Pittsburgh: Portätt av en stad; Realismus triumfer: Honoré de Balzac (1975); Kina* (six parts, 1978–79); *Med kameraet som våben* (1972); *Bilden som vapen* (six parts, 1979–82); *Bilden som vapen II* (seven parts, 1982–83).

MILOTA HAVRÁNKOVÁ (7 August 1945, Košice, Slovakia–)
Plný Čas (1980).

FRITZ HENLE (9 June 1909, Dortmund, Germany–)
Shango (1954), *Yanvallou* (1954).

HY HIRSCH (1911, Chicago–1961, Paris)
Even as You and I (1937, actor), *Horror Dream* (1947), *Clinic of Strumble* (1947), *The Adventures of Jimmie* (1950), *Divertissement rocco* (1951), *Come Closer* (1952), *Eneri* (1953), *Gyromorphosis* (1957), *Autumn Spectrum* (1957), *Defense d'afficher* (1958), *Chasse de Touches* (1959), *Scratch Pad* (1960), *Decollages recolles* (1960), *Le couleur de la forme* (1961), *Etude anatomique du photographes* (1961), *Recherche* (1961).

WALTER HIRSCH (12 April 1935, Leningrad, USSR–)
Huset (1970), *Jag heter Stelios* (1971), *Hello, Baby* (1974), *Den svenska tanten* (1983).

TANA HOBAN (1916, Philadelphia–)
Catsup (1967), *Beginning Concepts* (1973, TV series), *Where Is It?* (1980), *One Little Kitten* (1980).

THOMAS HÖPKER (10 June 1936, Munich–)
Washington: The New Rome (1973, TV), *Arabati* (1973), *Canada* (1974), *Rain in Arabati* (1975).

EIKOH HOSOE (18 March 1933, Yonezawa, Japan–)
Naval and Atomic Bomb (1960), *Tokyo Olympic Games* (1966).

GEORGE HOYNINGEN-HUENE (4 September 1900, Saint Petersburg, Russia–September 1968, Los Angeles)
Untitled (1927), *The Loves of Carmen* (1946), *Salome* (1946), *Passion* (1946), *Daphne: The Virgin of the Golden Laurels* (1951), *A Star Is Born* (1954), *Adventures of Ali Baba* (1954), *God's Monkey: Hieronymous Bosch* (1955), *The Rains of Ranjipur* (1955), *Bhowani Junction* (1956), *Les Girls* (1957), *Merry Andrew* (1958), *The Five Pennies* (1959), *A Breath of Scandal* (1960), *Heller in Pink Tights* (1960), *It Started in Naples* (1960), *Let's Make Love* (1960), *The Chapman Report* (1962), *A New Kind of Love* (1963).

MONIQUE JACOT (19 August 1934, Neuchâtel, Switzerland–)
La voix au chapitre (1975), *La vie qui va* (1981), *Surface sensible* (1983).

ART KANE (9 April 1925, Bronx, N.Y.–)
A Time to Play (1967), commercial director TV (1967–70)

WILLIAM KLEIN (19 April 1928, New York–)
Broadway by Light (1958), *Le grand Hernie* (1960), *Le grand Magasin* (1962), *Le Business et la Mode* (1962), *Barcelone* (1962), *L'Espagne: Tremblement de Ciel* (1963), *La circulation* (1963), *Les Élections* (1963), *Cassius le Grand* (1964), *Qui êtes vous, Polly Magoo?* (1966), *Loin du Vietnam* (1967), *Mister Freedom* (1968), *Eldridge Cleaver, Black Panther* (1969), *Float Like a Butterfly, Sting Like a Bee* (1969), *Festival Panafrican de la Culture* (1970), *Le grand Café* (1972), *Muhammed Ali, the Greatest* (1975), *The Model Couple* (1975), *Hollywood, California* (1977), *Grands soirs et petits matins* (1978), *The French* (1982), *Mode in France* (1985).

SERGIO LARRAIN (1931, Santiago de Chile–)
Vagabond Children (1963).

HELMAR LERSKI (Israël Schmuklerski) (19 February 1871, Strasbourg, France–29 November 1956, Zürich)
Rosa kann alles (1916), *Peter Lump* (1916), *Im Bewußtsein der Schuld* (1916), *Entehrt* (1916), *Am Abgrund* (1916), *Die Gräfin Heyers* (1916), *Der Knute entflohen* (1917), *Wenn Tote sprechen* (1917), *Ahasver* (1917), *Erloschen Augen* (1917), *Der Herr der Welt* (1917), *Die Memoiren der Tragödin Thamar* (1917), *Rächende Liebe* (1917), *Das Spitztuch* (1917), *Der Weg der Erlösung* (1918), *Kassenrevision* (1918), *Irrwege der Liebe* (1918), *Der Taktstock* (1918), *Das große Opfer* (1918), *Das Licht des Lebens* (1918), *Sei getreu bis in den Tod* (1918), *Gespenster* (1918), *Opium* (1919),

Nerven (1919), *Sterbende Völker* (1920), *Kinder der Finsternis* (1921), *Sie und die Drei* (1922), *Der falsche Dmitri* (1922), *Inge Larsen* (1923), *Das Wachsfigurenkabinett* (1923), *Neuland* (1924), *Die Perücke* (1924), *Der heilige Berg* (1925), *Ein Walzertraum* (1925), *Die Brüder Schellenberg* (1926), *Die Boxerbraut* (1926), *Die Abenteuer eines Zehnmarkscheins* (1926), *Dagfin* (1926), *Die Czardasfürstin* (1927), *Madame Pompadour* (1927), *Sprengbagger 1010* (1929), *Avodah* (1934), *Hebrew Melody* (1935), *Yaddei Hashemesh* (1940), *Anal* (1940), *Kupat Cholim* (1941), *Labour Palestine* (1941), *Balaam's Story* (1946), *Adamah/Tomorrow's Another Day* (1946).

HELEN LEVITT (31 August 1913, New York–)
Here Is China (1943), *The Capital Story* (1945), *In the Street* (1946–52), *The Quiet One* (1948), *The Steps of Age* (1950), *Another Light* (1952), *The Savage Eye* (1959), *The Balcony* (1963), *An Affair of the Skin* (1963).

ALEXANDER LIBERMAN (September 1912, Kiev–)
La femme française dans l'art (1936).

JEROME LIEBLING (16 April 1924, New York–)
Art and Seeing (1951), *A Tree Is Dead* (1955), *Pow-Wow* (1960), *The Old Men* (1965), *They Need These Days* (1966), *The Clouds* (1969), *89 Years* (1975), *High Lonesome: The Story of Bluegrass Music* (1993, advisor), *Fast Eddie and the Boys* (1994).

ELI LOTAR (January 1905, Paris–10 May 1969, Paris)
Les crevettes (1930), *Caprelles et pantopodes* (1930), *Ruptures de fibres* (1931), *Creosoot* (1931), *Las Hurdes* (1932), *Les maisons de la misère* (1938), *Aubervilliers* (1947).

DANNY LYON (16 March 1942, Brooklyn, N.Y.–)
Social Sciences 127 (1969), *The Destiny of the Xerox Kid* (1970), *Llanito* (1971), *El mojado* (1974), *Los niños abandonados* (1975), *Little Boy* (1977), *El otro lado* (1978), *Dear Mark* (1983), *Born to Film* (1981), *Willie* (1985), *The Media Man* (1994).

ROBERT MAPPLETHORPE (4 November 1946, New York–10 March 1989, Boston)
Underground films (1965–70), *Still Moving: Patti Smith* (1978), *Lady Lisa Lion* (1984).

MARY ELLEN MARK (20 March 1940, Philadelphia–)
Streetwise (1987), *American Heart* (1993).

CHRIS. MARKER (Christian-François Bouche-Villeneuve) (22 July 1921, Belleville, France–)
Les statues meurent aussi (1950, with Alain Resnais), *Olympia 52* (1952), *Toute la memoire du monde* (1956), *Dimanche à Pekin* (1956), *Lettre de Sibérie* (1958), *Le mystère de l'atelier quinze* (1958, narrator), *Les astronauts* (1960), *Description d'un combat* (1960), *Cuba Si!* (1961), *Le joli mai* (1962), *La jetée* (1963), *Le mystère Koumiko* (1965), *Si j'avais quatre dromadaires* (1966), *Rhodiaceta* (1967), *Loin du Viêtnam* (1967), *October 21, 1967/La sixième face du Pentagone* (1968), *Six cinetracts* (1968, codirector), *A bientôt, j'espère* (1969), *Le deuxième procès d'Arthur London*

(1969), *Jour de tournage* (1969), *On vous parle du Brésil: Tortures* (1969), *La bataille des dix millions* (1970), *Carlos Marighela* (1970), *Les mots ont un sens* (1970), *Le train en marche* (1971), *Vive la Baleine* (1973), *L'ambassade* (1973), *Le solitude du chanteur de fond* (1974), *Puisqu'on vous dit que c'est possible* (1974), *La spirale* (1975), *Le fond de l'air est rouge* (1977; released in Great Britain as *A Grin without a Cat*), *Junkopia* (1981), *Sans soleil* (1982), *2084* (1984), *A. K.* (1985), *Homage à Simone Signoret* (1986), *L'héritage de la chouette* (1989, TV, thirteen episodes), *Zapping Zone* (1985–94), *Berliner ballade* (1990), *Getting Away with It* (1990), *Photo. Browse* (1990), *Slon Tango* (1993), *Le tombeau d'Alexandre* (1993), *Le 20 heures dans les camps* (1993), *Petite ceinture* (1994), *Chaika* (1994), *Owl Gets in Your Eye* (1994), *Level Five* (1995), *Le facteur sonne toujours cheval* (1995).

ADAM MATKOCSIK (Poland–)
Ildiko (1981).

ELAINE MAYES (1 October 1938, Berkeley–)
The Clouds (1969), *Fall* (1972), *In Manhattan* (1974), *Hadley* (1976), *New York Walls* (1980), *New Wave Music* (1980), *Living in Hadley* (1981), *Silverlake Life: The View From Here* (1992).

SUSAN MEISELAS (21 June 1948, Baltimore–)
Living at Risk (1985), *Voyages: Nicaragua* (1987), *Pictures from the Revolution* (1991).

PEDRO MEYER (1935, Madrid, Spain–)
Pafnucio Santo (1975).

ELFI MIKESCH (31 May 1940, Judenburg, Austria–)
Ich denke oft an Hawaii (1978), *Das Klavier im Paterre* (1978), *Exekution: A Study of Mary* (1979), *Was soll'n wir machen ohne den Tod* (1980), *Macumba* (1982), *Canale Grande* (1983), *Die blaue Distanz* (1983), *Das Frühstück der Hyäne* (1983), *Mikado* (1983), *Committed* (1983), *Horror vacui* (1984), *Verführung: Die grausame Frau* (1985), *Ein Virus kennt keine Moral* (1986), *Der Rosenkönig* (1987), *Anita: Tänzerin des Lasters* (1987), *Die Jungfraumaschine* (1988), *Marocaine* (1989), *Positiv* (1989), *Annie* (1989), *A idade maior* (1991), *My Father Is Coming* (1991), *Malina* (1991), *Hey, Stranger* (1993), *Soldaten, Soldaten* (1993), *Erotique* (1994), *Verrückt bleiben, verliebt bleiben* (1997).

GJON MILI (28 November 1904, Kerce, Albania–14 February 1984, Stamford, Conn.)
Jamming the Blues (1944), *Raoul Dufy* (1951), *Stomping For Mili: Brubeck Jazz Quartet* (1955), *Eisenstaedt Photographs the Tall Men* (1955), *Tempest: Filming on Location* (1958), *Homage to Picasso* (1967).

MICHAEL MITCHELL (3 November 1943, Hamilton, Canada–)
Chipper (1973).

LÁSZLÓ MOHOLY-NAGY (20 July 1895, Bacsborsod, Hungary–
24 November 1946, Chicago)
Ein Lichtspiel: Schwarz-weiß-grau (1929), *Impression vom alten Marseiller Hafen* (1929), *Berliner Stillleben* (1930), *Großstadtzigeuner* (1932), *Architekturkongress*

Athen (1933), *The Life of a Lobster* (1935), *New Architecture at the London Zoo* (1936), *Things to Come* (1936), *Children's Workshop* (1940), *Interview with Students* (1942), *Work of Camoflague Class* [sic] (1942), *Student Exhibition #1* (1944), *Student Exhibition #2* (1944), *Design Workshops* (1942–44), *Students Working in Photo Room*(1945).

SARAH MOON (Marielle Hadengue) (17 November 1938, Britain–)
Approximately 150 TV commercials (1978–90), including *Anais Anais; Petit bateu: Dock; Macy's Towels; Eden Perfum; Cacharel: Black Lingerie; Mississippi One* (1991); *Contacts* (1994); *Henri Cartier-Bresson: Point d'interrogation* (1995); *Lumière et Compagnie* (1995).

MARTIN MUNKACSI (Marmorstein) (18 May 1896, Kolozsvar, Hungary–14 July 1963, New York)
TV films (1946–63, cameraman and lighting), *Bob's Declaration of Independence* (1954).

NIKOLAS MURAY (15 February 1892, Szeged, Hungary–2 November 1965, New York)
Amateur films (1936–45), *Frida Kahlo* (1942).

HANS NAMUTH (17 March 1915, Essen, Germany–13 October 1990, New York)
Jackson Pollock (1951), *De Kooning at the Modern* (1951), *Willem de Kooning, the Painter* (1966), *Josef Albers: Homage to the Square* (1969), *Henri Matisse: Centennial at the Grand Palais* (1971), *The Brancusi Retrospective at the Guggenheim* (1970), *Centennial at the Grand Palais* (1971), *Louis I. Kahn, Architect* (1972), *Calder's Universe* (1977), *Alfred Stieglitz, Photographer* (1982), *Balthus at the Pompidou* (1984).

PÅL-NILS NILSSON (7 July 1929, Rome–)
Horisont ett Kulturfönster (1963), *Movements* (1966), *Då, när jag var mannen på Oulavuolie* (1967), *Dans blir till: En film till Alvin Ailey* (1967), *Hemmavid* (1967), *Spelmansvardag* (1968), *Att skapa tradition* (1968), *Diego Blanco, gitarrist* (1968), *Vindelälven hotat vatten* (1969), *Leva för musik* (1969), *Tycker ni om Strauss?* (1969), *Thank you, massa* (1971), *Ralph Erskine* (1971), *Diktator eller Lekledare* (1972), *Hur ska det bli på Järva?* (1972), *Kvar i byn* (1972), *Nationalitet Okänd* (1972), *Maskin—maskindetali—människa* (1971), *Musik i Tvåan: Maskinmusik* (1973), *Glasdans* (1974), *Sverige i Sameland* (1974, 6 episodes), *Krishnas flöjt* (1975), *Var finns de land . . .* (1975), *Vad hände sen?* (1975), *Jag är Assyrier, mitt nomm är Ibrahim* (1976), *Balansen* (1976), *En levande skärgård?* (1977), *Korsnäsgården* (1978), *Raya* (1978).

GEORG ODDNER (17 October 1923, Stockholm–)
Week-End (1963), *Two* (1963), *Waiting for Eals* (1965), *Clarinet and Camera* (1965), *The Eternal Soldier* (1965), *The Emigrants* (1971), *The Surprise* (1971), *Dreamers on a Visit* (1978), *The Dreaming Child* (1978), *Spots of Life* (1981).

LENNART OLSON (21 December 1925, Göteborg, Sweden–)
Månland (1960), *Donaudeltat* (1960), *Röda badorter vid Svarta Havet* (1960), *Karneval* (1961), *Flamenco* (1962), *Fandango* (1962), *Basker* (1963), *Bonde i Baskerland* (1963), *Gangarm: En indier och hans famili* (1964), *Kathakali: Indisk dans*

(1964), *Konarak: Soltemplet* (1964), *Chitrakar: Målarkasten* (1964), *Jantar Mantar: Soluren som stannade* (1964), *Holi: Vårfesten* (1964), *Familien: En film från Bengalen* (1965), *Cyclon* (1965), *Bli skådeselare* (1966), *Byn i dalen* (1966), *Isaac vävare* (1966), *Folket i Oaxacadalen* (1966), *Helklo Bobby: En film om Robert Kennedy* (1967), *Kärlek 1: 1000* (1967), *Flim: A very important person* (1968), *Student i Lund* (1968), *Vara skådespelare* (1968), *Slaget om Lund: En dokumentärfilm om kommunal demokrati* (1968), *Genombrottet* (1968), *Förpassad, Påpassad, Inpassad* (1969), *Elvy Holmgen till exempel* (1970), *Bagru: En by i Indien* (1971), *Gangaram: En indisk bonde* (1971), *Indisk folkmusik* (1971), *Östpakistan: Tre månader efter katastrofen* (1971), *Bakåt Framåt: Bilder av Sverige 1972* (1972), *Två om kärlek I* (1974), *Två om kärlek II* (1974), *Strama tyglar* (1974), *Drakar* (1974), *En frykantig värld* (1975), *Land Policy* (1976), *Samba* (1977), *Främlingar* (1978), *Victor Jara* (1978), *Beethoven och Snogeröd* (1979), *Folkbildaren* (1980).

RUTH ORKIN (3 September 1921, Boston–16 January 1985, New York)
The Little Fugitive (1953), *Lovers and Lollipops* (1955).

GORDON PARKS (30 November 1912, Fort Scott, Kans.–)
Flavio (1962), *Diary of a Harlem Family* (1968), *The Learning Tree* (1968), *Shaft* (1971), *Shaft's Big Score* (1972), *The Super Cops* (1974), *Leadbelly* (1976), *Aaron Loves Angela* (1985), *Black Panthers* (1995).

ANTONIN PECH (21 October 1874, Cizicich, near Pilsen, Czechoslovakia–20 February 1928, Prague)
Hubička (1911), *Ponrepovo Kouzelnictví* (1911), *Rudi na Křtinách* (1911), *Rudi na Záletech* (1911), *Rudi se Ženi* (1911), *Rudi Sportsmanem* (1911), *Sokové* (1911), *Pro Peníze* (1912), *Svatojánské Proudy* (1912), *Pět Smyslů Člověka* (1913), *Prefatýn a jeho láska* (1913), *Zub za Zub* (1913), *Pomsta je Sladká* (1913), *Zamilované Tchýně* (1913).

KAREL PLICKA (14 October 1894, Vienna–6 May 1978, Prague)
Gajdoš (1927), *Batizovský Salaš* (1927), *Puchovská Dolina* (1927), *Hry Kysucké Mládeže* (1928), *Jaro na Podkarpatskej Rusi* (1928), *Za Slovenskym Ludom* (1928), *Po Horách, Po Dolách* (1929), *Zem Spieva* (1933), *Bedrich Smetena a Jablynická Sóla* (1933), *Jaro v Praze* (1934), *Stará Kultúra Slovenská* (1934), *Prezident Republiky u Nás* (1937), *Za Slovákmi od New Yorku po Mississippi* (1937), *Pán Prezident na Slovensku* (1945), *Večná Pieseň* (1945), *Vlast Vítá* (1945), *Barokní Praha* (1946), *Cesta k Barikádám* (1946), *Rolnícký deň vo Zvolene* (1946), *Nové Československo* (1949).

HERBERT GEORGE PONTING (1871, Great Britain–7 February 1935, London)
With Captain Scott in the Antarctic (1913), *Ninety Degrees South* (1933), *The Story of Captain Scott* (1936).

ENZO RAGAZZINI (8 December 1934, Rome–)
La macchia rosa (1969), *Pensare Brazil* (1971), *Impulsi* (1972).

CLAUDE RAIMOND-DITYVON (12 March 1937, La Rochelle, France–)
Est-ce ainsi que les hommes vivent? (1976), *Un jour comme les autres* (1977), *Basket* (1983).

ROBERT RAUSCHENBERG (22 October 1925, Port Arthur, Tex.–)
Canoe (1966).

MAN RAY (Emmanuel Radenski) (27 August 1890, Philadelphia–18 November 1976, Paris)
Le retour à la raison (1923), *Entr'acte* (1924, with René Clair), *Emak Bakia* (1926), *L'étoile de mer* (1927), *Anemic Cinema* (1927, with Marcel Duchamp), *Les mystères de château de des* (1928), *Essai de simulation de delire cinématographique* (1935, unfinished), *Dreams That Money Can Buy* (1947, with Hans Richter).

LENI RIEFENSTAHL (22 August 1902, Berlin–)
Das blaue Licht (1932), *Sieg des Glaubens* (1933), *Triumph des Willens* (1934), *Tag der Freiheit: Unsere Wehrmacht* (1935), *Olympia: Fest der Völker* (1938), *Tiefland* (1945–54).

MIGUEL RÍO BRANCO (11 December 1946, Las Palmas de Gran Canaria, Spain–)
La cage (1969), *Waiting for the Man* (1971), *Burning Gloves* (1971), *Dragon Trap* (1971), *Colony Records* (1971), *Electric Torture* (1971), *Trio electrico* (1977), *Memoria viva* (1978), *Aoliçao* (1980), *Nada levarei quando morrer aqueles que mim deve cobrarei no inferno* (1981).

HUMBERTO RIVAS (14 July 1937, Buenos Aires–)
Three short films (1974).

LEROY ROBBINS (14 June 1904, Saint Louis–24 January 1987, San Diego)
Advertising films (1930–31), *Imperial Valley* (1932, unfinished), *Dawn to Dawn* (1934), *Even as You and I* (1937) (with Roger Barlow and Harry Hay), *Suicide* (unfinished, 1935–38), *The Staff of Life* (1938), *The City* (1939), *Symphony in Stone* (1939), *School for Dogs* (1940), *Pipline* (1942), *Freedom to Learn* (1945), *Letter from Stalingrad* (1945), *Southern California Gas* (1946), *Survival in the Aleutians* (1948); *Confidential File* (1955, TV, sound only), *Stake Out on Dope Street* (1958), *The Untouchables* (1961), *Out of the Tiger's Mouth* (1962), *America, America* (1963), *An Affair of the Skin* (1963), *The Shepard of the Hills* (1964), *The Young Sinner* (1965), *Born Losers* (1967), *Hell's Angels on Wheels* (1967), *Psych-Out* (1968), *The Savage Seven* (1968), *Easy Rider* (1969), *The Plastic Dome of Norma Jean* (1970), *The Last Movie* (1975).

ALEXANDER MICHAILOVITCH RODČENKO (23 November 1891, Saint Petersburg, Russia–3 September 1956, Moscow)
Zurnalistka (1927), *Al'bidum* (1927), *Moskva v Oktjabre* (1927), *Čimizacija lesa* (1927), *Kem Byt?* (1927), *Vasha Znakomaya* (1927).

EDWARD RUSCHA (16 December 1937, Omaha, Nebr.–)
Premium (1974), *Miracle* (1975).

ROBERT SALTZMAN (10 June 1945, New York–)
Morocco (1967), *Wall Street* (1967), *Axel* (1969), *Roaches* (1969), *Joe and Jane* (1970).

LEENA SARASTE (3 August 1942, Helsinki–)
Reusenheben (1964), *A Wedding March* (1965), short documentary films (1967, film editor).

CHARLES SHEELER (16 July 1883, Philadelphia–7 May 1965, New York)
Shamberg film (1914?), *Katherine Baird Shaffer* (1919?), *Manhatta* (1921).

MICHAEL SNOW (10 December 1929, Toronto–)
A to Z (1956), *New York Eye and Ear Control* (1964), *Short Shave* (1965), *Wavelength* (1967), *Standard Time* (1967), ↔*Back and Forth* (1969), *One Second in Montreal* (1969), *Dripping Water* (1969), *Side Seat Paintings, Slides, Sound Films* (1970), *A Casing Shelved* (1970), *La region centrale* (1971), *Table Top Dolly* (1972), *Rameau's Nephew by Diderot (Thanks to Dennis Young) by Wilma Schoen* (1974), *Presents* (1980), *So Is This* (1982), *Funnel Piano* (1984), *Seated Figures* (1988), *See You Later* (1990), *To Lavoisier, Who Died in the Reign of Terror* (1992).

EVE SONNEMAN (14 January 1946, Chicago–)
Films (1973), *Canyon Cinematheque* (1974), *Ann Arbor Film Festival* (1974), *Bard College* (1976), *University of Rochester* (1976), *The Art Institute of Chicago* (1977), *Castelli Graphics* (1982), *Rheinisches Landesmuseum* (1982).

EDUARD STEICHEN (27 March 1879, Luxembourg–25 March 1973, West Redding, Calif.)
The Fighting Lady (1944).

RALPH STEINER (8 February 1899, Cleveland–13 July 1986, Thetford, Vt.)
City Film (1927), *H2O* (1929), *Silo* (1929), *People Playing Croquet* (1929), *Mechanical Principles* (1930), *Panther Woman of the Needle Trades or the Lonely Life of Little Lisa* (1931), *May Day in New York* (1931, with Irving Lerner), *Surf and Seaweed* (1931), *Granite/The Quarry* (1932), *Harbor Scenes* (1932), *Mechanical Principles* (1933), *G-3* (1933), *Cafe Universal* (1934, unfinished), *Pie in the Sky* (1934, with Elia Kazan, Irving Lerner, and M. D. Thatcher), *Hands* (1934), *The World Today: Sunnyside* (1935), *The World Today: Black Legion* (1935), *The Plow That Broke the Plains* (1936), *The People of the Cumberland* (1938), *The City* (1939), *Sarah Lawrence* (1940), *New Hampshire's Heritage* (1940), *Youth Gets a Break* (1941), *Troop Train* (1942), *Earth and Fire* (1950), *Seaweed, a Seduction* (1960), *Of Earth and Fire* (1968), *One Man's Island* (1969), *Glory, Glory* (1970), *A Look at Laundry* (1971), *Beyond Niagara* (1973), *Look Park* (1974), *Hooray for Light!* (1975), *Slowdown* (1975).

BERT STERN (3 October 1929, Brooklyn, N.Y.–)
Jazz on a Summer's Day (1968).

DENNIS STOCK (24 July 1928, New York–)
Efforts to Provoke, Quest, British Youth, One Little Indian, James Dean Revisited (1991).

PAUL STRAND (16 October 1890, New York–31 March 1976, Orgeval, France)
Manhatta (1921), *Manhattan* (1924), *Janice Meredith* (1924), *Crackerjack* (1925), *The Live Wire* (1925), *Betty Behave* (1927), *Where the Pavement Begins* (1928), *Redes*

(*The Wave*, 1934–36), *The Plow That Broke the Plains* (1936), *Heart of Spain* (1937), *Pay Day* (1938), *The People of the Cumberland* (1938), *Native Land* (1942), *It's Up to You* (1943), *Tomorrow We Fly* (1944).

KARL STRUSS (1886, New York–1981, Los Angeles)
Something to Think About (1920), *The Affairs of Anatol* (1921), *The Law and the Woman* (1921), *Fool's Paradise* (1921), *Saturday Night* (1922), *Fools First* (1922), *Rich Men's Wives* (1922), *Thorns and Orange Blossoms* (1922), *Minnie* (1922), *The Hero* (1922), *Poor Men's Wives* (1923), *Daughters of the Rich* (1923), *Maytime* (1923), *White Man* (1924), *Poisoned Paradise* (1924), *The Legend of Hollywood* (1924), *Idle Tongues* (1924), *The Winding Star* (1925), *Hell's 400* (1926), *Sparrows* (1926), *Meet the Prince* (1926), *Forever After* (1926), *Ben Hur* (1926), *Babe Comes Home* (1927), *Sunrise* (1927), *Drums of Love* (1928), *The Night Watch* (1928), *The Battle of the Sexes* (1928), *Lady of the Pavements* (1929), *Coquette* (1929), *The Taming of the Shrew* (1929), *Lummox* (1930), *Be Yourself* (1930), *One Romantic Night* (1930), *The Bad One* (1930), *Abraham Lincoln* (1930), *Danger Lights* (1930), *Kiki* (1931), *Up Pops the Devil* (1931), *Woman Love Once* (1931), *Murder by the Clock* (1931), *The Road to Reno* (1931), *Dr. Jekyll and Mr. Hyde* (1932), *Two Kinds of Woman* (1932), *Dancers in the Dark* (1932), *The Word and the Flesh* (1932), *Forgotten Commandments* (1932), *The Man from Yesterday* (1932), *Guilty as Hell* (1932), *The Sign of the Cross* (1932), *Island of Lost Souls* (1932), *Tonight Is Ours* (1933), *The Woman Accused* (1933), *The Story of Temple Drake* (1933), *The Girl in 419* (1933), *Disgraced* (1933), *Torch Singer* (1933), *Four Frightened People* (1934), *Belle of the Nineties* (1934), *The Pursuit of Happiness* (1934), *Here Is My Heart* (1934), *Goin' to Town* (1935), *Two for Tonight* (1935), *Anything Goes* (1936), *The Preview Murder Case* (1936), *Too Many Parents* (1936), *Sing, You Sinners* (1938), *Paris Honeymoon* (1939), *Zenobia* (1939), *Some Like It Hot* (1939), *Island of Lost Men* (1939), *The Star Maker* (1939), *The Great Dictator* (1940), *Caught in the Draft* (1941), *Aloma of the South Seas* (1941), *Happy Go Lucky* (1943), *Journey into Fear* (1943), *Riding High* (1943), *And the Angels Sing* (1944), *Rainbow Island* (1944), *Bring on the Girls* (1945), *Tarzan and the Leopard Woman* (1945), *Suspense* (1946), *Mr. Ace* (1946), *The Macomber Affair* (1947), *Heaven Only Knows* (1947), *The Dude Goes West* (1948), *Siren of Atlantis* (1948), *Tarzan's Magic Fountain* (1948), *Bad Boy* (1949), *Rocketship X-M* (1950), *It's a Small World* (1950), *The Return of Jesse James* (1950), *The Texan Meets Calamity Jane* (1950), *Father's Wild Game* (1950), *Tarzan's Peril* (1951), *Rose of Cimarron* (1952), *Tarzan's Savage Fury* (1952), *Limelight* (1952), *Lady Possessed* (1952), *Mesa of Lost Women* (1952), *Tarzan and the She-Devil* (1953), *Il piu comico spettacolo del mondo* (1953), *Il Turco napoletano* (1953), *Cavalleria rusticana* (1953), *Attila* (1954), *Due notte con Cleopatra* (1954), *Mohawk* (1955), *She Devil* (1957), *The Deerslayer* (1957), *The Rawhide Trail* (1958), *The Fly* (1958), *The Hot Angel* (1958), *Machete* (1958), *The Sad Horse* (1959), *Here Come the Jets* (1959), *The Rebel Set* (1959).

WOLF SUSCHITZKY (29 August 1912, Vienna–)
Julian Huxley films (1937), *Power for the Highlands* (1943), *Hello, West Indies* (1943), *Children of the City* (1944), *The Bridge* (1945), *No Resting Place* (1950),

Adventures in Sardinia (1950), *The Oracle* (1952), *The Bespoke Overcoat* (1955), *Sailor of Fortune* (1956, TV), *Charlie Chan* (1957, TV), *Cat & Mouse* (1958), *Cradle of Genius* (1959), *From Stone to Steel* (1959), *Lunch Hour* (1960), *The Small World of Sammy Lee* (1962), *Trinidad and Tobago* (1964), *The River Must Live* (1965), *Design for Today* (1965), *The Tortoise and the Hare* (1965), *Staying On* (1966), *Ulysses* (1966), *Carbon* (1967), *Poussin* (1967), *The Vengeance of She* (1967), *Les bicyclettes de Belsize* (1968), *Ring of Bright Water* (1968), *Claude Lorraine* (1969), *Ben Carter's Apples* (1969), *Entertaining Mr. Sloane* (1970), *Get Carter* (1971), *Something to Hide* (1971), *Living Free* (1972), *Theatre of Blood* (1972), *Moments* (1973), *Worzel Gummidge* (1979–81, TV), *Falling in Love Again* (1980), *Good and Bad at Games* (1983, TV), *Scenes and Songs from Boyd Webb* (1984), *The Young Visitors* (1984, TV), *The Chain* (1984, TV), *Claudia's Story* (1985, TV).

PEETER TOOMING (1 June 1939, Rakvere, Estonia–)
Uus aeg (1969), *Veel kord kevadest* (1969), *Laulupidu EXPO-70* (1969), *Koduküla* (1969), *Kui siit pilve piirilt* (1970), *Esti metloomad* (1971), *Läbinähtud nähtamatud* (1972), *Juhan Smuul* (1972), *Tiit Puura: Kolmat põlve sepp* (1972), *Aga kus on ema?* (1972), *Loomisrööm* (1972), *Otsin luiteid* (1972), *Tormipüha* (1973), *Kasulikud teod* (1973), *Eesti NSV* (1973), *Viljandi* (1973), *Võsastatud maad* (1973), *Juta Lehiste* (1973), *Tallinn kutsub* (1974), *Tere tulemast Tallinna!* (1974), *Orel* (1974), *Aastatega läbi Toompea* (1975), *Meie aeg* (1975), *Juhan liivi lugu* (1975), *Tugevad oma töes* (1976), *Eesti NSV* (1976), *Hea saak* (1976), *Hetked* (1976), *Tornimuusika* (1977), *Aastad* (1977), *Tallinn* (1978), *Maarjamägi* (1978), *Õiglane maa* (1978), *Fotorondo* (1978), *Oma pill* (1979), *Vitstooted* (1979), *Eksoodid* (1979), *Mees ja mänd* (1979), *Allika poole mineja* (1979), *Esti Foto* (1979), *Elamise lugu* (1980), *Söpruspuu* (1980), *Osa töde Simo Nõmmest* (1980), *Rada vabaks* (1981), *Linnaloom* (1981), *Virulased* (1982), *Kassilaane* (1982), *Tõnu Kaljuste täna* (1982), *Teekond mäe südamesse* (1983), *Rahva söda* (1983), *Olümpia I* (1983), *Lahemaa* (1984), *Leib* (1984), *"Kalevi" kolhoos* (1984), *Juudit* (1984), *Minsk* (1984), *Viiuliga* (1985), *Viru kolhoosi kogemustest* (1985), *Suvemängud Vinnis* (1985), *Kolhoos "Viru"* (1985), *Tiina* (1985), *Tsudnoje ozero* (1986), *Intiimne Adams* (1986), *Viro kolhoosi taidlejad* (1986), *Haljala kultuutimajas* (1986), *Vinni väljadel* (1986), *Vinni säru* (1986), *Reamehed* (1986), *See on Eesti!* (1986), *TREV-2* (1987), *Viru koolid* (1987), *Haljala keskkool* (1987), *MET* (1987), *Ehitajate suvemängud* (1987), *Suveöö unenägu* (1987), *Libahunt* (1988), *Norma 1988* (1988), *Norma puhkebaasid* (1988), *Norma traditsioonid* (1988), *Pärand* (1988), *Ärkamine* (1988), *Viru 40* (1988), *Lahkumnine Borodinist* (1988), *Kuidas elad Virumaa?* (1988), *Maa ja agronoom* (1989), *Juured* (1989), *Mörv katedraalis* (1989), *Meistriklass* (1989), *Rakvere TREV* (1989), *Fotomure* (1989), *Viru ehitab* (1990), *Virumaa metsakoondis* (1990), *Kuu* (1990), *Kangelasteu* (1990), *Concerto grosso* (1990), *Arstid Soomes* (1990), *Valuvesi* (1990), *On Virumaa virulaste hoida* (1991), *Tango* (1992), *Kaevurite pärl* (1992), *Tule mulle kellameheks* (1992), *Rabarong* (1992), *Kitseküla* (1993), *Eesti misjonärid Aafrikas* (1994), *Suur jalutuskäik Kilimandzarole* (1994), *Palmide alla!* (1994).

ED VAN DER ELSKEN (10 March 1925, Amsterdam–28 December 1990,
Warder, Netherlands)
Journey around the World (fourteen short films for AVRO-TV, 1959–60), *Van Varen*
(1961), *De Appel-iep* (1961), *Bewogen Bewegung* (1961), *Karel Appel: Componist*
(1961), *Dylaby* (1962), *Als twee druppels water* (1962), *Lieverdjes* (1963), *Grenzen
van het Leven* (1963), *Welkom in het Leven, lieve Kleine* (1963), *Op de bodem van de
hemel* (1963), *Heinrich Böll* (1964), *Een onvoltooide Reportage over Spanje* (1964),
Fietsers (1965), *Oberhausen, XI Westdeutsche Kurzfilmtage* (1965), *Trots Israel*
(1965), *Signalement van Peter Schat* (1966), *Mise en scène* (1967, TV series), *Orlow,
Turmac* (1968), *The Infatuated Camera* (1971), *Death in the Port Jackson Hotel*
(1972), *Paardeleven* (1972), *Spelen Maarrrr* (1972), *Een andere kijk op zwakzin-
nigheid* 1972), *Prins Bernhard fons helpt I* (1973), *Them & Us* (1973), *Het is niet wat
zij doen* (1977), *Avonturen op het Land* (1980), *Mr. Ed en de sprekende Film* (1980),
Welkom in het Leven, lieve Kleine (bis) (1982), *Een Fotograaf filmt Amsterdam*
(1982), *Bye* (1990).

JOHAN VAN DER KEUKEN (4 April 1938, Amsterdam–)
Paris à l'aube (1960), *Een zondag* (1960), *Even Stilte* (1963), *Yrrah* (1962), *Tajiri*
(1962), *Opland* (1962), *Lucebert, dichter-schilder* (1962), *De oude Dame* (1963), *In-
dische Jongen* (1964), *Blind kind* (1964), *Beppie* (1965), *Vier muren* (1965), *In't Nest
met de Rest* (1965), *Herman Slobbe* (1966), *Een Film voor Lucebert* (1967), *Big Ben*
(1967), *De Tijd Gest* (1968), *De Poes* (1968), *De snelheid: 40–70* (1970), *Beauty*
(1970), *Dagboek* (1972), *Het witte Kasteel* (1973), *Bert Schierbeek/De Deur* (1973),
Vietnam Opera (1973), *De Muur* (1973), *Het Leesplankje* (1973), *De nieuwe Ijstijd*
(1974), *Vakantie van de filmer* (1974), *De Palestijner* (1975), *Voorjahr* (1976), *Doris
Schwert/Frankfurt* (1976), *Maarten en de Bas* (1977), *De platte Jungle* (1978), *Sand-
wijtches* (1979), *De Meester en de Reus* (1980), *De Weg naar het Zuiden* (1981), *De
Beeldenstorm* (1982), *Iconoclaste* (1983), *De Tijd* (1984), *Speelgoed* (1984), *I Love $*
(1986), *The Unanswered Question* (1987), *The Eye above the Well* (1988), *Le masque*
(1990), *Face Value* (1991), *Bewogen Koper* (1993), *Sarajevo Film Festival* (1993),
Toni's Birthday (1994), *On Animal Locomotion* (1994), *Lucebert, Time and Farewell*
(1995), *Amsterdam Global Village* (1996).

WILLARD VAN DYKE (5 December 1906, Denver–23 January 1986,
Jackson, Tenn.)
Hands (1934), *Self-Help Cooperatives in California* (1935), *The World Today: Sunnyside* (1935), *The River* (1937), *The City* (1939), *The Children Must Learn* (1940),
Valley Town (1940), *Sarah Lawrence* (1940), *New Hampshire's Heritage* (1940), *A
Year's Work* (1940), *Tall Tales* (1941), *The Bridge* (1942), *Oswego Story* (1943), *Cow-
boy* (1943), *Steeltown* (1944), *Conference at Yellow Springs* (1945), *Pacific Northwest*
(1945), *San Francisco* (1945), *To Hear Your Banjo Play* (1946), *Journey into Medicine*
(1947), *The Photographer* (1948), *Mount Vernon in Virginia* (1949), *Years of
Change* (1950), *New York University* (1952), *Working and Playing to Health* (1953),
There Is a Season (1954), *Reflections of Boyhood* (1954), *Cabos blancos* (1954), *Excursion House* (1954), *Life of the Molds* (1957), *High Adventure with Lowell Thomas*

(1958), *Tiger Hunt in Assam* (1958), *Mountains of the Moon* (1958), *Land of White Alice* (1959), *Skyscraper* (1959), *The Procession* (1959), *Ireland—The Tear and the Smile* (1960), *Sweden* (1960), *Harvest* (1962), *So That Men Are Free* (1962), *Depressed Area* (1963), *Frontier of the News* (1964), *Rice* (1964), *Pop Buell: Hoosier Farmer in Laos* (1965), *Taming the Mekong* (1965), *Frontline Camera, 1935–1956* (1965), *Corbit-Sharp House* (1965), *The Farmer: Feast or Famine* (1965), *The Shape of Films to Come* (1968).

LUIGI VERONESI (28 May 1908, Milano–)
Caratteri (1939), *Viso e colore* (1940), *Film no. 4* (1940), *Film no. 5* (1940), *Film no. 6* (1941), *Film no. 9* (1951), *Film no. 13* (1981).

ROMAN VISHNIAC (19 August 1897, Pavlovsk, Russia–30 January 1990, New York)
Documentary on eastern European Jewry (1939), *The Worlds of Dr. Vishniac* (1959), *Living Biology* (1964, TV series), *The Big Little World of Roman Vishniac* (1972), *The Concerns of Roman Vishniac* (1972).

BRUCE WEBER (29 March 1946, Greensburg, Pa.–)
Broken Noses (1987), *Let's Get Lost* (1989), *Backyard Shift* (1992).

WEEGEE (Arthur H. Fellig) (12 June 1899, Zloczew, Poland–26 December 1968, New York)
Weegee's New York (1948), *Cocktail Party* (1950), *Windjammer* (1957), *Fun City* (1967), *The Idiot Box* (1967).

WILLIAM WEGMAN (12 February 1943, Holyoke, Mass.–)
Milk/Floor, Stomach Song, Randy's Sick, Pocketbook Man, Talking Fish, Out and In, Rage and Depression, Crooked Finger/Crooked Stick, Deodorant, Growl (these films were produced between 1970 and 1978); (1978), *Blue Monday* (1988); *The Hardly Boys in Hardly Gold* (1996).

WIM WENDERS (14 August 1945, Düsseldorf–)
Schauplätze (1967), *Same Player Shoots Again* (1967), *Silver City* (1968), *Alabama: 2000 Light Years* (1969), *3 amerikanische LPs* (1969), *Summer in the City* (1970), *Polizeifilm* (1970), *Die Angst des Tormanns beim Elfmeter* (1971), *Der scharlachrote Buchstabe* (1972), *Alice in den Städten* (1974), *Aus der Familie der Panzerechsen* (1974), *Falsche Bewegungen* (1975), *Kings of the Road* (1976), *Der amerikanische Freund* (1977), *Nick's Film: Lightning over Water* (1980), *Hammett* (1982), *Der Stand der Dinge* (1982), *Chambre 666* (1982), *Reverse Angle: New York* (1982), *Paris, Texas* (1984), *Tokyo-Ga* (1985), *Wings of Desire* (1986), *Notizen zu Kleidern und Städten* (1989), *Bis ans Ende der Welt* (1991), *In der Weite, so nahe* (1994), *Die Gebrüder Skladanowsky* (1995), *The End of Violence* (1997).

COLE WESTON (30 January 1919, Los Angeles–)
Escape to Reality (1973).

GEOFFREY L. WINNINGHAM (4 March 1943, Jackson, Tenn.–)
Friday Night in the Coliseum (1972), *Houston Astrodome* (1974).

MICHAEL WOLGENSINGER (17 September 1913, Zürich–)
Gottfried Keller (1939), *Mehr anbauen oder hungern* (1943), *Jugend Skilager* (1944), *Metamorphose* (1953), *Deka Dodeka* (1955), *L'après-midi d'un môme* (1955), *Schleifen Lisciare* (1964), *Dschai Nepal* (1964), *Sandorama* (1966), *Gunter Eich* (1971).

JOHN WOODMAN (1 July 1948, London–)
Apertures (1977), *Time Flow* (1977), *Light Movements* (1977), *Observational Series* (1978), *Beach Pan* (1979), *Bridge Farm* (1979), *Spider* (1979), *Reflections on My Shadow* (1980).

WILLY OTTO ZIELKE (also known as Victor Valet) (18 September 1902, Łódź, Poland–16 September 1989, Munich)
Bubi träumt (1931), *Hans Niklas, ein Münchner Original* (1931), *Arbeitslos* (1932), *Die Wahrheit* (1933), *Das Stahltier* (1935), *Olympia: Fest der Völker* (1938), *Verzauberter Niederrhein* (1954).

MARCOS ZIMMERMANN (1950, Buenos Aires–)
Cameraman for several feature films (1975–79).

Bibliography

Agel, Henri. *Robert Flaherty*. Paris: Cinéma d'Aujourd'hui, Editions Seghers, 1965.

Alexander, Stuart. *Robert Frank: A Bibliography, Filmography and Exhibition Chronology, 1946–1985*. Tucson: Center for Creative Photography, 1986.

Alexander, William. "Frontier Films: Trying the Impossible." *Prospects* 4 (1979): 565–69.

———. *Film on the Left*. Princeton: Princeton University Press, 1981.

———. "Paul Strand as Filmmaker, 1933–1942." In *Paul Strand: His Life and Work*, ed. Maren Stange. New York: Aperture, 1991.

Allan, Blaine. "The Making (and Unmaking) of 'Pull My Daisy.'" *Film History* 2, no. 3 (1988): 185–205.

Allara, Pamela. "Danny Lyon: From Photographs to Films: The Subject Imaged." In *Danny Lyon: Pictures from Films—Films from Pictures*. Medford: Tufts University, 1983.

Anonymous. "Some Amateur Movies." *New Republic* 58 (6 March 1929): 71–72.

Anonymous. "H_2O (1929)." *National Board of Review Magazine* 4, no. 10 (December 1929): 12.

Anonymous. *"Underground Printer."* *Film Art* 3, no. 9 (autumn 1936): 28.

Anonymous. *Film und Fotografie*. Zürich: Filmstelle VSETH/VSU, 1991.

Arnheim, Rudolf. "On the Nature of Photography." *Critical Inquiry* 1, no. 1 (September 1974): 149–61.

Auer, Michel, and Micheller Auer. *Encyclopedie internationale des photographs de 1839 a nos jours*. Hermance, Switzerland: Editions Camera Obscura, 1985.

Barthes, Roland. "The Photographic Message." In *Image/Music/Text*, trans. Stephen Heath. New York: Hill and Wang, 1977.

———. "Rhetoric of the Image." In *Image/Music/Text*, trans. Stephen Heath. New York: Hill and Wang, 1977.

————. *Camera Lucida: Reflections on Photography.* Trans. Richard Howard. New York: Hill and Wang, 1981.

Basque, Antoine de. "Robert Frank." *Cahiers du Cinema* 462 (December 1992): 89.

Bassan, Raphael. "Le laboratoire de Paolo Gioli." *Revue du Cinema* 383 (May 1983): 3.

Batten, Mary. "Notes on Rudy Burckhardt: Motion Seen." *Vision (Film Comment)* 1, no. 1 (spring 1962): 15–16.

Bazin, André. *What Is Cinema?* Trans. and ed. Hugh Grey. Berkeley: University of California Press, 1967.

Bensmaia, Robert. "From the Photogram to the Pictogram: On Chris. Marker's *La jetée.*" *Camera Obscura* 24 (September 1990): 138–61.

Beyerle, Mo. "Ästhetische Erfahrung und urbane Idylle: Jay Leyda as *A Bronx Morning* (1931)." *Amerikastudien/American Studies* 37 (1988): 75–84.

Bitomsky, Hartmut, and Manfred Blank. "Die fünf Windungen der Spirale: Gespräch mit Johan van der Keuken." *Filmkritik* 24, no. 5 (May 1980): 207–26.

Blakestone, Oswell. "HANDS (1928)." *Close-Up* 5, no. 2 (August 1929): 137–38.

————. "A Note on the Camera and Philosophy *(The Way).*" *Film Art* 4, no. 10 (spring 1937): 24.

Brookman, Philip. "In the Margins of Fiction: From Photographs to Films." In *Robert Frank: New York to Nova Scotia,* ed. Anne Wilkes Tucker. Boston: Little, Brown, 1986.

Browning, Irving. "Francis Doublier: Cameraman Fifty Years Ago." *American Cinematographer,* October 1944.

Burckhardt, Rudy. "How I Think I Made Some of My Films." In *To Free the Cinema: Jonas Mekas and the New York Underground,* ed. David E. James. Princeton: Princeton University Press, 1992.

Caditz, Judith Freulich. "Roman Freulich: Hollywood's Golden Age Portraitist." *Rangefinder,* July 1991, 46–47, 57.

Calder-Marshall, Arthur. *The Innocent Eye: The Life of Robert Flaherty.* London: Penguin Books, 1970.

Cameron, Ian. "I Am Writing to You from a Far Country . . ." *Movie* 3 (October 1962): 14.

Campbell, Russell. *The Cinema Strikes Back: Radical Filmmaking in the United States, 1930–1942.* Ann Arbor: UMI Research Press, 1982.

Canby, Vincent. "Films of Danny Lyon." *New York Times,* 3 November 1973.

Canton, Joseph Harris. *The Utopian Vision of Moholy-Nagy.* Ann Arbor: UMI Research Press, 1984.

Chabot, Jacques. "L'hypothese Marker." *Revue de la Cinematheque* 1 (May–June 1989): 4–7.

Cooper, Karen. "The Films of Danny Lyon: Visual Purist with Revolutionary Concerns." *Film Library Quarterly* 9, no. 1 (1976): 7–10.

Corliss, Richard. "Robert Flaherty: The Man in the Iron Myth." *Film Comment* 9, no. 6 (November–December 1973): 38–42.

Durgnat, Raymond. "Resnais & Co.: Back to the Avant-Garde." *Monthly Film Bulletin* 54, no. 640 (May 1987): 132–35.

Elder, Bruce. "Michael Snow and Bruce Elder: A Conversation." *Afterimage* 11 (winter 1982): 32–49.

Elsken, Ed van der. *Een liefdesgeschiedenis in Saint Germain de Prés.* Amsterdam: De Bezige Bij, 1956.

———. *Love on the Left Bank.* London: Andre Deutsch, 1956.

———. *Sweet Life.* New York: Harry Abrams, 1966.

———. *Once upon a Time.* Amsterdam: Fragment Uitgeverij, 1991.

Enyeart, James L. *Bruguière: His Photographs and His Life.* New York: Alfred A. Knopf, 1977.

Ertener, Orkun. "Filmen, als ob sich filmen ließe: Über das Bildersammeln und Filmemachen in Chris. Markers *Sans soleil*." *Augenblick* 10 (June 1991): 35–49.

Eskildsen, Ute. *Laszlo Moholy-Nagy: Fotogramme.* Essen: Museum Folkwang, 1996.

Eskildsen, Ute, and Jan-Christopher Horak. *Film und Foto der zwanziger Jahre.* Stuttgart: Verlag Gerd Hatje, 1979.

———. *Helmar Lerski, Lichtbildner.* Essen: Museum Folkwang, 1982.

Eskilden, Ute, and Terrence Pitts. *Danny Lyon: Photo Film.* Heidelberg: Edition Braus, 1991.

Ferereisen, Marie. "Raymond Depardon, Cineaste." *Revue de Belge* 30/31 (1990): 1–68.

Fischbein, Leslie. "*Native Land:* Document and Documentary." *Film and History* 14 (1984).

Flaherty, Frances Hubbard. *Elephant Dance.* New York: Charles Scribner's, 1937.

Flaherty, Robert. "Filming Reel People." *Amateur Movie Makers* 9, no. 12 (December 1934). Reprinted in *The Documentary Tradition: From Nanook to Woodstock*, ed. Lewis Jacobs et al. New York: W. W. Norton, 1971.

Flynn, S. K. "Bruce Weber Goes to Hollywood." *American Film* 12, no. 10 (September 1987): 25–32.

Frampton, Hollis. "For a Metahistory of Film: Commonplace Notes and Hypotheses." *Artforum* 10, no. 1 (September 1971): 32–35.

———. "Meditations around Paul Strand." *Artforum* 10 (February 1972): 52–57.

———. *Recollections/Recreations.* With an introduction by Susan Kane and an essay by Bruce Jenkins. Cambridge: MIT Press, 1984.

Frank, Robert. *The Americans.* With an introduction by Jack Kerouac. New York: Grove Press, 1959; Millerton, N.Y.: Aperture and Museum of Modern Art, 1968.

———. "A Hard Look at the New Hollywood." *Esquire* 51, no. 3 (March 1959): 51–65.

———. "Films: Entertainment Shacked Up with Art." *Artsmagazine* 45, no. 5 (March 1967): 23.

———. *The Lines in My Hand.* Tokyo: Yugensha, Kazuhiko Motomura; New York: Lustrum Press, 1972; Zürich: Der Alltag, 1989.

———. "J'aimerais faire un film." In *Robert Frank.* Paris: Centre National de la Photographie, 1983.

Frank, Robert, and Alfred Leslie. *Pull My Daisy.* New York: Grove Press, 1961.

Gassen, Heiner. "Filme über die Mächtigen: Raymond Depardon." *Epd Film* 3, no. 11 (November 1986): 10.

Gauthier, G. "Raymond Depardon, photographe et cineaste: Coincidences." *Cinemaction* 41 (January 1987): 137–43.

Geller, Evelyn. "Paul Strand as Documentary Filmmaker." *Film Library Quarterly* 6, no. 2 (spring 1973): 28–30.

Glassgold, C. Adolph. "H2O (1929)." *Arts* 15 (March 1929): 204–5.

Green, J. Ronald Green. "Slouching toward Bethlehem: Danny Lyon's Films." In *The Films of Danny Lyon* (brochure). Cincinnati: Cincinnati Film Society, 1985.

———. "Bleak Beauty: The Critical Reception of Danny Lyon's Films." *Afterimage* 15, no. 8 (March 1988): 14–18.

Greenough, Sarah. *Paul Strand.* Washington, D.C.: National Gallery of Art, 1990.

Greenough, Sarah, and Philip Brookman. *Robert Frank.* Washington, D.C.: National Gallery of Art, 1994.

Gray, Hugh. "Robert Flaherty and the Naturalist Documentary." *Hollywood Quarterly* 5, no. 1 (fall 1950): 41–48.

Grierson, John. "Flaherty as Innovator." *Sight and Sound* 21, no. 2 (October–December 1951): 64–68.

Gringas, Nicole. *Les images immobilisees: Proceder par impressions.* Montreal: Les Editions Guernica, 1991.

Hammen, Scott. "Sheeler and Strand's 'Manhatta': A Neglected Masterpiece." *Afterimage* 6, no. 6 (January 1979): 6–7.

Hight, Eleanor M., ed. *Moholy-Nagy: Photography and Film in Weimar Germany.* Wellesley, Mass.: Wellesley College Museum, 1985.

Horak, Jan-Christopher. "Film and Foto: Towards a Language of Silent Film." *Afterimage* 7, no. 5 (December 1979): 8–11.

———. "Discovering Pure Cinema: Avant-Garde Film in the 1920s." *Afterimage* 8, no. 1/2 (summer 1980): 4–7.

———. "Lerski et le cinema." *Photographies* (Paris) 8 (September 1985).

———. "The Films of Moholy-Nagy." *Afterimage* 13, no. 1/2 (1985): 20–23.

———. "Foto-Roman, Foto-Film: *La jetée.*" *Foto-Kritik* 21/22 (November 1986): 26–29.

———. "Modernist Perspectives and Romantic Desire: *Manhatta.*" *Afterimage* 15, no. 4 (November 1987): 9–15. Abridged version in *Paul Strand: His Life and Work,* ed. Maren Stange. New York: Aperture, 1991.

———. "Daddy Searching for the Truth: The Films of Robert Frank." *Afterimage* 16, no. 9 (1989): 8–13.

———. "That Danger of Unreason, That Threatening Space of an Absolute Freedom." In *Danny Lyon: Photo Film,* ed. Ute Eskilden and Terrence Pitts. Heidelberg: Edition Braus, 1991.

———. "The Penetrating Power of Light: The Films of Helmar Lerski." *Image* 36, no. 3/4 (1993): 40–53.

———, ed. *Lovers of Cinema: The First American Film Avant-Garde, 1919–1945.* Madison: University of Wisconsin Press, 1995.

———, ed. *Chris. Marker, der Fotograf.* Munich: Kamper/Tode/Gassen, 1996.

———. "Chris. Marker: Reality Bites." *Aperture* 145 (November 1996): 60–65.

Hübner, Christoph. "Filmen, Fotografieren, Schreiben: Johan van der Keuken und Wim Wenders als Fotografen." *Epd Film* 6, no. 8 (August 1989): 14–19.

Jacob, Gilles. "Chris. Marker and the Mutants." *Sight and Sound* 35, no. 4 (autumn 1966): 164–68.

Johnson, William. "History—His Story." In *Horses, Sea Lions, and Other Creatures: Robert Frank, Dave Heath, Robert Heinecken, and John Wood.* Belmont, Mass.: Joshua Press, 1986.

———. *The Pictures Are a Necessity: Robert Frank in Rochester, NY, November 1988.* Rochester, N.Y.: University Education Services, George Eastman House, 1989.

Joseph, Robert. "The Unimportance of Budget . . . *The Wave.*" *Hollywood Spectator* 13 (25 June 1938): 11.

Kamper, Birgit, Thomas Tode, and Heiner Gassen, eds. *Chris. Marker.* Munich: CICIM Verlag, 1997.

Klaue, Wolfgang, and Jay Leyda, eds. *Robert Flaherty.* (East) Berlin: Henschel-Verlag, 1964.

Kostelanetz, Richard, ed. *Moholy-Nagy.* New York: Praeger Publishers, 1970.

Kracauer, Siegfried. *Theory of Film: The Redemption of Physical Reality.* London: Oxford University Press, 1960.

Kramarski, Curt. "The Palestine Film for Palestine: An Interview with Helmar Lerski." *Palestine Post* 11, no. 2679 (12 July 1935).

Levitt, Helen. *A Way of Seeing.* With an essay by James Agee. New York: Horizon Press, 1981; Durham, N.C.: Duke University Press, 1989.

Levy, Jean. "L'audace et l'honnetete de la subjectivite." *Cinemaction* 41 (January 1987): 125–31.

Liebling, Jerome. "*Arbres et maison,* Botmeur, Finistère, 1950." In *Paul Strand: His Life and Work,* ed. Maren Stange. New York: Aperture, 1991.

Lopate, Phillip. "Rudy Burkhardt: Man with a Movie Camera." In *Museum of Modern Art Program Notes.* New York: Museum of Modern Art, 1987.

Lyon, Danny. *The Bikeriders.* New York: Macmillan, 1967.

———. *The Destruction of Lower Manhattan.* New York: Macmillan, 1969.

———. *Conversations with the Dead.* New York: Holt, Rinehart and Winston, 1971.

———. *The Paper Negative.* Bernalillo, N.M.: Bleak Beauty Books 1980.

———. *Pictures from the New World.* New York: Aperture, 1982.

———. *Merci Gonaïves.* Bernalillo, N.M.: Bleak Beauty Books, 1988.

MacDonald, Scott. "Ralph Steiner." In *Lovers of Cinema: The First American Film Avant-Garde, 1919–1945,* ed. Jan-Christopher Horak. Madison: University of Wisconsin Press, 1995.

Marker, Chris. *Coréennes.* Paris: Editions du Seuil, 1959.

———. *Commentaires 1.* Paris: Editions du Seuil 1967.

———. *Commentaires 2*. Paris: Editions du Seuil, 1967.

———. *Le fond de l'air est rouge*. Paris: Francoise Maspero, 1978.

———. *Le dépays*. Paris: Editions Herscher, 1982.

———. *Das Fremdland*. Trans. Roland Platte and Andreas Eisenhart. Berlin: Berl Galrev Verlag, 1985.

———. "Reecrire la memoire: *Sans soleil* de Chris. Marker." *Jeune Cinema* 149 (March 1983): 25–26.

———. "Sunless." *Semiotexte* 4, no. 3 (1984): 33–40.

———. *Silent Movie*. Columbus, Ohio: Wexner Center for the Arts, 1995.

Marsilius, Hans-Jörg. "Individualismus als Prinzip." *Film-Dienst* 46, no. 2 (19 January 1993): 40–41.

Martin, Marcel. "Flaherty." *Anthologie du Cinéma* 1 (1966): 121–72.

McCandless, Barbara, Bonnie Yochelson, and Richard Koszarski. *New York to Hollywood: The Photography of Karl Struss*. Albuquerque: University of New Mexico Press, 1995.

Metz, Christian. *The Imaginary Signifier: Psychoanalysis and the Cinema*. Bloomington: Indiana University Press, 1982.

Miller, Andrea Kaliska. "Films of Moholy-Nagy." In *Moholy-Nagy: Photography and Film in Weimar Germany*, ed. Eleanor M. Hight. Wellesley, Mass.: Wellesley College Museum, 1985.

Milne, Tom, and Julien Petley. "Candy Mountain. On the Road: Robert Frank." *Monthly Film Bulletin* 57, no. 672 (January 1990): 10–11, 28.

Moholy-Nagy, László. *Malerei Photographie Film*. Munich: Verlag Langen, 1925. English translation, *Painting, Photography, Film*. London: Lund Humphries, 1969.

———. "Zum sprechenden Film." *Internationale Revue* 2, no. 15 (October 1928).

———. "Die Optik im Tonfilm." *Filmd und Volk* 2, no. 6 (1928).

———. "Das Problem des neuen Films." *Bildwart, Blätter für Volksbildung* 8, no. 4 (1930).

———. "An Open Letter to the Film Industry and All Those Who Are Interested in Good Film." *Sight and Sound* 3, no. 10 (summer 1934): 56–57.

———. "About the Elements of Motion Pictures." *Design* 41 (December 1939).

———. *Vision in Motion*. Chicago: Paul Theobald, 1947.

———. "Problems of the Modern Film." In *Moholy-Nagy*, ed. Richard Kostelanetz. New York: Praeger Publishers, 1970.

Moholy-Nagy, Sibyl. *Moholy-Nagy: Experiment in Totality*. New York: Harper Brothers, 1950.

Moritz, William. "Americans in Paris: Man Ray and Dudley Murphy." In *Lovers of Cinema: The First American Film Avant-Garde, 1919–1945*, ed. Jan-Christopher Horak. Madison: University of Wisconsin Press, 1995.

Naylor, Colin. *Contemporary Photographers*. 2d ed. Chicago and London: St. James Press, 1988.

Peclet, Jean-Claude. "Das verpasste Rendez-vous: Fotografen und Filmemacher aus der Westschweiz." *Cinema* (Zürich) 30 (1984): 134–49.

Phillips, Sandra S., and Maria Morris Hambourg. *Helen Levitt.* San Francisco and New York: San Francisco Museum of Modern Art and Metropolitan Museum of Art, 1991.

Potemkin, Harry Alan. "Francis Bruguière." *Transition* (Paris) 18 (November 1929): 81–82.

Rafferty, Terrence. "Marker Changes Trains." *Sight and Sound* 53, no. 4 (autumn 1984): 284–88.

Regt, Evelyn de. "Once upon a time: Een biographie." In *Once upon a Time,* by Ed van der Elsken. Amsterdam: Fragment Uitgeverij, 1991.

Renov, Michael. "Thinking Film and Photography: A Conference Assessed." *On Film* 13 (fall 1984): 69–74.

Rodakiewicz, Henwar. "Documentary: A Personal Retrospect." *Film Library Quarterly* 2, no. 3 (summer 1969): 33–37.

Rony, Fatimah Tobing. "Victor Masayesva, Jr., and the Politics of *Imagining Indians.*" *Film Quarterly* 48, no. 2 (winter 1994–95): 20–33.

Rose, Barbara. "Kinetic Solutions to Pictorial Problems: The Films of Man Ray and Moholy-Nagy." *Artforum* 10, no. 1 (September 1971): 68–73.

Rosenblum, Naomi. "Paul Strand: The Early Years, 1910–1932." Ph.D. diss., City University of New York, 1978.

Rosenblum, Walter. "*The Quiet One.*" *Photo Notes* (spring 1949): 23–24.

Roth, Wilhelm. "Fotografieren, filmen, leben: Anmerkungen zu Robert Frank." *Epd Film* 6, no. 8 (August 1989): 20–23.

Schaub, Martin. "FotoFilmFotoFilm: Eine Spirale. Robert Franks Suche nach den Augenblicken der wahren Empfindung." *Cinema* (Zürich) 30 (1984): 75–94.

Schneider, Peter. "Umwege zum Film: Sechs Fotografen/Filmer aus der Deutschschweiz." *Cinema* (Zürich) 30 (1984): 95–133.

Senter, Terence A., ed. *László Moholy-Nagy.* London: Arts Council of Britain, 1980.

Singer, Ben. "Film, Photography, and Fetish: The Analyses of Christian Metz." *Cinema Journal* 27, no. 4 (summer 1988): 4–22.

Sitney, P. Adams. "A View of Burkhardt." *Film Comment* 1, no. 1 (spring 1962): 13–15.

Smith, Tom. *Moving Pictures: Films by Photographers.* New York: American Federation of the Arts, 1990.

Spielman, Yvonne. "Porträt Experimentalfilm 4: Elfi Mikesch." *Epd Film* 4, no. 11 (November 1987): 10–13.

Stange, Maren, ed. *Paul Strand: His Life and Work.* New York: Aperture, 1991.

Stebbins, Robert (also known as Sidney Meyers). "*Redes.*" *New Theater* 2 (June 1935): 11.

Stebbins, Theodore E., Jr., and Norman Keyes Jr. *Charles Sheeler: The Photographs.* Boston: Museum of Fine Arts, 1987.

Steiner, Ralph. "Revolutionary Movie Production." *New Theatre* (September 1934): 22–23.

———. *Ralph Steiner: A Point of View.* Middletown, Conn.: Wesleyan University Press, 1978.

————. *In Pursuit of Clouds.* Albuquerque: University of New Mexico Press, 1985.

Strand, Paul. "Les maisons de la misère." *Films* 1 (November 1939): 89–90.

————. *Time in New England,* edited by Nancy Newhall. New York: Oxford University Press, 1950; New York: Aperture, 1980.

————. "REALISM: A Personal View." *Sight and Sound* 18 (January 1950): 23–26.

————. "International Congress of Cinema, Perugia." *Photo Notes* (spring 1950): 8–11, 18.

————. *La France de profil.* Text by Claude Roy. Lausanne: La Guilde du Livre, 1952.

————. *Un paese.* Text by Cesare Zavattini. Turin: Tur Giulio Einaudi, 1955.

————. *Living Egypt.* Text by James Aldridge. Dresden: VEB Verlag der Kunst, 1969.

————. *Ghana: An African Portrait.* Text by Basil Davidson. New York: Aperture, 1976.

Sturken, Marita. "Frank Films On." *Afterimage* 8, no. 5 (December 1980): 18–19.

Thiemann, Birgit. "Die Relativität der Dinge und ihre Begriffe: Chris. Markers *Sans soleil.*" *Augenblick* 10 (June 1991): 25–34.

Toubiana, Serge. "Entretien avec Raymond Depardon: Le photographe sur le que-vive." *Cahiers du Cinema* 326 (July–August 1981): 3–4, 6.

Turim, Maureen. "Designs of Motion: A Correlation between Early Serial Photography and the Recent Avant-Garde." *Enclictic* 7, no. 2 (fall 1983): 44–54.

Tweedie, Katherine. *William Klein: Photographer, Filmmaker.* Rochester, N.Y.: Visual Studies Workshop, 1982.

Urrichio, William. "The City Viewed: The Films of Leyda, Browning and Weinberg." In *Lovers of Cinema: The First American Film Avant-Garde, 1919–1945,* ed. Jan-Christopher Horak. Madison: University of Wisconsin Press, 1995.

Van Dongen, Helen. "Robert Flaherty (1884–1951)." *Film Quarterly* 18, no. 4 (summer 1965): 3–14.

Van Dyke, Willard. "The Interpretative Camera in Documentary Films." *Hollywood Quarterly* 1, no. 1 (July 1946): 405–9.

————. "Documentaries of the Thirties." *University Film Association Journal* 25, no. 3 (fall 1973): 45–46.

Wenders, Wim. *Written in the West.* Munich: Schirmer Mosel, 1996.

Wolfe, Charles. "Modes of Discourse in Thirties Social Documentary: The Shifting 'I' of *Native Land.*" *Journal of Film and Video* 36, no. 4 (fall 1984): 13–20.

————. "The Poetics and Politics of Nonfiction: Documentary Film." In *Grand Design: Hollywood as a Modern Business Enterprise, 1930–1939,* by Tino Balio. New York: Charles Scribner's Sons.

Zuckerman, Art. "Focus on Willard Van Dyke." *Popular Photography* 56 (April 1965): 118–19, 127–29.

Zuker, Joel. *Ralph Steiner: Filmmaker and Still Photographer.* New York: Arno Press, 1978.

Index